HEALING THE
SACRED DIVIDE

HEALING
THE SACRED DIVIDE

MAKING PEACE WITH

OURSELVES, EACH OTHER,

AND THE WORLD

JEAN BENEDICT RAFFA

Larson Publications
Burdett, New York

ISBN-10: 1-936012-60-X
ISBN-13: 978-1936012-60-2
Library of Congress Control Number: 2012935984

Publisher's Cataloging-In-Publication Data
(Prepared by The Donohue Group, Inc.)

Raffa, Jean Benedict.

   Healing the sacred divide : making peace with ourselves, each other, and the world / Jean Benedict Raffa.

      p. ; cm.

   Includes bibliographical references and index.
   ISBN-13: 978-1-936012-60-2
   ISBN-10: 1-936012-60-X

   1. Other (Philosophy)—Religious aspects. 2. Difference (Philosophy)—Religious aspects. 3. Healing—Religious aspects. 4. Consciousness—Religious aspects. 5. Individuation (Philosophy)—Religious aspects. I. Title.

BL53 .R35 2012
200.19   2012935984

Cover art: Cicero Greathouse, *Mandorla I* (top) and *Mandorla VI*.
                www.cicerogreathouse.com

Published by Larson Publications
4936 NYS Route 414
Burdett, New York 14818 USA

larsonpublications.com

21 20 19 18 17 16 15 14 13 12
10 9 8 7 6 5 4 3 2 1

FOR OUR FAMILY'S NEWEST BABY BEARS:

CONNOR, JAKE, ALEX, SOPHIA, AND OWEN

CONTENTS

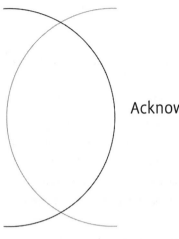

Acknowledgments

THIS BOOK, my third about the sacredness of the inner life, has undergone an eighteen-year gestation—most of it spent with my own mind and the musings of favorite authors. It takes equal parts audacity and humility to then expose one's subterranean universe to the light, and I would like to thank many people who have smoothed this daunting passage for me. Without them, this child of my soul would not have been born.

Some extremely kind and generous-spirited people spent much time and energy reading and commenting on earlier versions. Many of their comments and suggestions, offered with utmost wisdom and tact, have become part of this book, and for that they have my deepest gratitude.

Philosopher Dr. Michael Washburn wrote a thoughtful and thorough critique, sharing his extensive knowledge of psycho-spiritual development, highlighting terms and ideas needing clarification, and raising questions about issues to explore further. His belief in my work and affirming words about my writing tipped the scales in favor of one more rewrite.

Theologian Dr. E.J. Tarbox likewise wrote a detailed critique, giving special attention to theological issues. His very helpful comments and generous gift of the classic book, *Patterns in Comparative Religion* by Mircea Eliade, greatly strengthened my theories with understandings and connections I would otherwise have missed.

The eminent Biblical scholar Dr. John Dominic Crossan provided a third leg of foundational support. I am indebted to him for his observations about male/female dualism and his belief in dialectical capabilities as critical factors in human integration, wholeness, and health. Both were instrumental in reframing and titling this work.

Thank you also to Brittany Raffa, my brilliant niece and Dartmouth medical student, who provided invaluable insights from the perspective of the "average" (well, maybe not so much) reader, particularly about interesting passages which needed clarifying and tedious ones which needed shortening; to Tom Weiss for being such a receptive sounding board in our many discussions about the themes of this book, for pointing out avenues of thought I had not considered, and for the conversation that inspired the title; and to Randy Robertson for his encouragement to include more personal stories.

Ann Kennedy, founder of the Jung Center of Winter Park, Florida, and soul sister, made countless contributions to at least three earlier manuscripts. For many years her support and unwavering faith in me was a lifeline connecting me to other students and teachers in a creative, two-way flow of growing, learning, and healing. It still is. Thank you, dearest friend.

A special thank-you to the many benevolent network-building Spider-Grandmothers and Grandfathers who have believed in my worldview and have promoted, facilitated, and attended my classes, workshops, lectures, and seminars through the years, especially: Nell Martin, Justina Lasley, the Rev. Greer McBryde, Alice MacMahon, Dr. Anna Lillios, Joan Bailey, Charlotte Everbach, Therese Brooks, Barbara Sorensen, Que Throm; Anne and Lewis Doggett of the Center for Life Enrichment in Highlands, N.C.; Nancy and Dr. E.J. Tarbox of the Highlands Institute of American Philosophical and Theological Thought; Candace Boyd and her colleagues at the C.G. Jung Society of Sarasota; the C.G. Jung Society of Atlanta; and the Houston Jung Center.

Few have been more supportive of me and my work or more instrumental in the development of my thinking than the loyal and loving women of my women's groups. I send hugs of heartfelt gratitude to the members of my original Jungian study group for sparking and stoking my passion for Jungian psychology: Carolyn Coleman, Mickey Griffin, Jean Hess, Emmy Lawton, Jane McCartha, Jane Nies, and Sally Spencer. I send the same to my writer sisters Barbara Kennedy, Margie Pabst, Lenny Roland,

and Peggy Smith of The Purple Pros; to my current partners in Jungian study, Moonbeam sisters Dru Brown, Anne Doggett, Temple Hay, Nell Martin, and Helen Moore; and to my Matrix sisters Beth Black, Elizabeth Cohen, Mickey Griffin, Louise Sheehy, and Eileen Tatum. Every woman should be as fortunate as I to be upheld by a circle of such magnificent Wisewomen.

I would like to thank everyone who contributed original stories and poems for an earlier manuscript which was never published. Please know your gifts were not only much appreciated, but also made subtle contributions to this book. And I want all the lion-hearted seekers and dreamers who attended my classes or otherwise studied with me over the years to understand that much of this work is a direct result of your courageous seeking and generous sharing.

A heartfelt thank-you to my dear friend and gifted artist Cicero Greathouse for suggesting the mandorla image for the cover art and for his exquisite paintings which, in their own way, say as much about my subject as the words in this book.

While the term "eternal gratitude" is grossly overused at worst and theologically suspect at best, I can think of no words more adequate to express my feelings toward my literary agent Paul Cash for believing in me. Having the championship of someone with his depth of wisdom, tireless determination, and strength of character is one of life's greatest gifts. Thank you, kind ally and friend.

Paul, Amy, and everyone at Larson Publications have my deepest gratitude and respect for daring to print another book in this tide of so many in so many forms! You are truly an intrepid bunch and I dearly hope I prove worthy of your faith in me.

To my family—Julie, Matt, Tom, Robyn, and my precious grandchildren who are the love affair of my old age—thank you for being you, and for your unconditional love and support. You bring such joy into my life.

Most of all, always and ever, thank you, Fred, for sharing your life with me. I am the luckiest of women.

JEAN RAFFA
MARCH 2012

The message is unmistakable;
our own healing proceeds from that overlap
of what we call good and evil, light and dark. It is not that
the light element alone does the healing; the place where
light and dark begin to touch is where miracles arise.
This middle place is a mandorla.

—Robert A. Johnson

All opposites are of God,
therefore man must bend to this burden;
and in so doing he finds that God in his "oppositeness"
has taken possession of him, incarnated himself in him.
He becomes a vessel filled with divine conflict.

—Carl Jung

I have spread my dreams under your feet:
tread softly, for you tread on my dreams.

—W. B. Yeats

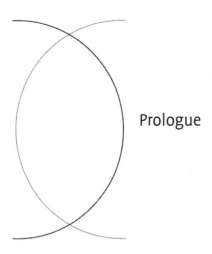

Prologue

IN THE DREAM I'm walking between railroad tracks that curve into a distant horizon. I see only earth, sky, and this hard metal road with rock-covered banks that fall away on either side into dark woods below.

I know this place. I walked these tracks with Daddy when I was five and we lived in Tallahassee. He wanted me to feel the magical allure of trains, and also know their danger. There were hobos in tent camps in the woods. I should stay away from them. I should stay away from the tracks, too. Little girls could get crushed by metal monsters that rode them.

Are there hobos in the woods now? Will a train come soon? Why am I here? Where am I going? Where's Daddy? I don't know. I only know I'm alone and must keep walking.

From behind me a voice calls, "Jean!" I turn, and there is Tonto.

"Come," he beckons. "Lone Ranger wants you." I'm thrilled. The Lone Ranger is my hero and he wants to see *me*! I push away a shadow of apprehension and follow Tonto. The Lone Ranger stands in a clearing. Behind him his magnificent white horse, Silver, munches grass contentedly. Beyond them, the dark woods. I feel wonder, excitement, curiosity. Beneath these, that tiny knot of anxiety.

"Stand there." The masked man points to a spot on the ground in front of the steep embankment. I obey and wait for the words that will reveal his regard for me, tell me why I'm here, confirm my mission.

The Lone Ranger pulls his gun out of its holster, aims at me, pulls the trigger, shoots. I feel the kick in my midsection, clutch my body at the point of impact, wait for the blood and pain. Is this it? Will I die now?

I wake up screaming, "Nooooo!" between great heaving sobs, outraged by this inconceivable betrayal from a man I've admired second only to Daddy. Mama rushes up the stairs into my bedroom and holds me in her arms.

"Shhh, you're okay. You're okay. It was only a dream."

Only a dream. That's when I tell myself, stunned with incomprehension but fierce in my determination, "This is important. I'm ten years old and I will never forget this dream!"

Readers of my book, *The Bridge to Wholeness: A Feminine Alternative to the Hero Myth*, already know this story. In the book I wrote next, *Dream Theatres of the Soul: Empowering the Feminine through Jungian Dream Work*, I mentioned the Lone Ranger again. Then, thinking I was done with him, I set him aside to address headier matters. I've been writing for years, hoping to round out those two books with a third that would complete them, but nothing quite gelled. I still had unfinished business with the Lone Ranger, Tonto, and Silver.

Actually, the Lone Ranger *did* give me my mission: *You want to know why you are here and where you're going? I'll tell you. These train tracks represent your spiritual journey. I've given you an experience that will shape it. Never forget the pain of being betrayed by the hero/god of your childhood—a lone, remote, and mysterious masked man who doesn't value your significance and holds the power of life and death over you. Remember this dream and become conscious of its fullest meaning. This is your life's work.*

He was right. I've been on a pilgrimage for self-understanding and spiritual meaning since I was seventeen and I still track the mystery of God in my dreams and waking life. Despite the warning in my Lone Ranger dream, my childhood image of God as a powerful heroic male dominated my spirituality well into adulthood. As I grew more confident in my femininity I began to wonder about the feminine aspects of Deity, but I never considered abandoning God's masculine side. What I have always sought is a deity of fully empowered masculinity and femininity.

Why does God feel so remote and impersonal? I wondered. *Why am I still afraid of him? Does God have a feminine side? What is it like? How would I be different if I had grown up with a God-image of integrated masculine and feminine energies? How would the world be different?*

Years of searching and questioning have unearthed some answers. This book offers what I know so far. Part 1 entertains some common assumptions that prolong God's divorce, a devastating development that began thousands of years ago and is still the norm for much of the planet. We explore eight ways of thinking about God that contribute to the dysfunctions of our culture, and consider alternatives that may better serve our deepest needs. Part 2 unwraps nine gifts of wisdom that an integrated God-image offers contemporary seekers.

Humanity's noblest dream is universal peace, justice, and love. We have pursued this dream throughout our history, but always we are stopped short by a vast chasm that separates us from ourselves, each other, and the world. As human life is sacred, so is this divide sacred. All physical life hinges on the tension between opposites—north pole/south pole, light/dark, summer/winter—and we are created in such a way that our psyches mirror this reality: in our left and right brains, conscious and unconscious selves, masculine and feminine sides.

Bible scholar Dr. John Dominic Crossan said to me in a letter, "We are, I think, incapable of not thinking dualistically." While this may well be true, it is also true that along with our thinking processes, our very consciousness is evolving. A primary characteristic of consciousness is that as we become more self-aware, we grow more aware of how significant "otherness" is. This ping-pong balancing effect whereby our growth in one area stimulates growth in another is hard-wired into our brains, and it, too, is sacred. Why? Because while we may never completely lose our dualistic perspective, we can establish mutually beneficial partnerships at every level, and these are our hope for peace, justice, and love.

The consciousness with which we distinguish the two poles of seeming opposites can't entirely separate them. Though it seems they are split apart they actually remain connected by an area that synergizes them, where each has some power but neither rules. This "divide" is a holy place full of miraculous potential and can be represented by the almond-shaped space created when two circles overlap.

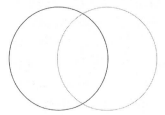

This place where our power to set ourselves apart yields to a dawning awareness of what we share with "other" is a *mandorla,* a holy place of healing where miracles occur. As you read these words from Jungian analyst Robert Johnson imagine two people, or two groups or nations or worldviews, coming together like this.

> The mandorla begins the healing of the split. The overlap generally is very tiny at first, only a sliver of a new moon; but it is a beginning. As time passes, the greater the overlap, the greater and more complete is the healing. The mandorla binds together that which was torn apart and made unwhole—unholy. It is the most profound religious experience we can have in life.[1]

The mandorla is creative synthesis, a symbol of partnership, conflict resolution, healing, and peace-making. No symbol is more apt for the inner work that heals splits in oneself, one's relationships, and how we understand what God wants of and for us. Making a mandorla of my own life has brought so much joy and meaning that I know it is holy work, a life-giving spiritual path relevant for seekers and healers today regardless of religious affiliation.

Please join me in weaving together life's opposites on a radical middle path to God.

Note

1. Robert A. Johnson, *Owning Your Own Shadow* (New York: HarperOne, 1991), 102.

PART 1

The Evolution of Our God-Images

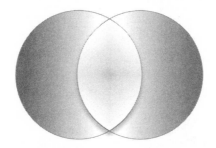

In the deepest recesses of our psyches a primal war is being waged between two compelling needs: our need to preserve the self-images our egos have so carefully constructed and our need to transcend the limitations our egos have imposed.

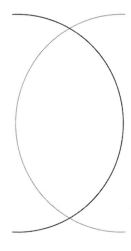

CHAPTER ONE

A God of Unconscious Oneness

This bliss connects us to everything and makes us
buoyantly alive. All our future plays out against this
primal innocent, infinitely pleasurable life

IN THE BEGINNING was sperm and egg. Of their
union a miracle occurred: New life was created and began to evolve. You are
that miracle. Within the fertilized egg that was you, everything you would
need to grow into a mature human being was already there—everything but
the food that would fuel you after you left the safe haven of your mother's
womb.

You didn't know it yet, but you would develop cells that would create
organs—lungs that would fill with oxygen, and a heart that would push the
oxygen-rich blood through your body. You would grow hands that would
hold and carry and caress, feet that would take you to unimagined places,
eyes that would see wonders, ears that would hear tender murmurs of love,
a mouth that would savor delicious foods, a stomach to digest them, and
a brain for thinking about these and other wonders.

You not only would evolve physically, but also grow psychologically
and spiritually. You would feel joy and sadness, pleasure and pain. You
would learn from these and build a personality that would process your
experiences and reflect on their meaning. You would become a thoroughly
unique individual, someone the world has never seen before.

Beneath all this a spiritual core would link you and every other human
on this planet with the Great Mystery—Mystery you would long to understand and yearn to be intimate with. Are you still yearning? If so, read on.
For this invisible part of you is the subject of this book.

Imagine for a moment that at conception your psychological and spiritual selves (or psyche and spirit) were like the insides of a chicken egg:

The white was your conscious, psychological self, closer to the surface, and the yolk was your unconscious, spiritual core. In the natural life of a fertilized egg the two parts merge and new life is created as a breathing, peeping baby chick. Metaphorically speaking, the same development is intended for our psyche and spirit. But in today's world, most "eggs" remain unfertilized and the white stays separated from the yolk.

Why do most of us live separated from our fuller selves? Why do we not grow into wise, integrated beings? Why does our desire to know and be known by God go unfulfilled?

The root problem is our lack of self-awareness and self-knowledge. Despite extraordinary advances over the long history of our species, most of us still don't know how or why our personal difficulties, lack of fulfillment, and discontent come about. Our families, societies, and religions are beset by the same ignorance. The time has come to understand that the solution to our separation from ourselves and God is *to think psychologically*. This is what brings consciousness, and full consciousness is the philosopher's stone, the long-sought secret to spiritual enlightenment.

Helping you discover the philosopher's stone is this book's goal. Part 1 gives important background information about why spiritual crises are rampant in today's world. Some of you will be surprised to find that the "enemy" is not an invasive "other" from outside the safety of your gates, but something within that needs attention. Understanding the true problem will help you make best use of Part 2. This section of the book describes the "mandorla mode" of psychological thinking that generates spiritual growth by bridging duality and creating consciousness. Erecting this bridge is a spiritual practice at the heart of each spirit person and every great religion, and anyone can begin it at any time.

Its construction progresses through three chronologically unequal "epochs" of self-awareness, each of which provides a support pillar for the next span. For most of us, the first is of relatively brief duration; the second is quite long (the whole of life for many people), and the third sometimes does not even begin. I am deeply indebted to Dr. Michael Washburn for this understanding and for his suggestions about how I might best express it.

Each epoch generates a specific form of consciousness that directly influences our personality and spirituality. Examining our life through the lenses of these three epochs reveals important features of psychological and spiritual thinking that are generally overlooked, not only in typical stage-theories but also by most religions. Most relevant to this book is our estrangement from profound sources of life and wisdom that are frequently associated with the feminine principle. I'll describe the first epoch here, and get to the others later.

Epoch I: Physical Consciousness

In the first epoch our awareness is limited to our five senses and the forces of physical instinct: bodily urges, unchecked emotions, and primitive images. As infants we are like hungry wolf cubs in a vast and comforting wilderness. We don't question our habitat or behavior or wonder if there is any other way to be; we simply act and react to physical stimuli without plan, reflection, or guilt. Every new object fills us with wonder, and every experience has special meaning just for us. We glory in our bodies, revel in the loving attention we get from our mothers and other caregivers, feel joy in our ability to make them respond to our antics with smiles or rush to our side at the slightest expression of need. Unburdened by self-consciousness and self-doubt, we are unthinkingly innocent of any wrongdoing because we have no moral code and feel no need to alter or repress anything about ourselves. We feel what we feel and we feel everything fully. We do not know that this is how it is with us, nor do we care, for we are at one with our bodies, ourselves.

In terms of how primitive humanity experienced this era of minimal self-awareness we might say that although anatomically modern *homo sapiens* had appeared on the planet, we had not yet reached full behavioral modernity. We did not realize we belonged wholly to the biological species we represented. Because our psyches were still in a "pre-natal" phase we shared directly in a life that was not our own, in what Mircea Eliade calls a "cosmico-maternal" life.[1]

In a child, this egoless, guiltless, free-and-easy state of instinctual behavior is natural and charming; but as we grow into adulthood it becomes increasingly dysfunctional. In fact, a lack of guilt or sense of responsibility combined with self-centeredness, emotional immaturity, antisocial behavior, and low impulse-control are characteristics of sociopaths. This is why we need egos, and why our egos need to grow in self-awareness: Learning to critique and control our more primitive tendencies is crucial to our survival.

Nonetheless, for one brief and magical moment in the life of every individual, Epoch I is heaven. In this glorious paradise where everything is about exploring the world with our senses and satisfying our physical needs there is no yesterday, today, or tomorrow. If we have a concept of time it is that we dwell in eternity. If we have a concept of God it is this bliss of oneness that connects us to everything and makes us feel buoyantly, vitally alive. Neither good nor bad, right nor wrong, Epoch I is simply everyone's earliest experience of being a human being. All our future psychological and spiritual growth plays out against this primal background of immersion in a maternal ocean of innocent, unconscious, infinitely pleasurable physical life.

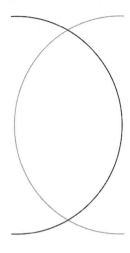

CHAPTER TWO

A Masculine God

He dwells atop a hierarchy of males and holds the power of life and death . . . so inferior are we that it is heresy to question his rules, no matter how arbitrary they seem.

AS I WRITE these words I feel a deep sadness about the world. This morning in my weekly dream group, a woman who used to be a social worker wept as she told us about visiting the home of an eleven-month-old baby girl who drowned in the bathtub while her drunken parents were arguing in the front yard because the father had sexually abused her. I rarely watch the news now because the epidemics, murders, rapes, death tolls from the wars, global warming—the list goes on—keep me awake at night. I fear for my grandchildren, worry about what the world will be like when they grow up.

I believe it's healthy to protect myself from too much toxic input from the media, but I also know it's neither healthy nor responsible to ignore the truth about what we're doing to each other and the world. Maybe things have always been this way and the more sheltered among us just didn't know. Maybe it was actually worse, and today things are better than ever. I really don't know. What I do know is that sometimes the situation feels hopeless.

Yet, for the most part, I don't think it is. The human spirit can grow and change. We have an inner need to improve ourselves—to be wiser, more balanced and noble, more responsible and compassionate. The lives of the world's most revered spirit people inspire us by proving it can be done. But most of us just can't seem to get it right: We don't know why we're the way we are, or why the world is the way it is, and we feel help-less to change any of it.

Some of us find hope in a supernatural deity that sees our problems and can fix them. From our limited perspective we try to imagine what this deity wants from us. Hoping for its goodwill and benevolent intervention, we try to please it. Whatever God may *actually* be, the God-images, beliefs, and practices of religion originate in our fears and desires—the normal fears and desires that accompany our growing awareness of ourselves—and our yearning to return to a barely remembered sense of being safe and at one with the Great Mystery of life.

When our primitive ancestors began to reflect on the Mystery, they may have assumed that because humanity is gendered, the gods must be as well. Earth was the foundation of existence and had an inexhaustible fruitfulness—it felt like a Mother. This experience shaped our earliest images of God. However, Mircea Eliade notes:

> In some cases, the sex of this earth divinity, this universal procreatrix—does not even have to be defined. A great many earth divinities . . . are bisexual. In such cases the divinity contains all the forces of creation—and this formula of polarity, of the coexistence of opposites, was to be taken up again in the loftiest of later speculation.[2]

Images of a Divine Androgyne of integrated masculinity and femininity appear throughout the world. Jungian analyst Dr. June Singer says they arise from the intuition "that the Ultimate Being consists of a unity-totality . . . [within which] exist all the conjoined pairs of opposites at all levels of potentiality."[3] In other words, our earliest God-images were expressions of our faintly remembered Epoch I experience of oneness. As a religious image, the Divine Androgyne was not about human sexuality, but about the potential for life's opposite energies to interact healthily within one unified, integrated being.

A slightly different expression of this idea appears in creation myths in which Earth Mother takes heaven as her partner and together the Divine Couple produces the gods and nurtures life. "The marriage between heaven and earth was the first hierogamy; the gods soon married too, and men, in their turn, were to imitate them with the same sacred solemnity with which they imitated everything done at the dawn of time."[4] The idea that all life results from a sacred marriage of two opposite yet complementary creative forces is as old as humanity itself. The feminine force appears always to foster a feeling of solidarity with the mothering earth, both as the whole place within which we find ourselves and as the inexhaustible power of creation. Moreover, the Goddess religions tended to generate long periods of peace in human affairs. For example, in Crete, the people

> appear to have been gentle, joyous, sensuous and peace-loving.
> From the evidence of ruins, they maintained, like the Maltese
> islanders, at least one thousand years of culture unbroken by
> war. The only other peoples we know of with such a long peace
> record—e.g., those of the Indus Valley and of Southern India—
> were also Mother Goddess cultures.[5]

Whether the earliest religions featured Earth Mother, the Divine Androgyne, or the Divine Couple, evidence suggests that reverence for the Sacred Feminine dominated religious thought for many thousands of years. Then about five thousand years ago the solitary Sky Father began to usurp the Great Mother's authority in the Middle East. Eliade notes that this Supreme God was not a daily physical and emotional reality like Goddess, but an intellectual concept. Idealized and aloof, he lived far from us and was essentially indifferent to our daily needs. Over time he grew increasingly uninvolved with human affairs.[6]

These changes occurred because our consciousness was evolving. Psychologically, we were leaving Epoch I and moving into a new era of self-awareness. The change gave rise to new religious forms with different priorities and perspectives on life. For example, as Sky Father gained supremacy "religious experience (already meager in the case of almost all the sky gods) gave place to theoretic understanding, or philosophy."[7] Learning to use our brains in more complex and abstract ways was natural and desirable. Unfortunately, wherever Great Mother was repressed, people tended to lose touch with themselves, Nature, each other, and their sense of life's sacredness.

For many people today who follow Judaism, Christianity, or Islam, God continues to be a separate, superior, human-like, dominant father. He dwells at the top of a hierarchy of males who serve him, he holds the power of life and death over us, and compared to him we are ignorant and powerless. In fact, so inferior are we to this omniscient, judgmental male that for many of us it feels like heresy to question him or his rules, no matter how arbitrary they might seem.

Insofar as they continue to elevate and idealize masculinity while disowning its destructive shadow (more on this later) and its complementary feminine partner, today's religions contribute to individual dysfunctions and the dysfunctional condition of our world. Fear of incurring the Sky God's disfavor stifles the biological compulsion to grow and change, to discover and empower our fuller selves. Our fear simply solidifies our position, and we retreat from life's inviting warmth into cold dogma. This effectively describes my own spiritual condition for many years.

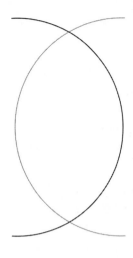

CHAPTER THREE

A Child's God

Deep beneath the adult surface layer, a childish emotional reality lives within as an insecure orphan child, afraid to leave the safety of her dark, locked room.

LIKE YOU, I got my first ideas about what is sacred from people around me. When I was ten, Grandma Benedict—with her marcelled white hair, perfect dentures, and smell of chamomile—came to visit while my father recovered from a heart attack. A devoted Baptist, she told me about Jesus and knelt with me by my bed as I invited him into my heart. She also taught me a prayer. It thanked God "for the shining sun above/for thy great and tender love," and asked him to make me more loving.

She talked about God's love for me. But some of her attitudes and actions suggested that God was a stern perfectionist, an aloof, no-nonsense ruler with no room in his heaven for fallen angels, bad children, or beloved dead pets. In fact, I'm pretty sure she believed heaven's gates would open only to good Baptists!

I also got mixed messages from Grandma Meengs, at whose Michigan farmhouse I spent many idyllic summers. While she was very kind, it was obvious that her God too was a strict taskmaster. He was appalled by people who drank liquor; would not allow certain activities on Sunday such as working, spending money for entertainment, going to movies, or playing cards; and found fault with women who didn't visit shut-ins once a week or wear hats and spotless white gloves to church every Sunday morning. He expected moral rectitude, self-discipline, and sacrifice from Grandma; and although she never said so, I could tell by the stoic resignation which could not disguise her disappointments that you mustn't expect God to give back much in return, at least not in this life.

The prayer Grandma Meengs taught me alerted me to the peril of dying in my sleep (*If I should die before I wake, I pray the Lord my soul to take*). When I asked her, though, she hastened to assure me that the possibility was very remote. Nevertheless, I should say my prayers every night to remind God that I wanted my soul to go to heaven. Apparently, God might forget about me otherwise, and I could fall, willy-nilly, into hell. I lay awake for a long time that night trying to reconcile a God of love with this new image of a careless, distant God who couldn't be counted on to remember to protect me while I was asleep.

From Grandpa Meengs, a lovely old Dutch man who put sugar on his sliced tomatoes and said "Hooer!" when he sneezed, I got the idea that God wanted to be thanked with long prayers before and after every meal, liked hearing the Bible read out loud before Sunday dinner, and wanted to see me in church every week. And God apparently preferred us to show our devotion and sincerity by singing hymns in three-part-harmony with gusto.

I don't remember my parents ever actually saying anything to me about God, but they believed in attending Sunday school and church regularly (Daddy went whenever he was home, which wasn't very often) and singing in the choir. Yet, despite the lack of spoken messages, my parents were my primary models for God.

Mama was an intelligent, hardworking, no-nonsense nurse admired by everyone who knew her. A woman of impeccable character with a Puritan work ethic and natural common sense, she expected a lot from herself and felt a deep responsibility to her family, friends, and community. Afflicted by a painful lack of social confidence, she shied from notice and acclaim, preferring to work diligently behind the scenes. After I left home she learned to type Braille and volunteered thousands of hours making documents for the blind and knitting baby caps and booties which she donated to the local women's hospital. She was kind, tolerant, and fair and loved my brother and me gently and unconditionally. Never once did she intentionally say a cruel word or make a promise she couldn't keep.

Daddy wasn't around very often to give her a hand, and Mama had a salary to earn and a job to keep. She had little time, energy, or inclination for much parenting beyond the basic necessities. At an early age I learned not to ask for anything out of the ordinary from her, whether it was baking cookies for class parties, driving me to the homes of friends, or attending the concerts and plays in which I performed. From when I was in second grade and my brother in fourth, we were on our own every day after school until early evening through necessity—the original latchkey children. From this I concluded that God had far more important things on his mind than me, and that the way to please him was to be good, responsible, independent, and self-sufficient.

Although my mother smoked for many years and even had an occasional glass of wine, she never smoked or drank in front of her parents who had been models for her own God-image. Thus I learned that I must not challenge God's rules or let him see uncomfortable truths about me, even if it occasionally forced me to hide a few little secrets. Otherwise (or so my childish mind unconsciously concluded), something terrible might happen: Maybe he'd think ill of me, be mad at me, or even stop loving and protecting me!

The most devastating message I learned about God from my mother was completely unintentional on her part. On her way to being the first woman in her family to have a college-educated profession, she adopted many values associated with masculinity—especially Warrior qualities like unbending dedication to her work, self-discipline, a Spartan lifestyle, independent self-sufficiency, and an unwillingness to impose on others or ask for help. She was introverted and emotionally reserved, and rarely expressed positive qualities she associated with femininity—such as softness, flexibility, vulnerability, strong feeling, emotional honesty, or a need for intimacy. When forced into situations that elicited these responses, she was visibly uncomfortable.

Indeed, it often seemed to me that she equated femininity with weakness, inferiority, and victimization. Like most people, she wasn't practiced in seeing herself objectively. I doubt she knew this about herself any more than she was aware of her assumption that men are more entitled than women, or that aligning oneself with masculine values is the way to stay safe and in favor with the powers that be. These were givens she never appeared to question. With no conscious awareness, she simply said "Yes" to the prevailing social and religious attitudes that favored maleness and

"No" to much of her feminine side. In doing so, she bequeathed to me the same God-image of male dominance and superiority that eroded her own hopes for wholeness.

I idolized my father. In my eyes he was perfect—my hero, a god. I have few memories of him because I saw him rarely and he died while I was eleven. But I do remember that as a policeman he believed in following the rules, especially rules about how to stay safe at home and on the streets. Naturally I concluded that following the rules was very important to God and the best way to stay safe in the dangerous world he had created.

Daddy was also a handsome, charismatic, self-confident singer, actor, and radio personality who charmed everyone with his good looks, playful sense of humor, and beautiful baritone voice. He loved literature, poetry, and music. When he was home recuperating from his heart attack, he filled the house with Gilbert and Sullivan operettas and read some of his favorite poetry aloud to me.

One day he took me to see a movie based on the opera *The Tales of Hoffman,* by Offenbach. As I was preparing for our outing he watched me struggling with my fine, thin hair. To me, styling my hair meant pinning it behind my ears with several bobby pins. After a while he suggested that I take out the bobby pins. He produced a tube of his Alberto VO5 pomade and combed a dollop of it through my limp mop. Then he stood back, eyed the pitiful results with bemusement, and told me something that, at the time, seemed deeply profound. "A woman's hair is her crowning glory," he solemnly pronounced. *This is an important thing for a woman to know,* my young heart fervently believed.

Another time he told me that a female newscaster on our new TV wasn't quite attractive enough because her eyes were too close together. Aha! Another moment of brilliant clarity. I felt honored that he confided these secret thoughts to me, and I treasured the few nuggets from the mystery of my father's masculine mind as laws written in stone by God atop Mount Sinai. From them I learned that God judges women's appearances and has certain standards about what makes them acceptable. God likes women to have glorious hair, be cultured, musical, well-groomed, and beautiful (preferably with wide-set eyes). Daddy would have loved Jackie Kennedy!

Once Daddy came upstairs to tuck me into bed and kiss me goodnight and, in a rare moment, gave in to my coaxing to sing me a song. Through that song I learned another lesson I never forgot: Daddy (and therefore God) loves little girls who are "sugar and spice, and everything nice" and who are always "Daddy's Little Girl." I was well-loved by this god-like man, and I was learning precious, valuable lessons about his (and therefore God's) expectations for me.

The summer before sixth grade we visited my father in another town where he was working. I was outside with several boys and girls having a carefree, rambunctious time diving, racing, and showing off in the motel pool when my parents called me inside. They had been watching and talking about me, and now they had something to say. Receiving personal attention from either of my parents was rare enough, but to be called into their joint presence was extremely unusual, like being summoned off the street to an unexpected audience with the Queen and King! I knew the matter must be of utmost importance, and listened intently.

I was a natural leader, with gifts and talents many children lacked, my father said. I should be careful, he warned, about not showing off, being bossy, or dominating situations too much. A little girl out there was having trouble keeping up with the rest of us. I should notice her, think about her feelings, try not to call attention to myself by outshining the others, try to include her and make her feel better about herself.

This was a crucial moment in my development. My eyes were instantly opened to an entirely new way of looking at myself and others. Overcome with self-consciousness, I realized for the first time that people were not only watching, but critiquing me, possibly even feeling bad about themselves because of me. I should think about their feelings and ignore my own. I should hide my strengths so as not to intimidate. I should be strong enough to make those kinds of sacrifices for others. Again, I felt as if I had gained a valuable piece of wisdom and I was grateful for it. I came out of the motel room a different child from the one who had so innocently pranced in.

After a moment's deliberation, I casually walked up to the little girl in the faded brown bathing suit and tentatively lied, "I like your bathing suit."

She seemed very pleased and grinned widely as she said something like, "Really? This old thing?" Then she bounced off happily to jump off the diving board, while I walked to the nearest chair and sat quietly so as not to attract notice.

I was stunned by my new awareness and felt uncomfortable about what I had done. I had just said something that wasn't true, but apparently with very good effect. What I said and did could make a difference to others! I could help people or harm them. What if in my ignorance I had spent the whole day out here innocently enjoying myself while making other children feel terrible about themselves without even knowing it? My God! The *mistakes* I could have made.

As I sat musing, my self-consciousness inflated like a bubble to the far reaches of the universe. Suddenly the world was filled with eyes, and I knew that all of them, including God's, were watching me. I felt as if I were being examined, cell by cell, beneath a critical, cosmic microscope. If I had to pick one moment in my life when self-consciousness took over and I left the innocent confidence of Epoch I behind, this would be it.

Soon, God was no longer a warm fuzzy feeling, but a collection of ideas. From my family I had learned that God first of all was a male who had nothing to do with my own body, my feelings or needs, or the joy and wonder I experienced in nature. He was an aloof, distant, powerful, all-seeing, overtly beneficent but secretly critical, gender-biased, judgmental, and untrustworthy King. He was a perfectionist who expected obedience, humility, hard work, high moral character, thoughtfulness, intelligence, beauty (from women), making nice (also from women), selfless service, and, of course, regular church attendance.

I was determined to give him these things to the best of my ability! In return, I would receive his approval (whew!), protection (maybe), and salvation (hopefully, if I worked really hard at it, but I would actually have no assurance of this until after I died). In between I should expect nothing else from him unless I did something wrong, in which case I would be notified and punished. He calls the shots and that's how it is. That was fine with me. After all, he was the King of Heaven; he was God.

This is a childish, Santa Clausy image of God. Based on a child's normal fears, vulnerability, and desire to please, it is a typical God-image of someone in the early stages of Epoch II. By puberty, most of us develop stronger egos with a measure of self-consciousness. Our new awareness of our individuality makes us less dependent on our personal mothers, but it does not necessarily cause us to question the God of our families. In fact, many of us never get around to that.

In my case, my God-image prevailed throughout my childhood and teenage years. When in young adulthood I became devoted to my religion, I brought this God-image with me. At a conscious level my spirituality underwent many changes in the coming years. But beneath the surface layer of intellectualization with which I came to identify as an adult, the same childish emotional reality—the same unconscious, needy attachment to the norms of my family—lived deep within me like an insecure orphan child who's afraid to leave the safety of her dark, locked room.

Why did this condition persist for so long? On to Chapter Four!

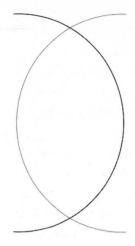

A Tribal God

If my family and church think I am good, I am; but if they think I am bad . . . I truly am . . .

I'M A LITTLE EMBARRASSED to admit that I had no knowledge of the subterranean realm that shaped my religious thinking—or any idea it was dominated by a child's God-image—until I approached midlife. I now realize that my God-image had remained stuck in pre-adolescence because of two traumatic events at age eleven that put the maturing of my ego on hold for many years. Then in midlife something unexpected happened. My inner adolescent, who had slept like a baby through my teens, began to wake up and notice how things really were. As I grew increasingly aware that my outer and inner lives were out of synch, a tension developed between God and me.

Wait a minute! When do I get to be an adult? I asked God. *Why do I always have to do things your way when everyone else breaks your rules all the time and gets away with it? When do I get to live my life the way I want to live it?* As the newly rebellious teenager in me reflected on my life (I was thirty-seven at the time), I began to realize just how much, to quote Jungian analyst Connie Zweig, "our early personal histories and unmet emotional needs influence our adult spiritual quests and religious desires."[8]

How does this apply to my life? Consider a few examples.

Trauma number one: Shortly after we visited Daddy at the motel my parents divorced. Did this influence my adult spiritual quest? Absolutely. In a heartbeat my comfortable immersion in a safe unconscious oneness morphed into a traumatic awareness of divided two-ness.

In junior high school I was so serious and self-conscious that I had little in common with my peers. While part of me yearned to be part of the mainstream teen culture, another part saw it as immature and shallow and compelled me to distance myself from it. After a while I secretly comforted myself with the notion that being a bit of an outsider confirmed my specialness in the eyes of God. Why did I think that? Well, didn't my heroes—God, Daddy, and the Lone Ranger—keep their distance too?

From college onward, an inner otherness occasionally snuck through my persona of earnest competence, idealistic resolve, and calm restraint. Sometimes this *other* felt as earthy, daring, and flamboyant as a gypsy. Sometimes it felt like a sad, lonely, insecure, and misunderstood orphan. In my thirties it began to feel like a dangerously angry bully—sort of like the Old Testament God of judgment and retribution I struggled to appease! Eventually my sense of being separated from God, others, and important parts of myself became so uncomfortable that I began a serious study of Jungian psychology with the hope of understanding and integrating my inner gypsy, orphan, and bully.

Trauma number two: Three months after my parents' divorce, Daddy died of his third heart attack and my primary exemplar for my God-image was dead. Is it any wonder I gave my heart to organized religion and clung to its assurance that its God was very much *alive* and truly loved me? For me it was all about the father God. The only times I thought about Jesus were Christmas and Easter and even then he didn't seem very important. I had no need for a baby or a suffering martyr. But I was desperate to restore the sense of safety a powerful and culturally sanctioned Father could provide, and to acquire it I did what my religion had done: I substituted mental abstractions for the physical imperatives which had previously defined my existence.

My mother was emotionally repressed and mistrustful of her femininity, and my father died when I was at an impressionable age. What does my history have to do with my adult spiritual quest? Just this: My most compelling needs have been to get in touch with my emotional realities, empower my femininity, and connect with sacred energies that are fully *alive* and close to me in the present moment.

If the motivations behind one person's quest differ from another's it is because of differing factors of personality and history. *Everybody* filters religious ideas through a lens of personal experience, and no two people have the exact same beliefs or God-image. But this is no cause for concern. The fact that spirituality is based as much on experiences as on input from religion in no way negates the truths of either element.

Every spiritual journey is personal, and every religion is grounded in the instinctual needs of the psyche. For example, our need to love and be loved fosters the belief that God is Love, as well as the goal of some Christians to have "a personal relationship with Jesus Christ." Our need for safety and protection fosters the belief that God is omnipotent. Our need for social interaction and connection gives rise to group worship and rituals. Each religion has its own beliefs, symbols, and ways of meeting universal needs. What matters most is not the details of our religions or personal journeys, but the great Mystery beyond the human limitations of time and space to which they point.

The goal of religion and the individual spiritual search is the same: to unite with, be at one with, the Mystery. We want to feel God, see the way God "sees," think the way God "thinks," behave the way God "behaves," love the way God "loves." Our success depends on our ability to open to the Mystery we call God. And unfortunately, our personalities and belief systems get in the way.

Here is one of the most important things I have learned about the spiritual quest:

If we want to know God we need to know ourselves well enough to see how and when we get in the way of receiving all of God.

In today's world one of the biggest barriers to receiving all of God is our fear of being ostracized by important social groups. One of these is our family. Another is our community of worship. Because of this fear many of us deny our own feelings and realities for years. Some never acknowledge them.

When I seriously began to question God in my late thirties, I had this herd mentality and didn't even know it. Beneath my fine ideals and carefully wrought beliefs was a set of emotional and instinctual assumptions of which I was completely unaware. Listen to the unconscious messages my gut was sending: *The tribe* (your family, mentors, teachers, government, religion, etc.) *is all-important. You are unimportant. The tribe's God-King is an all-powerful and all-knowing male. In comparison, you are powerless and ignorant. The better you are at adapting to the tribe's beliefs and the tribe's God, the better are your chances of survival. Period.*

The grown-up me didn't believe these things at a conscious level and I would have confidently contradicted anyone who suggested I did. But *without my knowledge* I was being influenced by my terribly insecure pre-adolescent "inner orphan" who believed them utterly. I had so little self-knowledge I was blind to her. But she was a very real complex of memories, emotions, ideas, and assumptions that covertly influenced my spirituality well into adulthood.

When I began a program of self-reflection I began to see that most of my religious practices were motivated by *fear*—fear of judgment from God and ostracism from my religious community. Sometimes God felt like a fierce and dangerous stranger whose retribution I feared, whom I had to obey and appease, who didn't value me as much as he valued others (especially men), and whose notice I sometimes hoped to avoid in order to stay safe.

From the age of seventeen I had a gnawing spiritual hunger that I looked to religion to satisfy. From then on I thought my reason for attending church and volunteering for so many boards and commissions was to give God what he wanted from me. But now I see that my unconscious motivation was not an altruistic desire to *serve* God but a need to *have the good opinion of* God, my ministers, and my fellow parishioners. My orphan was afraid that if I didn't go to church regularly, God might punish me, the preacher might be disappointed in me, and my religious community might think ill of me. I might even go to Hell!

I needed the approval of my "tribe" and its ideas about God. If my family and church thought I was good, I was; but if they thought I was bad, unworthy, lacking the necessary spirituality, or doomed to eternal damnation, it would mean I truly *was* bad, unworthy, lacking, and doomed. Again, I didn't believe this in any conscious way, but I now realize this is exactly what my hidden child believed.

Being an intelligent, well-intentioned, responsible adult does not automatically confer mature spirituality. As a college-educated, spiritually oriented woman I had a lot of information about my religion, but I didn't know myself or believe in the intrinsic value of my soul. With no models of psycho-spiritual maturity I had no understanding of how my personal psychology influenced my spirituality. I wanted to be spiritually mature and was doing everything I could to make that happen, except the one thing that would have worked: self-discovery.

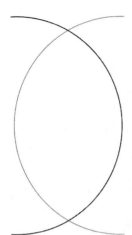

CHAPTER FIVE

A God Like Us

With an ego like this worshiping a God like that, is it any wonder most of us find it so incredibly difficult to open?

A MASCULINE GOD, a child's God, and a tribal God derive from a growing ego's tendency to see God in its own image. All three are typical God-images of Epoch II, especially in its earlier phases.

Epoch II: Ego Consciousness

Jungian analyst M. Esther Harding says this about the transition between Epochs I and II:

> Obviously we do not know how the ego arose in man. We have certain myths showing how ancient man thought about this problem, and we can observe the 81phenomenon in very young children today. Just as the individual child must undergo training and discipline, so too the primitive nature of man had to be housebroken and domesticated, restrained and adapted, if he was to advance in culture and in ability to control his environment.[9]

By around the age of three, most children's egos are strong and consolidated enough to think of themselves as separate individuals. This is when memory begins. We do not leave Epoch I behind at this point but we do begin to adjust our responses to our instinctual needs according to the demands of our environments and the development of our ego awareness. Recognizing our psychological separateness from Mother and our capacity for independent action doesn't always result in mature behavior, but it does make it *possible* for us evolve into the more mature form of self-awareness I call Epoch II.

The process is slow and gradual. Swiss psychologist Carl Jung reported that he was eleven when one day on his walk to school he stopped with the sudden revelation: "I am! I am what I am!" He realized that until then he had been living in a mist. I, too, experienced a rush of self-awareness at eleven; but I was thirty-seven before I woke fully from the fog in which I had been living and began to consciously differentiate myself from things.

Our egos have several spurts of increased self-awareness during Epoch II. Many of these awakenings are associated with developmental stages such as adolescence, young adulthood, and mid-life. At these critical junctures we confront new life challenges which make us aware of previously unknown needs and desires. The resulting inner conflicts help us see outdated reactions and assumptions, reflect on who we are and how we really want to live our lives, and dare to make new choices. At such times, most people gain valuable self-knowledge that furthers their inner growth; but fear and habit can hold us back, and we can get stuck at any time along the way. If this happens, our consciousness and religious thinking stop expanding even though our bodies and social behaviors continue to age and change.

Certain qualities of ego-consciousness are common in Epoch II. Among them are

- a sense of being separate from others;
- a primary emphasis on self-preservation and need-satisfaction, that is, self-centeredness and selfishness;
- the will to develop our individuality;
- an outer-referential focus on society and its conventions;
- resistance to and bias against otherness, including other people, other ways of thinking, other belief systems, and the disowned otherness of our psyches;
- anxiety about our self-worth;
- conflict between our longing to lapse back into the unconscious maternal matrix and the pressing need to prove ourselves in the eyes of the world.

What exactly is the ego? Carl Jung defined it as the organizing center of the *conscious* part of the psyche. Or we can simply say the ego is our conscious personality. This has three important implications.

First, as the ego emerges from Epoch I unconsciousness (or simply, *the unconscious*) it can become aware of only so much at a time. Its light starts out tiny and grows slowly. Everything about ourselves of which we are unaware, every primitive need and all our untapped potential, remains in the yolky unconscious. As we grow more self-aware in some areas of our lives, our attitudes and behaviors in other areas remain unconscious, unquestioned, and compulsive.

Second, our young ego doesn't realize it is becoming en*light*ened, or more conscious. We don't see that we're seeing more, and we don't reflect on this process. We simply absorb more light, willy nilly, without knowing how little we know or how much awaits our knowing. People around us can see how we're growing, but we can't. This is part of what being unconscious *means*: not knowing what's going on inside you or how you appear to others. Lack of objectivity about our true realities is characteristic of our egos until near the end of Epoch II.

Third, our differing personalities and experiences influence the development of consciousness. Every psyche does not enter Epoch II at the same age or attain the same degree of self-awareness. Once our egos attain enough mastery over our instinctual drives to acquire a certain level of security and self-esteem, many settle in comfortably and lose the need for more personal development and self-understanding. The demands and rewards of work and family life, social pressures and obligations, personal traumas, lethargy, and our natural resistance to the unknown tend to put a halt to expanding consciousness somewhere in Epoch II.

Hence, an Epoch II ego can be strong or weak, healthy or unhealthy, helpful or harmful, mature or immature, intelligent or ignorant, open or closed, caring or uncaring, static or growing. Some hunger for Spirit; some are not interested. Some fear the inner world; some can't get enough of it. The possibilities are endless.

The Masculine Orientation of the Epoch II Ego

A primary feature of Epoch II is the ego's preference for masculine values. If Epoch I is Mother's realm, Epoch II belongs to Father. It begins as a time of conflict when, in the words of philosopher Michael Washburn, "the father emerges both as a model of the independence the child desires and as a rival for the intimacy the child desires."[10] Whether or not a personal father or other adequate male model is available, children will try to satisfy their growing need to adopt masculine values by transferring their allegiance to teachers, peer groups, teams, nations, religions, or causes. Washburn explains,

> To the child, the father is the exemplary model of independent life—especially in the traditional patriarchal household, where he is . . . a sovereign master. Accordingly, the child senses that if it can win the father's acceptance it can enter the father's world and thereby share in the father's independence and extricate itself from dependence upon the mother.[11]

Epoch II ego-consciousness probably emerged about 50,000 years ago, but in the Middle East it began to make a big difference in human behavior around 5,500 years ago, somewhere between 3500 and 3100 B.C.E. This coincides with the appearance of writing—specifically, the first cuneiform figures in Sumeria—as well as the ascendency of the Sky God, the beginning of the demise of Goddess, and the onset of dominator cultures and hero myths.[12]

Once we choose the Father's world of work over the Mother's world of dependency (with little awareness or understanding of our choice), we usually put our conflicts on hold for a while. But during adolescence most egos receive a new charge of self-awareness and face traumatic new realities: Our bodies are growing and changing in alarming ways; we have opinions, needs, and talents that differ from what our parents expect of us; we want to become independent and express ourselves more openly; people are watching and judging us; our actions affect others for good or evil; someday we will die.

These new conflicts elicit an intense need to further develop our individuality. Although the genders experience this growing self-awareness differently, the gap is narrower than we might think.[13] During this time the healthy ego of either gender flexes its wings, struts around the nest, and begins to call forth "masculine" values such as will power, independence, self-initiative, self-discipline, competition, achievement, and ambition. It does this partly to gain favor in Father's world, and partly in service to four main goals for which all of humanity naturally strives: lawful order and moral virtue, power and success, release from delusion, and love and pleasure.[14]

Dualism and the Epoch II Ego

With ego consciousness, everything becomes about us. Things no longer just exist: they exist for *us!* They are good or bad for *us!* All things which were once one, are now split in two. Dualism arises naturally as we separate from Mother's realm and begin to differentiate ourselves. We start figuring out how we are like her and how we're not, what we can and can't do, who will help us and who won't, and so on. In other words, we sort things into pairs of clearly defined opposites: that which is desirable, or "good," and that which is undesirable or "bad." If we felt relatively safe and comfortable during Epoch I, we usually identify with the "good" and repress the "bad."

Good and bad differ among individuals and tribes. Naturally, *our* group—the one that's familiar, bolsters our egos, and makes us feel safe and acceptable—is good. *Their* group becomes at least suspect and sometimes bad. Likewise, as individuals we disown whatever we don't like about ourselves, don't want to be, or don't want to know about ourselves. We don't think about what we're doing or wonder why we're doing it, it just comes naturally. But whenever we repress an inner quality that feels important to us to fit in with a group ethos, we lose touch with our golden core.

Before, it was all about the great warm, floaty, androgynous Mom. In Epoch II it's increasingly about Mom and *me*, Dad and *me*, Dad and Mom, male and female, self and other, us and them, King and Queen, good and evil, spirit and body, life and death, God and *me*. Seeing differences, taking sides, and conforming to new standards we consider better than ones we want to leave behind brings hope and makes us feel we have some control. By about the age of eleven when we attain mature cognitive ability, dualistic thinking is our solid default mode and our ego is firmly established as the center of the psyche (and the universe, for most egos!).

Dualistic thinking is neither good nor bad in itself. It's simply the ego's natural mode in this stage.

Repression and the Epoch II Ego

A third dominant feature of the Epoch II ego is repression, toward both self and other. The dark side of dualistic thinking creates bias, prejudice, suspicion, hostility, fear, aggression, and repression. Most Epoch II egos contain their repressive tendencies without causing undue damage or harm. But there are always some people who obsess over the "masculine" qualities so highly prized during this phase that they become inordinately repressive to "feminine" otherness. Unwilling to consider opposing points of view or budge from entrenched polarized positions, they can become so self-righteous and closed-minded that they gravitate, like the Sky God onto which they project these qualities, toward agitation, divisiveness, domination, and war.

Egos like this might be strong enough to keep growing, and often are well-intentioned. But as long as they put their consciousness in service to repression, *and as long as they cling to their position as the sole "deity" within the psyche,* they will not recognize their imbalances. The most powerful and repressive of these Epoch II egos are the major culprits in the dangerous dramas playing out on the world-stage today. In their psychological ignorance, many of them fervently believe they are God-centered; but in truth, they are firmly entrenched in Epoch II egocentricity.

In empowering our ego and masculine qualities we are obeying the evolutionary imperative to gain access to this aspect of our potential. Fish gotta swim. Birds gotta fly. People gotta grow up and become conscious. Epoch II is an essential phase of psycho-spiritual development and a profound improvement over Epoch I. We all have to experience it, and most of us function relatively comfortably and healthily in this realm throughout our lives. Nevertheless, during Epoch II, vast amounts of our psychological inheritance, the majority of which we associate with Mother, remain buried in a dark, pre-conscious, reservoir to which we deny ourselves conscious access.

The same is true of our spiritual inheritance. In the West and in the

Middle East our separating out from the personal mother is accompanied by a rejection of Sacred Mother, but this doesn't destroy her. In fact, Eliade was convinced that until very recently a sub-stream of Goddess religion still flowed in peasant cultures of the West. Why? Because the Sacred Feminine is an archetypal reality in the human psyche.

As long as humans exist, Mother Queen will be as vital to us as Father King. Repressing her simply forces her underground, where she continues to impact our thoughts and deeds in ways we don't understand and can't control. An unexamined Epoch II bias against feminine values in our own time, for example, strongly influences our views of women and how we live our lives.

Not even acute psychic pain can guarantee victory over habitual repression. The masculine orientation of the Epoch II ego is so deeply tied to conventional beliefs about what is real, important, virtuous, and capable of bringing safety, power, and success that sometimes not even the strongest and most mature egos take the leap into conscious, integrated wisdom. There is not a firmly entrenched Epoch II ego on the planet that welcomes the reality and power of the disowned feminine or wants to admit that our repression of her is the underlying cause of so much discomfort. In the deepest recesses of our psyches a primal war is being waged between two compelling needs: our need to preserve the self-images our egos have so carefully constructed and our need to transcend the limitations our egos have imposed.

The proof of the Epoch II ego's extreme need to preserve, indeed, to glorify its self-image whatever the cost is its willingness to kill and die for the God it creates in its own image. The Epoch II God is just like us. It is oriented toward masculinity, thinks dualistically, has the same beliefs about good and evil as we do, prefers our particular tribe, and represses otherness to the point that it is sometimes compelled to destroy the things our tribes fear and despise. With an ego like this worshiping a God like that, is it any wonder most of us find it so incredibly difficult to open to the unknown otherness in our unconscious?

This brings us to a final distinguishing factor of Epoch II: conflict. Chapter 6 highlights a major conflict experienced by almost every Epoch II ego: the opposition between masculinity and femininity.

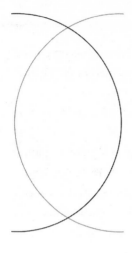

CHAPTER SIX

A Gender-Biased God

You repressed a talent, didn't develop important skills, passed up opportunities because of biases of people you grew up with. From denial, embarrassment, hidden anger, or wounded pride, you don't want to believe how much you've missed out on.

FOR AS LONG as I can remember I've struggled with the idea that God is a male. Many spirit persons don't think of God as a supernatural gendered being, but many ordinary people do. Everywhere we turn, religious language still speaks of He or Him and tells us we are His. As a child I found this curious. By midlife I was finding it annoying. Now I think it's just plain silly, because this way of thinking limits our ability to open to all we really are and what the Mystery really is about.

Still, there are levels of spiritual awareness. And there are times when describing the Mystery in terms of gender can be helpful, as it was for our early forbears. When it comes to seeing our assumptions and biases, it still is. To that end, this chapter offers two lists: one containing concepts associated with the "Feminine Principle" and another for the "Masculine Principle."

I put these terms in quotes because I might as easily say the so-called masculine and feminine principles. There of course are males and females, but both physically and psychologically many people find themselves somewhere between the two. Some feel like one gender living in the body of the other. Some have physical attributes associated with both genders. And we all have psychological attributes associated with both genders.

Scientists have long understood that in the physical world the interaction between polarities is what keeps our planet stable and functioning smoothly. Yet until very recently, few people with Epoch II ego-consciousness have thought of human behavior in the same way. Freud broke new ground when he noted that "man's instinctive nature is divided between the instinct for self-preservation and the instinct for species-preservation."[15] He wrote,

> The individual does actually carry on a twofold existence: one to serve his own purposes and the other as a link in a chain, which he serves against his will, or at least involuntarily.[16]

We can associate the instinct, or drive, for self-preservation with the "masculine" striving for knowing, competing, and individuating, and the drive for species-preservation with the "feminine" urge toward relating, creating, reproducing, and evolving. Note Freud's observation that the individual serves the drive for species-preservation against his will: No ego starts out wanting to shoulder responsibility for anyone but itself!

People broadly accept this basic polarity and use the terms *masculine principle* and *feminine principle* as metaphors or category heads under which to classify all phenomena. The terms persist because they serve a useful purpose: They *symbolically* express "the energic power behind all of the other polarities."[17] This is the basis for my lists, using these terms as metaphors for pairs of opposites in every psyche. None of the qualities at either pole is inherently good or bad, but any of them can be taken to negative extremes if we obsess over it and repress its partner. All have positive value for both genders—whether you are a female or a male you have the potential to develop every quality listed.

The associations I give for masculine and feminine have generally held sway in mainstream Western thinking for two millennia; but earlier, and in other parts of the world now, we find many differences. For example, while Westerners today usually associate the sky with masculinity and the earth with femininity, ancient Egyptians symbolized the sky as the goddess Nut and the earth by the god Geb. Likewise, whereas traditional Tibetan Buddhism sees compassion as a masculine virtue and wisdom as feminine, the current Western trend is toward the opposite associations.

Such anomalies prove my point about the metaphorical value of the terms. The sky is no more literally masculine than the earth is literally feminine, and both genders are equally capable of being wise and compassionate. Epoch III thinkers know this and lose the need for such classifications. But associating phenomena with masculinity and femininity can be helpful in our Epoch II efforts to better understand ourselves and our ideas about God. It provides a basis to help explore the truth of our opinions and discover philosophical contradictions and solutions. Developing this dialectical ability is crucial to our psyche's integration and wholeness.

Why Emphasize the Differences between the Opposites?

My goal is to dissolve gender stereotypes, not promote them. I am not a proponent of dualistic thinking. I don't think that all men (or all women) are alike. I don't believe men and women should be judged or treated by different standards. I don't consider either gender more valuable or less equal than the other, or prefer the qualities associated with one to those of its opposite. I do not believe that our roles in life should be prescribed by our society's attitudes toward gender. All that is Epoch II thinking, and a source of spiritual blindness.

I separate the terms into two camps to give a visual illustration of the Epoch II recipe for conflict—its tendency to perceive opposites from a perspective that divides them and judges one side as more or less desirable. This kind of dualistic thinking is so deeply embedded in our psyches that in the language of numerology two represents conflict!

Try to look at the pairs of words listed under *Drive for Self-Preservation* and *Drive for Species-Preservation* not as stereotypes or gender descriptors, but as a rough composite of *everyone's* psychological and spiritual potential. Notice how aligning yourself with one side creates a divide in you that separates you from the positive qualities of its opposite. Use this awareness as an opportunity to see the value of both sides.

The Importance of Your Associations

My classifications are archetypal and cultural, not personal. I have not made them up, but culled them from a variety of sources over years of research. If your own associations for some of them differ greatly from what I offer, don't discount your personal responses. In fact, it's essential that you pay close attention to your emotional reactions and differing associations. Whether or not they are shared by others, they are true for you because of your history; recognizing them can lead to valuable insights that will expand your self-awareness, a primary goal of this book.

If you find yourself seeing one list as good and the other as bad, or if you feel defensive or smug about some of these associations or have a particularly strong emotional response like anger or resentment, there could be several possible reasons. One might be that you aren't using my distinction between gender (men and women) and the masculine and feminine principles (fully present as potentials in each of us, regardless of biological gender).

When I first learned, for example, that reason has generally been associated with masculinity and emotion with femininity it made me mad. I didn't like it and didn't want to believe it. My family valued reason over emotion and so did I. I told myself that being a woman didn't mean I was any more emotional than some of the men I knew, and I rejected the stereotype of the unreasonable, emotional female with all my being.

Why did I have such a strong response? Two reasons: First, I was in the grip of dualistic tribal thinking and didn't want to be associated with something my family thought of as undesirable. Of course there's nothing inherently negative about emotion or positive about reason; it all depends on how they are used. Moreover, I was just as emotional as anyone else. But I didn't know I was because I had repressed so much of my emotional life. I didn't want to be emotional, so I was particularly sensitive to any suggestion that I was. Ironically, the intensity of my emotional response proved the lie of my denial!

The second reason I responded so strongly to this particular pair of opposites is because I was thinking of the term *feminine* as a synonym for women. I didn't know yet that women have a masculine side and men have a feminine side. Associating emotion with femininity isn't the same thing as stereotyping *women*. It's merely an indication of how civilizations have tended to view the feminine *principle*, which is a metaphor for the drive for species-preservation—not a quality associated only with females. In the everyday world of human behavior, women can be eminently reasonable and men can be wildly emotional.

Another reason for a negative response could be that the biases of your group of origin forced you to repress deeply meaningful skills or talents such that your failure to develop your fullest potential has caused you pain and/or resulted in missed opportunities. Whether out of denial, embarrassment, hidden anger, or wounded pride, maybe you simply don't want to believe how much you've missed out on. If that is so, I hope you realize it's never too late to claim the life you were born to live.

A pronounced emotional reaction could also be rooted in a problem with one of your parents or caregivers. For example, if your mother was cold or cruel, or if she abandoned you at an early age, leaving you to be raised by your father who was a very nurturing parent, you might associate such terms as "connection," "relationship," "intimacy," "softness," and "nurturance" with masculinity while having negative associations for feminine qualities and women in general. Conversely, if you had a hard-working, productive, logical, focused mother and an absent, overly aggressive, or unduly passive father, you might have negative associations for men and some of the masculine qualities.

So pay attention now! How do you really feel about the following associations the West has long held for masculinity and femininity?

The Feminine and Masculine Principles

Drive for Species-Preservation	*Drive for Self-Preservation*
The Feminine Principle	The Masculine Principle
Relationship	Individuality
Connection	Separation
Intimacy	Distance
Descent	Ascent
Shared authority	Hierarchical authority
Internal guidance	External guidance
Being	Doing
Fertility	Productivity
Creativity	Manifestation
Nurturance	Assertion
Receptivity	Penetration
Passivity	Activity
Submission	Dominance

Drive for Species-Preservation	*Drive for Self-Preservation*
Emotion	Logic
Ethic based on caring	Ethic based on justice
Instinct	Reason
Nature	Science
Diffuse awareness	Focused consciousness
Mystery	Clarity
Subjectivity	Objectivity
Imagination	Supposition
Experience	Belief
Symbol	Fact
Image	Word
Practicality	Idealism
Process-oriented	Product-oriented
Verbal	Mathematical
Unconscious Nature/Matter	Conscious Spirit/Mind
Non-ego	Ego
Heart	Head
Oriented to the big picture	Oriented to detail
Holism	Polarity
Collective	Individual
Concrete	Abstract
Physical reality	Esoteric ideal
Body	Spirit
Earth	Sky
Moon	Sun
Dark	Light
Depression	Inflation
Completion	Perfection
Psychology	Spirituality
Chaos	Stability
Change	Permanence
Internal	External
Enfolding	Unfolding
Right hemisphere of the brain	Left hemisphere of the brain

Drive for Species-Preservation	Drive for Self-Preservation
Both/And	Either/Or
Cyclical	Linear
Magnetism	Dynamism
Soft	Hard

You may have noticed that a crucial pair of opposites is missing from this list. If awareness of our separateness from our mothers is the initial impetus for psychological growth, it is awareness of our capacity for good and evil that generates spiritual growth. Since we cannot discuss spiritual growth without addressing this pair, it is the subject of the next chapter.

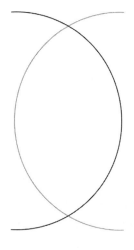

CHAPTER SEVEN

A Conventionally Moral God

Evil is not located in a supernatural entity, a particular person or nation, or one side of an argument. It resides in an ego that is implacable in its certainties, ignorant of its destructive tendencies, and closed to further growth.

OF ALL THE OBSTACLES to spiritual maturity, dualistic thinking about God's moral code is perhaps the most difficult to deal with and the most dangerous to humanity. For many seekers, the classic conflict between good and evil is the name of the religious game, and everything—including human life and the fate of our planet—depends on who wins. *If my God has a different conception of right and wrong than yours, then the hell with you! You deserve to have your brains blown out.*

Am I right? In this way of thinking, the highest priority isn't to live and act with compassion but to have correct beliefs. Right there you know you're talking about Epoch II because you're all about mental abstractions and either/or judgments.

Unlike the majority of their peers, the men who founded the great patriarchal religions had evolved beyond Epoch I. Ever since Eve ate the apple there have been serious seekers who consider heady issues like what is right and what is wrong, what is God and what is Devil. The founding patriarchs had developed healthy egos and acquired consciences. And because they were trying so hard to be the good guys, they reasoned that evil must exist somewhere out there in the dark world of otherness. It couldn't be in *them*.

Based on their growing self-reflective awareness and the dualistic thinking it spawned, they chose what they considered to be the good in every pair of opposites and formed their God-images around these words, qualities, and concepts. This kind of thinking was necessary if humanity was to become more conscious and morally responsible. But they misused it when they assigned the label of *evil* to the rejected opposite. This tendency of every Epoch II ego is the reason for Jesus's notable and widely ignored suggestion [Matthew 7:4, 7:5 and Luke 6:41, 42] to look not for the mote in thy neighbor's eye but for the log in thine own.

For example, instead of seeing the Great Mother as an opposite but equally valid aspect of Creation, they portrayed her as a threat to growing consciousness. Goddess represented their former Epoch I condition of instinctual behavior and moral irresponsibility, whereas the new solitary masculine God symbolized their hope of evolving toward a "higher," more perfected and enlightened consciousness. Terrified of losing the ground they had worked hard to gain, many of them believed they had to destroy Goddess's worship and replace it with their new bias toward God. And since they feared their own feminine sides, they demonized Goddess. This is why femininity is still associated with the unconscious and, for some people, dangerous and even evil aspects of the psyche.

For the past five thousand years, Goddess has been the overarching symbol for what patriarchal religions of the West and the Middle East have rejected. She is the whore male authorities have projected onto every defenseless woman who has been stripped of her autonomy, used for their purposes, and then abandoned to fend for herself. She is the witch they tortured and torched for stirring their terror of feminine power. She is the devil who tempts us to sin, the seductress who infiltrates our fortresses and weakens our resolve, the heretic who threatens to expose the pathology of our pat beliefs, the nemesis of every pious do-gooder who acts from the head and not the heart.

But before she was a symbol of evil, she represented something very good indeed: loving and creative partnership between the opposite energies of life. By demonizing her we subverted our hopes for wholeness. By integrating her we can break out of the dualistic prison that bars our growth.

But wait a minute, you may be thinking: *If evil is the opposite of good, and if we're supposed to integrate the opposites, are you telling me I need to condone evil as well as good? I'm sorry, but that's just wrong!*

This issue is a major stumbling block for every thinking seeker. Here's the bottom line: The opposition of evil-versus-good belongs in a separate category all its own.[18] Why? Because unlike the others, which are morally neutral expressions of naturally occurring energies, good and evil are dualistic *judgments* about the *worth* of these energies. Over the centuries patriarchy has judged the feminine side of many of these pairs evil and the masculine side good. As philosopher Michael Washburn noted to me in a letter, "This is a horrendous category mistake, but it has successfully disguised patriarchy's *judgment* of women by making it seem as if it were a *fact* about women."

Okay, I get it that we can wrongly judge things evil that are not, but surely there is evil in the world, you might argue. *And we know it when we see it. Isn't there some standard we can all agree on that will help us overcome personal biases and think maturely about this?*

Good question! Dr. Lawrence Kohlberg and Dr. Carol Gilligan of Harvard University have devised and tested theories about moral reasoning that should be of some assistance.[19] The following is a condensed summary of their combined findings.

Three Levels of Moral Reasoning

Level I: Pre-Conventional

According to this theory, we all start out at Level I. Here we reason that *bad* is whatever gets us punished and prevents us from getting what we want, and *good* is whatever keeps us from being punished and provides what we want. To people who think like this, it's okay to lie, steal, and cheat as long as we are clever enough not to get caught. This thinking is natural and normal in young children, but prisons are filled with adults who never grew beyond this immature, self-serving morality.

Level II: Conventional

The Level II emphasis is on the conventional values of our families and social groups. *Bad* and *good* start out being whatever gains the disapproval or approval of our parents. Then they gradually come to be defined by whether we do our civic duty or experience guilt if we do not. Estimates are that the moral reasoning of about sixty percent of the population is based on this way of thinking: It emphasizes the importance of gaining your family's and society's approval, having a conscience, doing your duty, acting responsibly, keeping laws, and making personal sacrifices for the good of your family and community. Some of us think of this as the highest form of morality, but there is more.

Level III: Post-Conventional

For the approximately twenty percent who move on to Level III, moral reasoning transcends local rules and boundaries to enter a universal arena. People at this level don't leave conscience, law, or duty behind. Rather, they use their maturing understanding to work out a personal ethic that is not prescribed or enforced by anyone else and applies to everyone and everything.

We enter this level when we come to see that *s/he* is a person too, and s/he deserves fair and equal treatment. *Bad* then becomes anything that violates human rights and good is whatever affirms them. However, it eventually dawns on us that evil is even more than the violation of human rights going on *out there:* it is the absence *in me* of love or caring; it is when *I* do not respect the life, sovereignty, or significance of otherness. It is when *I* feel hatred. When *I* feel superior or more entitled. When *I* do not see the log in my own eye. Most of all, it is when *I* do not act with fairness and compassion toward every form of life, including myself and my fellow human beings.

The ultimate *good* then becomes whatever I can do to promote justice and engender love using the principle of nonviolence to create the most possible benefit and cause the least possible pain or harm to others. At this level of reasoning, morality is no longer about pointing out and destroying the evil in them. It is about cultivating genuine love in me and acting in accordance with this love in everything I do. This is a fulfillment of the noblest moral potential of humanity.

So What?

Now here's the problem. Level II moral reasoning is closely linked to Epoch II ego-consciousness. While both are vast and vitally necessary improvements over Level I and Epoch I, they are also both easily seduced into complacency by collective thinking. During Epoch II we are pleased to have left our youthful selfishness behind and we enjoy society's sanction. We may be attracted to Level III morality when we come across it; but unless we are personally embroiled in a difficult moral dilemma that forces us to question our values, it is easily set aside. Indeed, some more repressive Epoch II egos tend to set "self-indulgent navel-gazing" against our ideals of hard work, self-sacrifice, responsibility, and duty. This polarizing attitude toward self-exploration can stop our growth.

For most people in Epoch II, conforming to societal norms and rules never presents serious problems. Sometimes we question our group's standards and work diligently to change rules that seem unfair, but for the most part we are content to conform. Indeed, a certain amount of conformity is the necessary glue that holds societies together and protects their members. Most of us realize this and try our best to do the right thing without undue rebelliousness or, at the opposite extreme, becoming unthinking slaves to convention.

But when our natural resistance to change is combined with a painful personal history and powerful repressive forces in society, conventional thinking can engender a moral fanaticism that actively seeks to enslave and destroy those whose moral values and religious beliefs differ from ours. In today's world this kind of thinking justifies terrorism and ethnic "cleansing." In the past it enabled God-fearing Christians to enslave Africans and obliterate the cultures of Native American "pagans." Thus "we" who do not recognize and speak out against moral fanaticism in our own culture are as culpable as "they" who remain silent in theirs. To stand by and do nothing simply adds another brick to the wall that blocks humanity's evolutionary march to mature morality.

Currently, Epoch III consciousness and Level III moral reasoning face powerful opposition from fanatical defenders of traditional values and religious orthodoxy. We see fierce conflict between the comforts of conventional thinking and the allure of the headier fruit of individuation, moral maturity, and spiritual liberation. Those whose struggles between hurting and caring go deepest, who can tolerate the tension between the opposites the longest, who are most open to change and most willing to go the distance—these people are going to love *this* apple when they bite into it! Nothing tastes better to a maturing mind and spirit than expanding consciousness.

Our concepts of good and evil grow and change as we grow and change, and that is a very good thing. Just as we are programmed to grow in self-awareness, we are *supposed* to evolve from self-centered personal concerns, through local concerns, and into universal ones in which we genuinely care as much about the welfare of all others as we do about ourselves. If we become too entrenched in Epoch II moral certainties and project them onto an equally rigid God of conventional morality, we are our own worst enemies and a threat to others.

So in answer to my earlier question—*If evil is the opposite of good, and if we're supposed to integrate the opposites, are we supposed to condone evil as well as good?* Absolutely not. We are not to condone evil in ourselves or in others. We are to *integrate* the evil within us *into our awareness,* which is the only way to defuse it.

In other words, we are to stop pointing the finger and scapegoating others and start recognizing our own capacity for evil: the critical and judgmental thoughts, the desires for revenge, the small lies and subtle deceits, the betrayals of those who trust us, the blame we heap on others while excusing ourselves, our prejudice against people who are different, our thoughtless acts, our indifference toward the pain and misfortunes of others, our secret selfishness and sense of superiority. Seeing the evil within ourselves humbles us and replaces blame with understanding, hatred with tolerance, fear with trust.

There are two sides to every conflict, and there is self-serving as well as mature reasoning on both sides. Evil is real, but it is not located in a supernatural entity, a particular person or nation, or one side of an argument. Evil resides in an ego that is implacable in its certainties, ignorant

of its destructive tendencies, and closed to further growth. The Rt. Rev.
Larry Maze says,

> For a contented ego, all things big and small matter only with
> regard to their impact on me and whatever it is that matters to
> me. . . . The God-Satan duality exists within our own being where
> there is a constant conversation going on between Self and ego,
> between what lies in the shadow and in the light. It is that conver-
> sation alone that transforms the dark shadow.[20]

Tolerating the tension of dialogues between our inner opposites is our
key to moral maturity. The Epoch II King's laws and punishments can no
more bring lasting peaceful attitudes and actions to a closed mind than a
Sunday morning sermon can change the inveterate Monday evening thief.
Like the hellfire and brimstone sermon, threats may help some people do
the right thing for fear of retribution; but in moments of crisis, rules have
little power to sway the raging shadow of an unconscious person.

The research of Kohlberg and Gilligan uncovered one more factor
crucial to this discussion. From the masculine perspective the supreme
moral value is justice; from the feminine, it is caring. But this does not
have to be an either/or situation. Can we not honor both? Governments
and legal systems have tried their best to honor the King's ethic in society, but injurious class distinctions, economic injustices, and all manner
of crime persist. The psycho-spiritual solution to our moral problems is
to consciously develop our Queen and integrate her standards with those
of the King.

Our ability to care in this way depends on a radical change of heart.
And changes in heart go hand in hand with ego change. Current research
indicates that if you can change the way you think, you will change the
way you feel. Few things in this world are as powerful and life-altering
as an ego willing to engage in mental training. As a result of committed
psycho-spiritual practices, spirit persons from every age and culture report
spiritual awakenings that cause permanent change. Science is proving it.

For example, neuroscientist Mario Beauregard writes of certain meditation practices that "people can change profoundly and irreversibly after

these experiences. The change is generally interpreted as being for the better because the person becomes very loving and forgiving."[21] Likewise, *Newsweek* science writer Sharon Begley reports on an ongoing dialogue between neuroscientists and the Dalai Lama about the plasticity of the human brain: The research reveals how mental training in adults actually alters the brain's structure and function so that more of its "real estate" is devoted to the new qualities—such as openness to God and compassion for otherness—that are being nurtured.[22]

We have good reason to hope. It is possible for us to develop mature moral reasoning. But to do so we must accept that just as surely as evil resides in others it also resides in us. I will speak more about this in Chapter Nine and in Part 2.

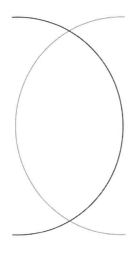

CHAPTER EIGHT

An Outer Other God

*Our ego wants to be King of the psyche. Its
unwillingness to open to inner otherness, to share
its home, is a rejection of the Great Mystery . . . it
sabotages our desire to complete ourselves . . .*

A YOUNG Epoch II ego reasons that since God lives
in Heaven, God does not live on Earth. It follows that spiritual authority
on Earth comes only from spiritual professionals who are somehow closer
to God than the rest of us are. We may hear people say God lives in us,
and we may try to believe it; but to an Epoch II ego this is a very difficult
idea. After all, if God lived within us, wouldn't we know it? Wouldn't we
feel it?

For most of us most of the time, God is not a palpable, everyday reality
but a separate entity to appreciate through mental abstractions, not personal experiences. But it doesn't have to be that way—as a symbol from
the animal kingdom may illustrate.

In many times and places throughout the world, bears have carried
spiritual significance for humans. When bears hibernate in the winter they
fall into a sleep so deep that they appear to be dead; yet, in the spring they
emerge from their caves as if resurrected. Thus, bears symbolize spiritual
awakening and rebirth.

Other spiritual meanings derive from how mother bears raise and
initiate their cubs. Deeply nurturing and fiercely protective, they display
the very best aspects of maternity, not only because they are so effective
at preserving the life of their young, but also because they show us how
to leave fear behind and begin the journey to the sacred within. Here's a
story along those lines that affected me deeply.

• • •

The mother bear is one of the most tender, nurturing, and fiercely protective mothers in the animal world. In the spring when she emerges from her den, she brings with her at least one new cub if she gave birth during the hibernation. One of the first and most difficult lessons she teaches her baby is to stay hidden and quiet high up in a tree while she searches for food. It is essential that the cub remain in the tree, for if she climbs down and wanders around alone it is only a matter of time before she will become lunch for a ravenous adult male bear.

Having no idea of the danger that awaits, in those first few days out of hibernation the cub tries to climb down and follow her mother. When this happens the mother swats her child firmly and chases her back up the tree. Finally the poor baby stays, afraid of being alone, but more afraid of her mother's disapproval. Soon she learns to trust that if she stays there long enough, Mother will eventually come back. Then the joyful cub can climb down and together they will eat, play, and snooze until it's time to bed down for the night.

The mother and cub follow this routine for about two years. During this time the dutiful cub learns her lessons well from the good mother.

Then one day the mother bear trees her cub as usual. She goes out into the woods as usual.

And she never comes back.

The sun's rays lengthen. Twilight arrives. The baby waits in the tree. She is hungry. She is lonely. She is afraid. After a while she even becomes angry. How dare her mother stay away so long? Still she waits. Night falls. She hears strange and terrifying noises in the woods and there is a gnawing hunger in her belly. But she has learned her lessons well, so she waits for her mother like a good little bear.

Here is the terrible truth that the young bear must learn: In order to survive and grow into a mature bear who will eventually become a nurturing mother herself, she must commit an act of disobedience against the good mother. She must climb down from the tree.

The moment when the baby bear climbs down and wanders off to make her sad and lonely way through the dangerous forest, is the moment she accepts her royal birthright. No longer will she be a naive and innocent little princess. She has no choice but to grow up. The queen of her universe is dead. Long live the new queen.

• • •

Although it may seem cruel, the mother bear's abandonment of her cub initiates its journey into maturity. The young bear's predicament parallels the ego's path of awakening to the sacred authority of our own soul and the compelling need to act on it. Very often this awakening is brought on by sufferings in love relationships which force us to take our inner lives seriously and find within ourselves the love we seek. Until this happens, the breadth of our choices and depth of our potential are obscured by a single-minded focus on getting love and approval from outer others.

Our separation from our inner realities is a natural consequence of the ego's progress through Epoch I to the stage in Epoch II when, having disowned our feminine sides, we project the good mother (symbolized by the mother bear) onto society, which then becomes the new good mother we serve. The most reliable indicator of our ego's readiness to grow into Epoch III is when we awaken to the fact that this profoundly wise and powerful inner feminine authority actually dwells with us, and are willing to commit an act of disobedience (inner or outer) against the good mother of society to follow this inner guidance. This applies for both women and men.

The mother bear often appears in art, myth, fantasy, and dreams to symbolize this potent feminine force which dwells in a cave-like chamber of the unconscious and periodically emerges to initiate us into more mature spiritual levels. For example, some inundation (flood) myths in which the old world is destroyed to set the stage for a new one feature bears associated with moon goddesses.[23] Psychologically, this refers to a psyche that has been flooded with powerful and painful emotions which create new awareness and motivate change. Jung associated this transforming activity with the Mother archetype.

In alchemy, bears were considered the *nigredo* (or dark, transforming phase) of the mysterious *prima materia*.[24] This represents loss of libido, depressions, and dark nights of the soul which are brought about by unwelcome incursions of repressed unconscious contents (experienced by the masculine-oriented ego as foreign and other, and therefore feminine) which threaten to drag us down into the muddy abyss of despair.

In Christianity the mother bear often represents virgin birth since she supposedly gives shape to her young as she licks them; and "in both Greek and Latin the word for bear is of feminine gender, reflecting the bear's positive motherly qualities (especially the ethical and caring aspects)."[25] These associations refer to the benevolent, nurturing aspects of femininity, which in myth, alchemy, and history is often represented by the Queen archetype.

The Queen's initiatory strategies have the same purpose as those of the mother bear: They are intended to awaken us to a more expanded, mature, and empowered way of living. But like the baby bear, the Stage II ego has come to rely on habit, familiarity, and the sense of safety its solitary perch in a lofty tree provides. From there, like the Outer Other God it has created for itself, it can observe life without actually having to become fully immersed in it. For this reason, facing its true vulnerability is very painful and almost always rigorously resisted. But it is exactly this descent from mental abstractions into physically experiencing the joys and sorrows of life, this coming down to earth to meet the sacred, that is our introduction to Epoch III consciousness and the fuller Mystery we seek.

Opening to the Inner Other

Just as our bodies have a mysterious imperative to grow and develop physically, so our psyche has a mysterious compulsion to evolve. We don't know *why* this is, we just know it is. Carl Jung thought of the psyche's compulsion to evolve as the archetype of Divinity, and he saw it as both the core and circumference of our being. He named this archetype the Self with a capital S and defined it as our God-image. Also known in various times and cultures as the Big Self, the Sacred Self, the Higher Self, the Christ within, the Diamond Body, and so on, this evolutionary energy consists of two integrated streams: one masculine (Animus/King) and one feminine (Anima/Queen).

Remember that "masculinity" and "femininity" here symbolize together the principle of opposites that underlies all that is sacred to us: the miracle of life and all the mysterious forces that engender and sustain it which we call the drives for self-preservation and species-preservation. In Taoism the feminine principle is known as *yin* and the masculine as *yang*. In *kundalini* yoga they are visualized as two channels—called *ida* (the feminine subtle channel controlling the left side of the body) and *pingala* (the masculine subtle channel influencing the right side of the body)—that twine separately around the spinal column and merge at seven energy centers called *chakras*.

When our ego begins to separate from the personal mother during Epoch II, we are also separating from the Sacred Self and its two integrated forms of energy. Having experienced the extraordinary "superhuman" powers with which we were so intimately connected during Epoch I, our immature egos create an image of an outward and omnipotent heavenly deity, and project into/onto that the powers we cannot claim for ourselves. With our newly conscious masculine orientation we tend to think of this God as the ideal King, a supreme ruler who is also a perfect Warrior, Scholar/Magician, and Lover. What we don't realize is that our tendency to see God this way originates in the masculine archetypes of the Self and personifies our Animus.

At the same time, associating the feminine "superhuman" powers of the Self with our personal mother from whom we wish to separate, our growing ego tends to leave most of her "superhuman" aspects behind. But the Sacred Feminine lives on in the feminine archetypes which comprise our Anima. The primary one is the Queen, the feminine authority of the psyche. The others are Mother, Wisewoman, and Beloved. All of these are maternal and transformational to varying degrees. What we are just beginning to understand in today's world is that *these* are the archetypal energies that initiate us into experiencing the sacredness of our souls.

It takes us a long time to understand this. Both reason and intuition tell a maturing ego that whatever God might actually be, God surely does not view the universe through the eyes of human ego-consciousness. God is not familiar and safe like our opinions, bodies, families, neighborhoods, religions, nations, and ethnic groups. God is not just on our side, loving only who and what we love, fearing and hating who and what we fear and hate.

God is intimidating.

God feels dangerous.

God scares us.

God is *Other*.

This makes sense to most of us. What doesn't make sense is that *God is also Self*. Most people pull back in alarm when first introduced to this idea. *What? Are you trying to tell me I'm God? Or equal to God? But that's heresy! Hubris! The worst kind of arrogance!* This is the shocked reaction I got from a minister who came to me for help with a big dream. After years of Jungian studies and personal dreamwork I had become so accustomed to the idea that I couldn't understand why he found it so appalling. I understand now. His was the natural response of an anxious Epoch II ego that is afraid of being swallowed up by the feminine unconscious and has no internal connection to the Self.

John (not his real name) was a charming, sincere, and well-meaning elderly man devoted to serving God and his church. His fascination with his dream coupled with his strong desire to understand it spoke to his deep yearning for spiritual meaning and wisdom, but intellectually he seemed unable to entertain the possibility that these things could be found inside him. Why? Why indeed. Consider some of the ideas his church had drummed into him:

He was born in sin.

He is unworthy of God's love.

Pride is one of the seven deadly sins.

His ego is sinful and needs to be humbled.

His natural instincts are sinful and need to be repressed.

His desire to think well of himself is the worst kind of pride.

To earn God's love he needs to be God-centered, not self-centered.

Since he is sinful and God is not, God does not live in him
but in Heaven.

All these ideas are rooted in dualistic thinking. All assume the worst about us and the best about a separate, abstract God that is fundamentally other than us. All are well-intentioned reactions against archetypal evil and the feminine principle with which we sometimes confuse it. None consider the possibility that archetypal good could also live in us, and that we are capable of knowing it intimately. All are symptomatic of psychological ignorance, self-hatred, fear, and unconsciousness.

John's desire to serve God, combined with his beliefs about God, had shaped his self-image. He saw himself as a humble man who cared about others. But the John I experienced was a very controlling, dismissive, self-centered man whose "humility" felt more like an act meant to cover up an embarrassing sense of superiority than an authentic way of being.

He longed to know what his dream could mean, but resisted efforts to help him better understand himself—which, of course, was the whole point of his dream. Perhaps part of why he didn't want to look within was that he had bought into the conventional wisdom that self-study indicates self-centeredness, and partly because it threatened his self-image. What if he found other, even less desirable qualities like pride, selfishness, or thoughtlessness inside him? Maybe even narcissism? His need to protect his self-image and prove his worthiness, combined with his compulsion to hide his unworthiness, took up so much of his mental energy that he had little left for noticing reality—let alone exploring hidden contents of his psyche. But that's not so unusual is it? Aren't most of us like that?

Why do we work so hard to avoid the truth? What *is* this terrible truth that our ego doesn't want to see? Simply this: The Epoch II ego is oriented to the drive for self-preservation, which is oriented to power. This is the fundamental reality that religions try to keep in check when they emphasize our sinfulness, unworthiness, and need for humility. The idea that God lives in us is a huge threat to our ego because our *ego* wants to be King of the psyche! We *like* being the supreme authority. We like knowing the answers and being in control. We like feeling superior. We do not want to share our home or authority with a dangerous *Other*. And we definitely do not want some strange power we don't know or understand restricting us, meddling in our business, or worse, knowing who we really are. This is the truth I saw seeping out from behind John's carefully constructed mask.

And here's another, more shocking truth. What John didn't know was that beneath every Epoch II ego's attachment to the masculine drive for self-preservation and power, our feminine drive for species-preservation is also at work. And what is her basic orientation? In a word, sex. His sexual attraction to a forbidden woman was the subtext of his dream and the instinct demanding to be heard through it; but because of this minister's beliefs about the split between "higher" spirit and "lower" matter, the eroticization of all life that the Sacred Feminine inevitably brings with Epoch III awareness made him deeply uncomfortable.

It's important to note here that both Freud and Jung understood the primal influence of sex on the psyche. The difference was that Freud believed sexual trauma and repression was the cause of mental illness and that understanding this would help the sufferer adjust to the requirements of everyday living. Unlike Freud, Jung believed there is a spiritual component to the psyche which, by being made conscious, can transform the individual from one who merely copes to one who discovers the meaning of his/her life and lives with authenticity, joy, and passion. Jung saw the sexual instinct in its broadest spiritual sense of opening oneself to the natural, physical processes of life and uniting with otherness to complete ourselves and preserve our species. By employing his masculine side in inner work that empowered his feminine side and made room for her in his conscious orientation to life, Jung *psychologically* united his masculine and feminine drives. This inner marriage ushered his ego into Epoch III integrated consciousness which understands that sexual and spiritual energy are two expressions of the same life force.

To the average Epoch II ego the drives for self-preservation and spe-cies-preservation often seem utterly incompatible. We want to complete ourselves by experiencing the love and joy of ecstatic union with other-ness, but we don't want to give up control or make sacrifices for the sake of others. So because our egos secretly want to be in charge, and because we're bound to dualistic thinking, the only way we know to reconcile the two drives is to see God as *Outer Other*—an invisible heavenly deity with whom we can never possibly become intimate (and who, conveniently, is very easy to forget) *because of our unworthiness*—and we cling to this idea like a life-preserver! Or else we scorn traditional God-images altogether because they seem primitive and superstitious to our modern scientific minds.

In either case, the Epoch II ego would much rather believe in—or disdain—a masculine god, a child's god, a tribal god, a god like us, a gender-biased god, a god of conventional morality, or a separate god of otherness than to actually do the difficult work of uniting with the unknown otherness of our own souls. But this is exactly what is required of one who aspires to psycho-spiritual maturity.

The heartbreaking reality for a well-meaning seeker is that our ego's unwillingness to open to inner otherness is ultimately a rejection of the Great Mystery. It is our resistance to knowing our fuller selves that sabotages our desire for a deeply meaningful spiritual life. Since the incomplete God-images to which we have been so devoted are actually idols that we ourselves have constructed and maintained, it is up to us to tear them down, toss them out, and stay open to the genuine evolutionary energies that want to replace them.

Psychological openness will not expose us to the influence of a supernatural "devil" as so many people fear, but simply show us our own capacity for evil. Moreover, it will create a welcoming space for the rejected feminine otherness of our soul, encouraging her to enter, look around, and unite in friendship with our ego and every other aspect of our being. The inevitable outcome will be an integrated God-image which we no longer experience as Outer Other but as Inner Beloved: the sacred core and circumference of our beings and our connection to the universal One Being.

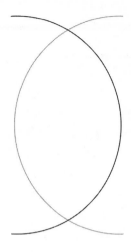

CHAPTER NINE

A God of Integrated Consciousness

Honoring the feminine principle and integrating the opposites into our personalities, world-views, and God-images is the next and necessary step toward increased consciousness . . . and the only lasting solution to individual and global strife.

THE CONFLICT experienced by an Epoch II ego (recall p. 48) gives rise to anxiety. Many of us get so used to living with anxiety that we lose awareness of it, even as it continues to drive our behavior from behind the scenes. But after a time of devoting most of our energy to attaining our ego's outer goals, a burst of consciousness can bring our anxiety to light in uncomfortable ways.

We begin to feel dissatisfied with ourselves and our lives, unfulfilled by our accomplishments and acquisitions, weary of our anxious compulsion to expend vast amounts of energy on things that feel meaningless, and concerned about how we want the rest of our lives to be. We question things we took for granted and are tempted to make choices we never considered before. What was familiar feels foreign, relationships that were happy and healthy become unstable, hope gives way to hopelessness. The world that was juicy and bursting with promise seems at times dreary, flat, and dead.[26] The psychological explanation for this is that our Stage II ego's belief that we are in control of our lives is being severely challenged by the Anima/mother bear who is ready to emerge into consciousness so she can empower us to become our whole selves.

In Jung's generation and my own, this kind of awareness rarely made a life-changing impact on people before midlife and was associated with declining abilities, awareness of our mortality, and a growing desire to spend our remaining time with authenticity, deep feeling, meaning, and purpose. Although some people handle this wake-up call badly, most manage these mental and physical changes with little difficulty, making new choices to explore interests they've put on hold for too long, and approaching the years leading toward and beyond retirement with hope, optimism, and pleasure in their new freedom.

From a historical perspective we can see that the Epoch II ego is evolving and the mid-life crisis may one day become a thing of the past. Technology has dissolved tribal boundaries and cultural differences to an unprecedented degree. In many parts of the world young people of both genders are freer than ever before to embrace differing values and beliefs without undue fear or pressure to conform. Today there are people in every nation of the world who have been exposed to mandorla messages about the importance of overcoming our resistance to the otherness in ourselves and each other since they were born. As a result, some are transitioning into Epoch III at younger ages.

Regardless of when or how it happens, growing pressure to seek relief from uncomfortable inner forces we don't understand and can't ignore presents the opportunity to complete ourselves. I believe that many who question their God-images and explore their "dark" sides are unusually sensitive to the psychological repression of the Anima and the societal dominance of women. Sensing that their suffering originates in their own unconsciousness, they begin the work of seeking out and healing inner divides. Those who persist discover that this journey of expansion and self-exploration eventually ushers them into Epoch III, an era of individuation, reunion with the feminine principle, and integrated wisdom.

Epoch III: Integrated Consciousness

Epoch III is a realm of potentially limitless consciousness in which we no longer project our own ego-consciousness onto a God outside us, but open to all that God may be and develop an inner relationship with God. With earlier levels of self-awareness, we didn't ask for admittance, we just walked in. But Epoch III is the seeker's domain and despite the crises that invite us to explore it, it will not open to us unless we knock.

Descending into the unknown and honoring its truths is daunting. It can also be painful because the ego is suffering the trauma of dying to "the world's" opinions. This psychological death is often accompanied by a lack of psychic energy, a sense of alienation from the world, unstable relationships, mood shifts, depression, extreme anxiety, impulsiveness, potentially self-damaging behaviors, intense and inappropriate anger, emptiness, boredom, identity disturbances, and so on.[27]

These common symptoms point to a purging and opening of the ego that must occur before new psycho-spiritual life can be born. This often starts with reassessing society's conventional moral and religious ideas, rejecting those which no longer serve their growth, and integrating new ones that do. Help can be found in various forms of mental training that explore the non-egoic realm. Some people use spiritual practices such as prayer, meditation, contemplation, and mindfulness to observe their thinking and come to terms with negative or compulsive thoughts and worries. Dreamwork, bodywork, psychotherapy, art, reading, writing, study, and active imagination likewise help us retrieve repressed material and identify and control toxic mental events and emotions as they arise.

At a conscious level this work might be motivated purely by a desire to alleviate our discomfort; but as Carl Jung discovered through fearless and lengthy exploration of his unconscious self (a three-year journey recorded in his extraordinary *The Red Book*), it nevertheless has the consequence of activating the Self. As Washburn states, "In dying to the world, the ego also dies to the God-image it had projected upon the world,"[28] and a new and deeper faith is born. Opening to the reality of the indwelling Sacred ushers us into a fresh new realm suffused with sacred meaning. Entering this realm is not a function of any particular religion or set of beliefs, but a natural unfolding of the potential for growth in every soul.

In the Middle Ages many Jewish, Muslim, and Christian mystics experienced an Epoch III increase into the Divine Unity of God and used the art of alchemy to explore its deeper meaning.[29] For them, transforming base metals into gold was a metaphor for perfecting the spirit by transforming fixed, solid aspects of the personality (so sure of their rightness that they are essentially dead) into a fresh, childlike openness.

Jung noted that in the ultimate phase of the work this leads "to the union of opposites in the archetypal form of the *hierosgamos* or 'chymical wedding.' Here the supreme opposites, male and female . . . are melted into a unity purified of all opposition and therefore incorruptible."[30] The alchemists called this the sacred marriage of the King and Queen, and saw it as the key to comprehending the Ancient Mysteries, the lost wisdom that brings enlightenment.

Whereas Epoch I is about Mother and Epoch II about Father, Epoch III belongs to the Self, or Divine Couple. Their relationship develops within us as we consciously integrate opposites that were formerly separated. This is the growth into individuation and wholeness that is the goal of psychology, and the way of enlightenment of which spirit persons speak. It is our *magnum opus,* the most beautiful work of art a human can create and the fulfillment of our greatest potential: to become the unique, creative beings we really are. Completion of this work brings many benefits, including affirming self-knowledge, deeply satisfying personal meaning, freedom from the compulsion to please or impress, the joy of clearly seeing the underlying patterns of our lives from a cosmic perspective, a sense of connectedness to nature and all of life, and benevolent thoughts and actions guided by a conscious immersion in the Divine Unity.

Where Are We?

Alchemists, like Gnostics and other ancient wisdom-keepers before them, wanted to liberate individuals from false concepts and preprogrammed ideas and open their eyes to greater self-knowledge and self-trust. But the true spiritual essence of their work had to be veiled in esoteric symbols and language to avoid destruction by the established religious order of their times. A millennium later, repressive elements in society still wage war against the liberation of the human spirit.

Currently the bulk of humanity appears to be in Epoch II, although some individuals have not yet left Epoch I and others have attained Epoch III integrated consciousness. Despite the sincere efforts of many governments and religions to bring healing and peace, much of our world is tormented by a malaise of fear, anxiety, hopelessness, frustration, and violence. The basic reason? We are incomplete. Why? Because we are unable, and in some cases unwilling, to grow beyond Epoch II ego-consciousness. And because we are incomplete, *our "God" is incomplete.*

We are still suffering from the primal trauma of our sacred parents' divorce. Like profoundly wounded, self-absorbed adolescents we mask our fears with bluster, cling frantically to like-minded peers, struggle to prove our worth, and lash out at intimidating otherness. Our gang wars are going global and our colors are sending challenging signals to the world. Unless a critical mass of us evolves into Epoch III soon, we are very likely to terminate all growth in a global World War III. Our hope lies with Epoch III thinkers and leaders who think psychologically, feel and act spiritually, and earnestly strive to heal all divisiveness.

We have among us Epoch III theologians from every religion. They have experienced how a lack of self-knowledge and rigid adherence to limiting beliefs about an incomplete God sabotage our birthright of wisdom, compassion, joyous vitality, and spiritual meaning. They are horrified to see that instead of helping, some aspects of the beloved religions to which they have devoted their lives are sowing the seeds of our destruction. With a deep hunger for truth and enormous courage, these modern heroes are unlocking the doors to increased consciousness by speaking openly against psycho-spiritual imprisonment.

Epoch III consciousness asserts that God is *not* dualistic: God is *unified duality.* Or to put it another way, God is *unity in multiplicity.* Insofar as any group—religious or otherwise—fosters the integration of opposites to engender greater openness and understanding, it contributes to the healthy development of its members and our progress toward creating love, justice, and world peace.

Where Do We Go from Here?

In preceding chapters we saw many aspects of the dominant god of Western and Middle-Eastern culture, whose rejection of the Sacred Feminine expresses our own incompleteness as Epoch II egos. In Part 2, I will explore how God can learn from Goddess and how, correspondingly, we can open to the Anima to acquire greater integration of the feminine and masculine principles, both in our God-image and in ourselves. Preparing the temple of our psyche for this sacred marriage requires an understanding of the basic principles which underlie this book.

First, this book is about psychological and spiritual development in the universe within, not about gender or sexuality in the outer world. The essential task of the spiritual journey is to become transformed through a union of *inner* pairs of opposites. While this will naturally have consequences in the outer world, it will not affect our gender or sexual orientation.

Second, if you remember nothing else from this book, remember this. Honoring the feminine principle and integrating the opposites into our personalities, world-views, and God-images is not a foolish idea promoted by a bunch of angry libbers longing for a sentimental regression to a Golden Age of matriarchal power and psychological innocence! It is the next and necessary step toward increased consciousness in which our egos become less self-centered and more God-centered, and the solution to individual and global strife.

Finally, the Mystery we call God transcends all human perceptions. This means that no one religion has a corner on spiritual maturity. It's not a function of law, faith, or belief. It's not about how you describe God, how well you know scripture, how hard you pray, how many rules you keep, how many souls you save, or how many good deeds you do. It doesn't matter how, when, where, or how often you worship God. You can't buy spiritual maturity by giving money to the temple, synagogue, church, cathedral, mosque, ashram, or poor. And you can't obtain it merely by being good. Why? Because spiritual maturity is a direct result of our ability to integrate divides in loving union. Ultimately, spiritual maturity is a function of enlightened *consciousness*.

Only consciousness.

Consciousness is very difficult to describe. If it were easy, our problems may have been solved long ago. For now, the simplest definition I can give is that consciousness *is knowing what is in your unconscious.* "Well, thanks," you may be thinking, "that clears it right up!" Don't worry. I'll say much more about this in Part 2.

In the words of Jungian analyst Edward Edinger, "The union of opposites in the vessel of the ego is the essential feature of the creation of consciousness."[31] In other words, our psycho-spiritual maturity depends on our ability to become *aware* of the otherness we have divided ourselves out from and then open up to let it in. As we listen to its claims with patience, objectivity, and tolerance we begin to unite the opposites. In doing so we nurture the God of oneness in our hearts. This is the most profound spiritual truth I know.

To acknowledge the principle of opposites is not to succumb to dualistic thinking. The world of matter will always appear dual to ordinary human perception, but the limitations of one-sided thinking can be transcended with consciousness. The ultimate spiritual realization is the unity of all creation, a unity that is fueled by ongoing interactions between pairs of equally valid and empowered opposites. When one truly understands that this interaction creates and sustains life, one can no longer persist in valuing one pole while repressing the other.

Uniting opposites is a three-step process in which you train yourself to

- *discriminate*: recognize pairs of opposites whose division creates conflicts for you, distinguish the differences between them, and become aware of your biases against either side,

- *cultivate* understanding and compassion for the otherness you have disowned, and

- *integrate* the positive aspects of rejected otherness into your thoughts and behavior as appropriate and needed.

As we develop mature consciousness the ripple effect takes over, and without even trying we become agents for healing in everything we do. This is how we ease the imbalances in the world: by healing them in ourselves. This is how we become mature spirit persons: by opening to all of ourselves and all of God.

Psychological integration births spiritual integration. Together, they create the sacred marriage. The offspring of this marriage are nine gifts of spiritual wisdom: holistic perception, transforming light, acceptance of the shadow, emotional integrity, partnership, balance, sovereignty, meaning, and mandorla consciousness. Like human children, these gifts do not arrive fully mature, but take time to develop. Thus, while our bodies will inevitably decline, our souls can celebrate the sacred marriage throughout the remainder of our lives.

Are you ready to begin the work for which you were born?

Notes

1. Mircea Eliade, *Patterns in Comparative Religion* (Lincoln and London: University of Nebraska Press, 1996), 244.

2. Ibid., 262.

3. June Singer, *Androgyny: The Opposites Within* (Boston: Sigo Press, 1976), 6.

4. Eliade, *Patterns in Comparative Religion*, 239.

5. Ibid., 213.

6. Ibid., 63.

7. Ibid., 110.

8. Connie Zweig, *The Holy Longing: The Hidden Power of Spiritual Yearning* (New York: Jeremy Tarcher, 2003), 13.

9. M. Esther Harding, *Psychic Energy: Its Source and Its Transformation*, 2nd ed. (Princeton, NJ: Princeton University Press, 1963), 197.

10. Michael Washburn, *Transpersonal Psychology in Psychoanalytic Perspective* (Albany: State University of New York Press, 1994), 69.

11. Ibid.

12. Leonard Shlain, *The Alphabet Versus the Goddess* (New York: Penguin/Compass, 1998), has a fascinating theory about how the creation of the alphabet generated changes in the brain and influenced humanity's god-images.

13. Washburn, *Transpersonal Psychology in Psychoanalytic Perspective*, 76–95.

14. These are the four "ends" of Indian philosophy as cited in Joseph Campbell's *The Masks of God: Oriental Mythology* (New York: Penguin Books, 1962), 21.

15. This theory was initially brought forward by Viktor Tausk and Sabina Spielrein as reported by John Kerr, in *A Most Dangerous Method* (New York: Vintage Books, 1994), 474.

16. Sigmund Freud, "On Narcissism: An Introduction," in *Yearbook of Psycho-Analysis*, vol. 6, ed. and trans. James Strachey, with Anna Freud (1914; London: The Hogarth Press, 1957), 78.

17. Singer, *Androgyny*, 5.

18. I wish to thank Dr. Michael Washburn for this extremely helpful insight.

19. You can find a thorough summary of Kohlberg's theory in Thomas Armstrong, *The Human Odyssey: Navigating the 12 Stages of Life* (New York: Sterling Publishing Co., 2008).

20. Larry Maze. "Ego-Self Conversations and the Problem of Evil," *The Rose* (Athens, GA, Emmanuel Church), 15 (winter–spring 2009), 27.

21. Mario Beauregard and Denyse O'Leary, *The Spiritual Brain: A Neuroscientist's Case for the Existence of the Soul* (New York: HarperOne, 2007), 38.

22. Sharon Begley, *Train Your Mind Change Your Brain* (New York: Ballantine Books, 2008).

23. J.C. Cooper, *An Illustrated Encyclopaedia of Traditional Symbols* (London: Thames and Hudson, 1978), 18.

24. Ibid.

25. Boris Matthews, trans., *The Herder Symbol Dictionary* (Wilmette, IL: Chiron Publications, 1978), 20.

26. I credit many of these and some of the following insights to Michael Washburn.

27. Washburn, *Transpersonal Psychology in Psychoanalytic Perspective*, 183–216.

28. Ibid., 234.

29. For fuller discussions of alchemy, see June Singer, *Androgyny: The Opposites Within* (Boston: Sigo Press, 1976), and Edward Edinger, *Anatomy of the Psyche: Alchemical Symbolism in Psychotherapy* (La Salle, IL: Open Court, 1985).

30. C.G. Jung, "Introduction to the Religious and Psychological Problems of Alchemy," in *Psychology and Alchemy*, 2nd ed., *Collected Works*, vol. 12 (Princeton, NJ: Princeton University Press, 1968), 37.

31. Edward F. Edinger, *The Creation of Consciousness: Jung's Myth for Modern Man* (Toronto: Inner City Books, 1984), 21.

PART 2

NINE WISDOM GIFTS OF
AN INTEGRATED GOD

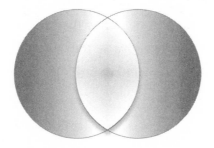

We've been afraid that if we look within we'll discover the unworthiness of our true selves. We thought self-examination would make us even more egocentric than we already are! We thought questioning our old beliefs and opening to new ideas would send us straight to Hell! What we never could understand is that making the unconscious conscious is a spiritual path in which the masculine ego works in partnership with the Deep Feminine, and that together they lead us into the sacred realm where we become Godcentric.

When you make the two One,
and when you make the inner as the outer
and the outer as the inner,
and the above as the below . . .
then you will enter the kingdom.

—*The Gospel of Thomas*
Saying 22: 4, 7

Without the God there is no Goddess,
And without the Goddess there is no God.
How sweet is their love!
The entire universe is too small to contain them,
Yet they live happily in the tiniest particle.

—Jnaneshwar
The Nectar of Self-Awareness[1]

THE FIRST GIFT
HOLISTIC PERCEPTION

The greatest threats to our world today are rooted in repressive, extremist factions that believe in the infallibility of words written long before we had even an inkling of the big picture . . . and feel these words must be defended with their lives. Preferring words to the mysteries they point to is like reading *Gourmet* magazine while the kids are starving!

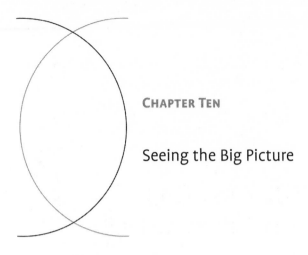

CHAPTER TEN

Seeing the Big Picture

WHATEVER GOD might be, our ideas about God originate in the mystery stew of our physical and psychological inheritance. They evolve through personally meaningful experiences of sacred energies that rock our world and blast away at our defenses. Our God-images are also influenced by the words of others. If the words are not written down, our stories, ideas, and images of God grow organically, becoming more expansive and complex with changes in location, time, teller, and listener. But when words are carved in stone they become unyielding; and with the passage of time they begin to dwarf the mysteries to which they point until we forget what the soul really feels and the spirit really needs.

For many seekers in the West today, religion is about as nourishing as fast-food take-out. Judaism, Christianity, and Islam worship a masculine God associated with logos, or cosmic reason, which finds its expression in words. The association easily devolves into rigid mental abstractions: a cluster of concepts meant to explain our relationship to the Mystery, and a set of ideals intended to help us live more ethically.

There's nothing wrong with words, concepts, or ideals. This book is full of them. But abstractions are easily separated from realities. And when the masculine tendency to maintain power and protect turf kicks in, the abstractions become dogma. We end up with a piece of territory staked out with barbed wire around it and a "No Trespassing" sign out front, then heaven help anyone who disagrees or interferes. Smite the heretics! Wipe the infidels off the face of the Earth! Destroy every man, woman, and child!

How do you show the sense of a God who loves everything he created yet endorses killing babies and outsiders? You use words in the interest of survival. First, you obsess over your masculine drive for self-preservation and project it onto your God-image while repressing your feminine drive for species-preservation. In the condition of near paranoia that ensues, it's easy—necessary, really—to demonize otherness. Then, claiming divine inspiration (after all, ensuring your survival really does feel like a spiritual imperative), you write down your case against the demons so everyone can read it, gird your loins for battle, and, pointing to those holy words as your authority, start destroying your enemy—all the while feeling self-righteous and justified. When a religion or nation does this, it is a sacred cause. When an individual does it, s/he's institutionalized.

The written word has enormous power. It was key to Moses's success in uniting his people under one god. The plagues visited upon Egypt, the escape across the Red Sea, the pillar of light, the manna from heaven, the staff that turned into a serpent, the exhortations to be grateful and good—none of these kept the Israelites from worshiping their old deities. But when Moses came down from the mountain with two stone tablets with Ten Commandments on them, Judaism became a fully established religion. Likewise, Christianity and Islam were isolated, provincial cults until their scriptures legitimized them and ensured their survival.

Images have enormous power as well. This is partly because they are more sensory, concrete, and primal than words—the human brain recognized and created images long before it made up alphabets. When we read or hear a word, it sometimes takes a moment to sink in, or doesn't sink in at all. But when we see an image we respond automatically—it goes directly to our instinctual, emotional selves without first being rerouted through our thought-process.

Something else about images makes them especially potent: Images are the language of our souls. To paraphrase the fourteenth-century Christian mystic Meister Eckhart, when our souls want to express themselves, they project images outward and then enter into them. The Rev. Jerry R. Wright, a Jungian analyst, says,

> Creation, then, is really images. That tree is an image. That flower

is an image. That water is an image. And so are we. We are images
into which God's spirit has entered. If we want to know what is
holy, we pay attention to the images all around us in the outer
world and to the images that find us in our dream world. In the
image is the Life. We cannot know . . . the mystery of God in its
essence, but what we can know are the images into which God has
entered. As we engage the image, we are in fact having an experience of God.[2]

Sometimes we encounter an image that has such profound relevance
to our immediate issues that our hearts respond with powerful feeling. We
feel shaken to the core, touched by something beyond ourselves. This is
when we know that an image has been entered by God. Joseph Campbell
has called this experience "a profoundly felt, inward knowledge of the
transpersonal imperatives and quality of life. . ."[3] Words tend to give us
mental concepts about God; images are far more effective at providing
personal knowledge and experiences of God.

Images are a way of communicating. Like music, they transcend language, race, age, gender, nation, politics, and religion. An image that calls
forth similar emotions in everyone reminds us of our similarities. You don't
have to believe in Great Mother to be moved by the extraordinary statue of
Artemis of Ephesus who wore the testicles of sacrificial bulls strung around
her neck, or to be impressed by the magnificent caryatids that hold up the
porch of the Erechtheion temple on the Acropolis in Athens. You don't
have to believe in the God of Christianity to be awed by Michaelanglo's
painting of creation on the ceiling of the Sistine Chapel.

You don't need an outer authority to tell you when an image is spiritually relevant to you. Your body and emotions alert you to God's presence
in that image. This happens because images and emotions come from the
unconscious, physical, natural self.

This power that images can have over us is unacceptable to an ego that
is trying to extricate itself from unconsciousness. Animals dream in images.
Animals experience fear, loyalty, lust, love, and other emotions. The major
goal of a developing ego is to transcend its animal self to become more

conscious. This is why the ego prides itself in creating words and abstract ideas: because the ability to do so is proof of superior intellect which, it is assumed, is proof of one's growing consciousness.

This is why the first thing the worshipers of the Sky God did when they conquered the Goddess-worshiping cultures was to spread new stories. They extolled their abstract, heavenly, imageless male God as the only god (*You shall have no other gods before me*) and forbade the making of images (*You shall not make for yourself a carved image—any likeness of anything that is in heaven above, or that is in the earth beneath, or that is in the water under the earth* . . .). To have permitted images or worship of the female aspects of Deity would have diminished the Sky God's growing power—and, by association, the growing authority of the males in the religious hierarchy.

The earliest Epoch II males knew that, with the shift from Epoch I consciousness, they had gained a lot of ground over their previous animal natures. They also believed/feared they had a lot to lose if they gave in to them again. The most fearful and repressive among them therefore fought the hardest in the struggle to define God, and they won. Thus, when God became a single, solitary male, words became holy, images became idols, and feminine power was fractionalized and forced underground. Out of sight, out of mind. After a few thousand years, Goddess was effectively effaced from collective consciousness in the Middle East and the West.

The proliferation of words and images in today's world is changing all that. Photography, television, and computers bring people more opportunities to participate in the feminine mysteries than ever in history. It is hard to ignore otherness when it's in your face every day. We've felt the serpent tongue of fear in our guts when looking at photos of the mushroom cloud over Hiroshima and the broken icebergs calving off the Ross Ice Shelf. We've gasped in awe at NASA's photo of Mother Earth floating in space. We've wept at televised scenes of mutilated soldiers and abused children.

Science and technology are showing us our potential for good and evil in unprecedented ways. On every part of the planet, on every continent and in every nation, our awareness is rapidly expanding and our one-sided worldviews and religious beliefs are being challenged. We're getting it that there are some places in the world where good and gentle people get along perfectly fine with values and beliefs completely different from our own, and other places where the same values we espouse beget unimaginable violence and cruelty. We're getting it that our world is in trouble, that we need each other, that we're one giant interrelated system—and that, as badly as we might want to deny it, we are not always (in all ways) the good guys.

We simply can't discount the fact that the major religions in the West and the Middle East were founded on the authority of words written exclusively by males about 1400 (Islam), 2000 (Christianity), and 3600 (Judaism) years ago, before anyone had even an inkling of the big picture. Nor can we deny that many believers in these religions still take these words as literal truths that must be defended with their lives. But when it comes to spirituality, preferring words to the mysteries they explicate is like reading Gourmet magazine while the kids are starving!

The religious clashes that threaten our world today do not derive from Buddhism with its goal of enlightened oneness, Hinduism with its pantheon of gods and goddesses who model human archetypes and the cycles of life, Taoism which emphasizes balance between the feminine and masculine principles, Jainism which recognizes the sacredness of all life, or Shinto's great love and reverence for nature.

The greatest threats to our world today are rooted in repressive, extremist factions of religions that worship a male god and believe in the infallibility of his written words. Each of us can take steps to counteract this regressive influence by examining the artificial divides created by our own fearful egos. We can begin by integrating the opposites of word and image.

Integrating Word and Image

To train yourself to be as literate about images and symbols as you are about written words:

- Pay attention to the symbols in your dreams.

- Consult a good symbol book for their possible metaphorical meanings. If the description of a symbol doesn't resonate, ignore it. But if it gives you an "Aha," you're onto something important about yourself.

- Look around. What are the symbols with which you surround yourself? Use your symbol book to see what they say about what's important to you.

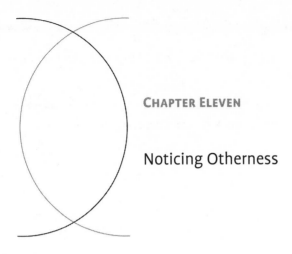

Noticing Otherness

WHEN I READ, study, or write, I concentrate so hard that I'm almost oblivious to my surroundings. It can be so difficult for me to "resurface," that I deserve my mother's epithet of "one-track minded."

When I walk into a party, though, I notice myriad things almost simultaneously without focusing on anything in particular: smells, sounds (speech, music, the clatter of dishes), colors, shapes, designs, lighting, people and their body language, textures, views, furniture arrangements and decor, and so on. While I may remember only a few of these things later, at the time I experience them they all feed into my brain to give a generalized impression of the mood or ambience. This information, in turn, influences my thinking, emotions, and behavior in that setting.

In her book, *Knowing Woman*, Irene Claremont de Castillejo calls these two ways of getting information *focused consciousness* and *diffuse awareness*.[4] She associates focused consciousness with men and diffuse awareness with women. While this notion could be rooted in subtle differences in male and female brains, I'm a walking example of someone who uses both. Focused consciousness is emphasized in our education and expected in our work, but the faculty of diffuse awareness is rarely taught. I believe both are crucial to mature spirituality and would like to address this imbalance.

We are in a condition of diffuse awareness when we withdraw our focus from the particulars of a situation to become engrossed in the big picture. Engaging it this way is a natural ability with four primary components: *listening* (as opposed to speaking), *appreciating* (as opposed to criticizing or judging), *empathizing* or feeling (as opposed to reasoning), and *questioning* (as opposed to blind acceptance and/or authoritarian telling).[5] All these powers require being receptive and are therefore associated with the feminine principle, and all are integral to sacred experience.

The diffuse form of *listening* is akin to what classical Greeks termed *pronoia*, or anticipatory awareness. This is the kind of attention we use in many forms of meditation. It is an unfocused yet alert mode of curious, non-judgmental awareness featuring such things as a relaxed body, a quiet open mind, a slightly tilted head, softened senses, gently crossed eyes, loosened jaw. Removing our focus from things that are bright, bold, and loud, we hear tiny sounds, feel subtle changes in the atmosphere, notice gentle movements around and within us that would otherwise go unobserved. Perceiving through this softer lens helps us experience our connection with otherness and see through appearances into the heart and soul of matters.

The *appreciating* aspect of diffuse awareness travels an emotional gamut from affectionate regard to extreme states of pleasure, delight, awe, wonder, and ecstasy. These emotions often emerge spontaneously when we relax our minds to worship, meditate, listen to music, or enjoy beauty. The most extreme forms of appreciation arise naturally in mystical states in which we abandon ourselves to life, joyfully conscious that we are conscious, blissfully aware that we are the witness who watches.

Empathizing derives from the Greek *empatheia*, or passion. Empathy is a heart-level response to another being. It not only respects the significance of otherness, but actually unites with it in a real communion of shared feeling. We develop empathy as our focus shifts from the need to differentiate ourselves from others to a need to connect. True empathy resonates in others and warms and uplifts them. It is built on the compassion we acquire by accepting and forgiving ourselves for our own flaws.

Finally, by *questioning*, I mean what philosophic Greeks called *ennoia*, or internal reflection. This is an open, thoughtful approach to otherness— other people, other ideas and opinions, other belief systems, other ways of perceiving. It is not defensive, rebellious, or confrontational, but truly interested in exploring, learning, and growing. A guarded, fearful ego uses questions to undermine, confound, intimidate, and keep at bay the otherness it perceives as enemy. A strong, cohesive ego uses questions to open doors into new realms of understanding and experience.

How we think influences how we perceive God. This, in turn, influences how we act toward others. In its extreme forms, dualistic thinking tends to separate the most mysterious and compelling energies of the universe into Good and Evil. Relying obsessively on words and focused thinking that isn't balanced with a respect for images and diffuse awareness can entrench these divides until they become irreconcilable. This is why we need to be more aware of one-sided ways of thinking and open ourselves to a broader, more holistic awareness.

Holistic thinking makes connections and builds bridges. The bridge between focused consciousness and diffuse awareness is mindfulness. It honors information from images as much as words, from diffuse awareness as much as focused consciousness, from the unconscious as much as the conscious self. Integrating these opposites develops more brain power and contributes to the formation of a God-image with a broader, more cosmic view of humanity.

The next chapter imagines what such an integrated God-image might be like.

Integrating Focused Consciousness and Diffuse Awareness

- Cultivate diffuse awareness by taking a walk outdoors whenever you can for the purpose of emptying your mind of thoughts and attending to input from all five of your senses: hearing, sight, taste, touch, smell.

- Clear your mind of everything but sensory input. Don't focus or strain. Relax and let your eyes soften and cross very gently. Just notice, feel, appreciate.

- Did you learn anything new about yourself and your surroundings?

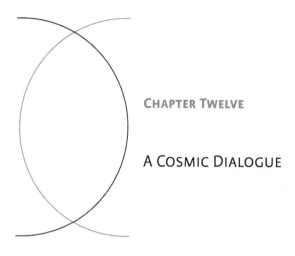

CHAPTER TWELVE

A COSMIC DIALOGUE

God sits in his heavenly study, poring over a volume of holy words. Looking down at Earth now and then, he gets more and more agitated. Goddess walks in, just back from a busy day with their children in the place that's absorbing his attention.

God looks up at her and, pointing to that spot on Earth, says, "You know, honey, things are going crazy down there. I gave them _____ *(fill in the blank with Moses, Jesus, Mohammed, or another spiritual leader you favor)* about _____ (3600, 2000, 1400, . . .) years ago. They recorded his words in this book, and now only a few of them respect the words or keep the laws. I think it's time to remind them who's boss."

Goddess ponders for a moment, then replies. "I think you've been sitting up here alone with your scrolls and books for way too long! Spending most of my time with the children, as I do, I see that's happening everywhere, not just there. Our children are growing up. Their childhood beliefs are outdated, and many of the rules they needed a long time ago no longer serve their needs."

"What are you talking about? They're naughty children. They need rules. If the religions were good enough for their founders, they should be good enough for them. Besides, I don't like change," God says. "I like how it was."

"Well, dear, do you really like fathers selling their daughters into slavery? Parents stoning their children at the city gates for overeating or drinking? Should people really be killed for blaspheming? Wives beaten if they argue with their husbands? Times have changed; humans have changed; you and I have changed. But many of our children don't realize we're still growing and want them to keep growing, too. Maybe it's time to stop emphasizing rules and beliefs and start encouraging them to pay attention to what's happening in and around them. Maybe it's time to help them develop more understanding and love for each other."

God thinks about it. "We tried that a while back. They haven't gotten the message."

"Well, just hearing about love isn't enough to change them. They have to *experience* it. They need to experience us as loving parents who want them to grow up, instead of critical bosses who want to keep them in line."

"And how do we make that happen?"

"They've had a few thousand years of learning about you from teachers, religious leaders, and other authorities outside themselves. They see you as their Sacred Father who loves them and wants them to be good; but sometimes your words feel far removed from their realities, and you live so far away that they have little hope of ever really knowing you. I think they're ready to start remembering me, their Divine Mother who is always in their souls. Then they can begin to feel our love instead of just hearing about it."

"I see where you're going," God says. "You're suggesting their religions should emphasize creating balance and union within themselves and in their relationships, just as we're getting better at this with each other. As long as they look to me alone to save them, they'll keep ignoring the parts of themselves that cause their problems. But as Mediatrix, you can ignite their inner spark, the part of us that some of them call the Christ within. Yes, you're right. I think they're ready to discover the inner Kingdom. Or should I say, 'Queendom?'" he says with a glint in his eye.

Goddess smiles at her beloved husband. "I suppose there can be many names for the same thing. But whatever they call it, experiencing us for themselves, and feeling connected to our energy, is what will make for lasting change."

God returns his wife's smile. "I love that about you. Always seeing the connections and causing the transformations. The best among them have always known me through you whether they realized it or not. You're absolutely right. The children have focused on me alone for too long. The time has come for them to know their Sacred Mother—my beloved partner—as I do."

They embrace, then Goddess returns to her work on Earth. This time she's on the lookout for seekers who are creating intimacy with otherness, the ones most apt to recognize her and accept her. God looks on and smiles, feeling refreshed by their discussion, warmed by the positive results of their synergy, and filled with renewed hope for their children.

CHAPTER THIRTEEN

The Divine Feminine as Holistic Perception

THE EPOCH II masculine God-image is associated with polarized thinking and discriminating seeing, both of which are essential to mature cognition. Looking at things holistically is a specialty of the feminine side of deity, and is equally essential to mature cognition. We tend to think of the Father God as being partial to *us: our* family, *our* team, *our* religion. But we need to remember that our Mother loves *all* her children. Aware of the big picture and averse to conflict, she acts to create understanding and promote harmony. Wisdom comes from integrating both ways: being able to see and distinguish the individual parts while at the same time understanding their importance and knowing how they fit and work together.

To get the big picture we have to open our minds to new information and new ways of taking it in. Most of us at the conscious level take only our own culture's generally agreed-upon truths seriously; but our minds and bodies are always sending us subtle messages, like an uncomfortable feeling or a momentary insight that contradicts an old belief or shows us something unsuspected about ourselves. Other messages come by way of physical sensations and symptoms, illnesses, accidents, a strong response to disturbing or compelling images in waking life or dreams, and all sorts of feelings, needs, instincts, visions, urges, compulsions, temptations, emotions, attitudes, anxieties, fears, intuitions, and synchronicities (meaningful "coincidences") that cause aberrant blips on our radar screens. We can think of these as messages from the Divine Feminine who is prodding us to grow beyond youthful one-sidedness.

Our brains can't process every bit of information all the time, so we select what we stop to think about and what we automatically dismiss. Many of us ignore our personal realities in favor of conventional certainties, and let valuable insights and opportunities slip by because of fear or "reason." The spiritual journey requires us to recognize Goddess's voice when it slips through the cracks in our rock-solid personalities and belief systems.

The Greeks personify mental powers beyond the norm as the Muses, nine daughters of Zeus and Mnemosyne, Goddess of Memory. They embody divine inspiration that wells up from deep caverns of the unconscious and prompts extraordinary creativity in music, art, literature, speech, science, etc. Recognizing these Muses is a metaphorical nod to the Divine Feminine's contributions to human thought and culture.

Although I've never seen a full and detailed description of the Muses' powers, I'm fairly certain they would include the faculties in the following table. When these become part of the consciousness we live with, they reveal a much bigger picture than we usually see—not just of humanity's fullest cognitive potential, but of what is truly sacred.

The Nine Daughters of Holistic Perception

Mythos (Analogical Thinking)	The language of symbol, image, metaphor, imagination, emotion, and personal meaning that gives entry to the spiritual realm. The ability to see meaningful similarities and underlying connections between things, to use imaginative ways to express the soul's truths, and to create something original by combining separate, apparently unrelated elements. This way of thinking includes, but is not limited to, the faculties below.
Diffuse Awareness	A "soft-eyed," unfocused yet attentive form of internal reflection composed of listening, appreciating, empathizing, and questioning.
Emotional Awareness	The ability to recognize, express, and maintain healthy control of emotions in ways that promote personal mental health and positive relationships.

Relationship Awareness	Understanding the dynamics of relationships, being receptive to otherness, and knowing how to nurture healthy, honest, harmonious intimacy.
Nature Awareness	Feeling at one with Nature, recognizing and respecting her energies, and knowing how to interpret her messages.
Intuitive Awareness	Acquiring knowledge and foreknowledge through attention to and respect for inner promptings and outer phenomena.
Body Awareness	Feeling at home in our body, being attentive to its energies, knowing how it communicates with the ego and otherness, and being able to decipher its messages.
Gnosis or Mystery Awareness	Spiritual understanding rooted in personal experience and spiritually meaningful imagination and intuition.
Self Knowledge	Recognizing the reality and power of the unconscious, understanding and accepting the contents of the personal unconscious, and partnering with the power and authority of the Self.

All these "feminine" ways of knowing and seeing will appear throughout this book as we explore the importance of integrating various opposites and share stories that illustrate their lessons. I often will combine metaphorical and literal meanings, dreams and other inner events with outer life, and personally meaningful symbols with myths and historical facts. This is not sloppy thinking, but a deliberate combining of different brain functions to bring more psychological satisfaction and spiritual meaning than any one way of thinking does by itself.

The following story about my first glimpse into a greater picture of God and myself than the one furnished by my family tells of my own initiation into holistic thinking. It came by way of an experience of sacred energies that were utterly foreign to anything I had associated with Deity. I associate them now with the Divine Feminine.

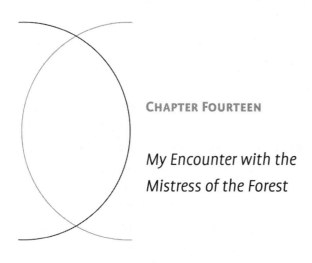

CHAPTER FOURTEEN

My Encounter with the
Mistress of the Forest

MY PARENTS' DIVORCE and father's death shortly afterwards did a real number on my sense of safety. To compensate for my new vulnerability, I developed independence and insensibility into an art form and wore them like a uniform to cover my fears and insecurities. By seventeen I prided myself in being able to take whatever I was given, no matter how difficult, all alone and with no emotion, drama, excuses, or self-pity.

With no name or explanation for how I perceived myself, no conscious awareness of having assumptions about how I should live, I was completely aligned with the masculine values of my culture. My God was unquestionably male and I had quite a bit of head-knowledge about him. I had attended Sunday school and church most of my life. I knew many Bible stories and said grace before meals. Yet none of these things actually made any difference in my life. The symbols and images of my religion were outside of me. They had no personal significance or transforming power. My head may have been connected to God, but my heart and soul were completely uninvolved.

This is not to say that I was unaware of a benevolent life-force. As a very young child I often felt the wonder and mystery of life when playing outdoors, but I didn't associate this joyful sense of awe with the God I learned about from my family and church. That God was a masculine authority in adult society, a God of words, rules, and stories from distant places and times, a God of formal rituals whom one approached only in man-made churches. He had to do with beliefs, not feelings; creeds, not experiences; buildings, not nature; historical religious events in faraway places, not natural everyday ones here and now.

Then in my seventeenth summer my church's youth group leader asked my mother to be the nurse at church camp for two weeks and invited me along as a counselor. Since entering junior high school I had been spending more time indoors: The heat in central Florida, especially during the summer, can discourage all but the most intrepid of nature lovers. But the Ocala National Forest is a wonderland of pure springs, cool pine groves, dense palmetto thickets, and soggy cypress swamps. Going to camp there brought me back in touch with something I had almost forgotten.

Margaret Walstrom was a confident, dedicated, and gifted youth group leader. A tiny woman with boundless energy and a cheerful disposition, she believed that she could bring out the best in teenagers by giving them responsibility and then trusting them to do the right thing. She wasn't the slightest bit intimidated by rowdy teenage boys or giddy pubescent girls. With daughters of her own, she understood young people and knew how to keep us in line without making us feel guilty or rebellious. She was also deeply spiritual. Her God was nothing like the distant God of the other adults I knew. He was very real and practical, fully interested and fully involved in the everyday affairs of human beings—even the things that went on at church camp.

That first summer I was only three years older than the oldest campers, but unlike Mrs. Walstrom I was intimidated by them. I was totally inexperienced in practically everything I was expected to do; but having found great comfort in my mask of stoic competence, I *really* didn't want to admit my insecurities or ask for help. One of my major concerns had to do with a skit my study group was supposed to present in the talent show at the end of the week. We were to pantomime actions to a musical version of the creation story while wearing white sheets lit with an eerie black light ("Let there be light!").

I had never cast, costumed, produced, or directed a dramatic production and had no conception of how to go about it. By the middle of the week I realized that, if I didn't get some help, my group's sloppy performance would expose my ineptness to the whole camp. This was totally unacceptable. Better to let one person see behind the mask than the whole group! So one day during practice time, I set aside my pride and admitted to Mrs. Walstrom that I wasn't sure I could pull it off.

This was all the opening she needed. She said something like, "Just ask for help from the Holy Spirit. He will enter your heart if you ask him to. He is a helper and a guide, and he will show you what to do." Then she walked off briskly to another group.

I was interested and impressed. This was an aspect of God I hadn't heard about, and the idea of getting personal help from him appealed to me. I went off alone, sat on the ground and leaned against a tree, and prayed as sincerely as I could for the Holy Spirit to enter my heart and help me with these responsibilities. I waited, but just as when I gave my life to Jesus ten years earlier at my grandmother's urging, I felt nothing, saw nothing, heard nothing.

I had expected something dramatic, not quite a bolt of lightning or a burning bush, but something obvious and physical from outside myself. Maybe I hadn't prayed right. Or maybe this was all just wishful thinking. I had to admit there was a part of me that secretly believed nothing would happen. Disappointed but still hopeful, I went back to my group.

The next morning I led the girls from my cabin into the woods for our morning prayer walk. We started every day by taking our Bibles outdoors. Each person would find a special spot where she would read the scripture and meditation assigned for the day and then pray about them. That morning I rested back against the rough bark of a tall pine tree. It felt special to be outdoors so early, and I relished the peace and beauty around me as I prepared to read the scripture for the day. It was part of Jesus's Sermon on the Mount in Chapter 5 of the book of Matthew. At first I read like I always did, without really paying attention, and then I came to verse thirteen:

Ye are the salt of the earth; but if the salt have lost his savour, wherewith shall it be salted? It is thenceforth good for nothing, but to be cast out, and to be trodden under foot of men.[6]

"Wait a minute," I thought, a light slowly beginning to glimmer in my mind. "*I* am the salt of the *earth*. I am like salt, which makes food taste better. I am something good, something that makes the world a better place.

But if there's something wrong with me, if I'm not doing my job and making things better, then the earth will not be as good as it should."

The metaphor of salt resonated with me. With increasing excitement I read the fourteenth verse, then the fifteenth and sixteenth.

> 14 Ye are the light of the world. A city that is set on a hill cannot be hid.

> 15 Neither do men light a candle, and put it under a bushel, but on a candlestick; and it giveth light unto all that are in the house.

> 16 Let your light so shine before men, that they may see your good works, and glorify your Father which is in heaven.

This was absolutely amazing. I *understood*! The Bible wasn't just a compilation of meaningless words meant for other people. These verses were talking to *me*. They were telling me that I was a good person, that God knew me, and that I had a responsibility to be the best I could be, to help others. I should let the light of my soul shine through so that we all could be blessed and our Father would be glorified. For an amazing moment I felt as if some dark and empty space inside me had suddenly been filled with brilliant light. Before this the scriptures had held no meaning, but now I could see.

Suddenly I realized: This is it! This is the work of the Holy Spirit. Because of this deceptively simple, yet intensely meaningful interior event, God was no longer just a concept but a reality. I felt that God knew me and wanted to help me; it was just that "his" way of communicating with me was very different from what I had expected—it was far more subtle, an inner awareness rather than an outer event. I wouldn't see burning bushes or hear voices, but I could expect to *feel* God's presence by reading the scriptures and then noticing a meaningful inner quickening. This heightened awareness of the sacredness in me was so captivating that I was determined not to lose it.

At seventeen, this new awareness of my inner life applied only to religion, and religion was a separate compartment that had nothing to do with the rest of me. Like many females of my era, I believed male authority figures had a much greater claim on me than I did. The whole idea of *self* was associated then with negativity: self-centeredness, self-importance, selfishness, self-servingness, self-righteousness, pride, egoism, and lack of humility. It didn't occur to me to take personal needs other than my spiritual ones seriously; but those were sanctioned by my family, so I took them very seriously indeed.

Consumed by a powerful hunger to learn more about the sacred otherness I had discovered, I responded the only way I knew how to, through masculine mental activity: logic, intellect, self-discipline, and study. I began to read the Bible intensely. Over the next few years I read the New Testament three times, verse by verse, chapter by chapter, underlining passages, writing down meaningful phrases, carefully gleaning insights about what God wanted from me and trying to apply them to my life. I couldn't even begin to conceive in those early days that the Father/King wasn't the only aspect of God involved in nurturing my spirituality. I see now that the Mother/Queen was crucial to the awakening of my spiritual nature that summer.

The Queen was the part of Mrs. Walstrom and the Divine Feminine that, like the mother bear, recognized the spiritual readiness and potential of my soul. I knew a lot *about* God by that summer, and the time had come for me to *experience* God. I had acquired religious *beliefs*; it was time to acquire a religious *attitude*. I honored the authority of a masculine God *external* to me; now I was ready to glimpse the spiritual authority *within* me. I had *heard* that the God/King loved me, but until the Goddess/Queen began to stir, I had never actually *felt* that love.

Because of my Christian background I believed I had been touched by the Holy Spirit, and—like Mrs. Walstrom—I believed that Spirit was masculine. It was many years before I would discover that many early Christians considered the Holy Spirit to be feminine. They called her Sophia and thought of her as "the collective archetype of the entirety of cosmic and individual life, growth, and development. . . . [who] is most closely associated with the nature and fate of humanity: the initial differentiation and subsequent individuation of the soul and its union with spirit."[7]

I can't say it better: an "initial differentiation" between myself and the sacred energies of the universe, accompanied by a first baby step toward the individuation of my "soul and its union with spirit." These big words are a textbook description of what happened to me that day.

After my encounter with the Mistress of the Forest, I was no different from many newly turned-on Christians. I clung like a tick on a dog to the beliefs of the church under whose aegis I had tasted the new blood of spiritual meaning for the first time. Something wonderful lived in the wilderness of my soul and I knew it. It would take another ten years of dancing around it before I would be ready for the Divine Mother's second gift, the gift of transforming light.

Notes

1. Andrew Harvey, *The Essential Mystics: The Soul's Journey into Truth* (Edison, NJ: Castle Books, 1996), 51.

2. Jerry R. Wright, "The Image and the Mystery," *The Rose* (Athens, GA, Emmanuel Church), 15 (winter-spring 2009), 7.

3. Joseph Campbell and Charles Muses, *In All Her Names: Explorations of the Feminine in Divinity* (San Francisco: HarperSanFrancisco, 1991), 63.

4. Irene de Castillejo, *Knowing Woman* (New York: G.P. Putnam's Sons, 1973), 15.

5. Nancy Kline, *Women and Power* (London: BBC Books, 1993). Kline does not specifically link these components with De Castillejo's quality of diffuse awareness as I do, but sees them as four attributes of feminine communication that are markedly different from masculine modes.

6. This and the following verses are from the *Holy Bible*, King James version, Matthew 13–16.

7. Stephan A. Hoeller, *Jung and the Lost Gospels: Insights into the Dead Sea Scrolls and the Nag Hammadi Library* (Wheaton, IL: Theosophical Publishing House, 1989), 112.

THE SECOND GIFT
TRANSFORMING LIGHT

The Woman of Light's message is not, "*You are so special and spiritual that I have decided to bless you . . .*" It is, "*You are a very unconscious, if well-meaning, soul who lives in a dense fog. . . . My light dwells within you, but you have to find it and make it grow. Hopefully this vision of your light will motivate you . . .*"

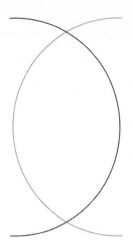

CHAPTER FIFTEEN

Becoming Conscious of the Unconscious

IN JUNGIAN psychology the ego is considered the organizing center of consciousness. There's no doubt the ego can be a problem, but it doesn't need to be destroyed. Rather it needs to grow strong and mature enough to explore and integrate the non-egoic (unconscious) realm on its own terms, so we can become more authentic, individuated, and conscious.

Growing consciousness humbles the ego because it realizes it shares the psyche with entities more powerful than itself. As it redirects its energies to the universe within, it is not killed, but rather *dies to the world*. In other words, it stops judging itself or measuring its worth by the standards or opinions of others. While losing its identification with the world initially feels like death to the ego, it actually presages a spiritual rebirth. This is because only when the ego stops trying to prove itself to others can it step aside and allow the Self its rightful place in the center of the psyche.

Our goal is to stop being unconscious of our true natures. This is both a psychological and spiritual task.

Psychologically, we need to understand what drives our personalities, makes us unique, and contributes to our problems and successes: our talents, interests, passions, dreams, hopes, repressed emotions such as fear and guilt, assumptions, thought processes, physical differences, health issues, behavioral responses to various stimuli, and so on. If we can't see what influences our functioning, we can't heal our dysfunction. If we don't know who we are and what we love, we have little hope of becoming individuated and fulfilled.

Spiritually, we need to be aware of what eases our suffering, elicits genuine reverence, promotes love and compassion, provides purpose and meaning for our lives, and fills us with wonder and awe. Some of our spiritual needs are met by communal observances, others by private and deeply personal rituals. Neither is inherently more important than the other; the point is to know and honor what truly feeds our spiritual nature, promotes our spiritual growth, and connects us to the Mystery.

The Ego's Relationship to the Self

The closest connection we have to the Mystery is our spiritual core, the Self. It compels us to evolve to completion through masculine and feminine drives, each with distinct patterns of archetypal energy that further our development.

A few words about how I use the terms spirituality and religion in this context may be helpful. I see spirituality as the human *experience* of, and felt appreciation for, the Sacred Mystery as mediated by the Self, and religion as an abstract *belief system about* the Sacred Mystery. Religions are based on the ego's intuitive awareness of universal spiritual realities, but these realities are not necessarily experienced by all who adhere to a particular religion. Thus, a religious person is not necessarily spiritual.

In Epoch I we have no need for religion because we experience the Sacred Mystery all the time, even though we don't consciously realize it. When Jung visited a very primitive tribe in Africa, for example, he asked them about the meaning of what appeared to him to be religious rituals; they had no idea what he meant by the term *religious* because they had no formal, organized belief system. The rituals they performed to honor the Mystery were unconscious and habitual, taken for granted by all without question or reflection.

Many spiritually oriented Epoch II egos sense the Mystery but rarely understand in any life-changing way that they share the same home with it. Thus during Epoch II we create, organize, and join religions because we like clarity, reason, order, and social approval, and because we need assurance of our self-worth and self-preservation, either here or in the hereafter.

In Epoch III, our ego returns to its spiritual core whether it intends to or not, simply by working to bring more light to the unconscious. In deliberately doing so, it establishes what Jung called an ego-Self axis upon which two-way communication occurs between the ego and the Self. This shift of focus from the outer to the inner world frees us from the need for worldly validation. Thus, the Epoch III ego is always deeply spiritual, but it may or may not be conventionally religious.

Every religion is founded on the rock of the Self. The Self prodded Abraham to be hospitable to strangers and Moses toward greater spiritual openness, social responsibility, and justice. Buddha at its prompting sought release from delusion through self-knowledge and consciousness. Jesus sought compassion and social justice. Mohammed sought communion with Divine Unity. All these spirit persons were motivated by the same spiritual core.

The fact that many Westerners today have no problem accommodating Eastern philosophies is a testament to our growing capacity for holistic thinking, which knows that our differences matter less than the commonality of our spiritual goals. But we can't see our commonalities when we are unaware of the reality of the Self. And we can't become aware of the Self until our egos become intentional about exploring the unconscious.

So let's take a closer look at the ego's role in creating consciousness.

The Ego's Role in Creating Consciousness

In *A New Earth* Eckhart Tolle defines the ego as "*a dysfunctional relationship with the present moment.*"[1] I love this and find it enormously helpful! A Jungian might add that the ego's dysfunctional relationship with the present moment decreases as its ability to stay conscious in the present moment increases.

Here's an example of what I mean. When I'm feeling frustrated because I'm doing something I feel I have to (say, empty the dishwasher) but would much rather be doing something else (for example, writing), my ego is in a dysfunctional relationship with the Now. However, when I *notice* my frustration and don't want to keep feeling it, my ego is becoming more conscious. If I then realize I can *choose* to wallow in childish frustration or stop and look into what's happening, my ego is staying conscious. If I go a step further and choose to *accept* this responsibility and focus on the task at hand instead of fighting it, and if my frustration vanishes as a result and I actually experience some pleasure doing this simple job, I've accomplished something very important. My ego hasn't died, but for those few moments functioned with Epoch III consciousness by deciding to face reality and stop expecting to have its own way all the time!

Note that this is the same three-step process of uniting opposites outlined in Chapter Nine: *discriminating, cultivating understanding and compassion,* and *integrating.* First, I become aware of, or discriminate my bias against one pole in a pair of opposites—that is, I realize I'm frustrated at having to empty the dishwasher now because I'm thinking of what I want to do in the future (the next few seconds), which is to sit down at my computer and write. Next, I choose to *cultivate understanding and compassion* for the rejected pole—in this case, for the present moment, the job at hand and the grumpy, irresponsible child in me that doesn't want to do it. Finally, my ego decides to accept these realities and *integrate* them into my awareness by being intentional and present with this job instead of rushing through without thinking. In just a few seconds, my ego moves from ordinary ego-consciousness into integrated consciousness.

Depending on my circumstances, I sometimes go through this process several times a day, and sometimes never even get to step one! But this is a huge improvement over my younger years when I had little awareness of what was going on inside me and my only option for dealing with my dysfunctional relationship with the Now was to shut up, grit my teeth, and get on with it. That really isn't a pleasant way to get through life, but it's a daily reality for many of us with Epoch II egos.

What makes the leap from ordinary ego-consciousness to integrated consciousness possible is the mindfulness I've deliberately cultivated. The "shut up, grit my teeth, and get on with it" mode is a focused and obsessively Warrior-like determination that traps me in a habitual rut and blinds me to other ways of responding. But years of meditation have instilled a new habit of mindfulness that diffuses my focus and helps me consider my options.

My frustration in this example is a symptom of an unconscious assumption I'm still cherishing, and with which my ego hasn't come to terms. Somewhere in my unconscious a spoiled little princess feels like she shouldn't have to clean out the dishwasher but should get to do exactly what she wants to! My ego doesn't think this consciously; it's far too busy identifying with its ideals of self-discipline, duty, and mind over matter. But something inside me—I call this something my princess because it's easier to recognize that way—does think this way. She is what sets up the conflict that gives rise to my frustration. Focusing all my attention on accomplishing whatever my ego is determined to suffer through is a choice to keep my princess buried in my unconscious. And as long as she stays there, she'll continue to kick up a fuss whenever she feels like it.

But here's the pithy core of it: I don't like feeling that frustration; I don't *want* to live that way. So I take my frustration seriously and try to figure out where it's coming from. With practice, I get better at noticing and reassuring my princess that she'll get to do what she wants to as soon as I finish this necessary job. Watching my frustration dissipate is more than enough reward for the effort it takes to be mindful!

Integrating Conscious and Unconscious

To train your ego to become more aware of what's going on in your unconscious:

- Set aside twenty to thirty minutes a day (or as often as you can) to meditate.

- Sit in a quiet place. Close your eyes and be very still.

- Pay attention to your breath. You might think to yourself, "Breathing in. Breathing out."

- If you notice a thought, feeling, physical sensation, or emotion, accept it, then mentally brush it away and return to following your breath.

Did you acquire any insights about yourself?

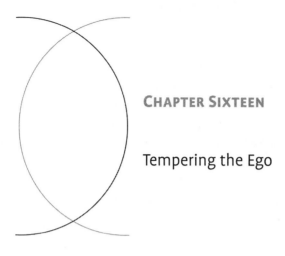

Chapter Sixteen

Tempering the Ego

THE EGO is neither good nor bad. In fact, about the only generalizations we can make about it are that

- once a young ego separates from the maternal matrix it tends to gravitate toward anxiety, conflict, dualistic thinking, fear, repression, and masculinity;

- it is more conscious of itself than it was during Epoch I, but less conscious than it will be if it continues to evolve into Epoch III;

- the way it manifests in individuals can run the gamut from extreme confidence to extreme self-doubt; solidity to fragility; strength to weakness; receptivity to repressiveness; happiness to misery, etc., and

- it can choose to stay stuck in immaturity, which is easier, if usually more uncomfortable, or it can choose to continue growing, which is harder, but infinitely more satisfying.

If the ego isn't inherently bad, why does it get such a bad rap (as in egocentric, egotistical, egomaniac, and so on)? Because of its tendency to become easily inflated or puffed up with self-importance. Most of us get this way some of the time; some of us are this way most of the time. An inflated ego may serve a person quite well in many ways, but in the long run it doesn't bode well for psycho-spiritual maturity, social harmony, or healthy relationships.

Our egos need to be confident enough to protect us and help us fulfill our needs. They also need to be conscious enough of how we think, feel, and act to choose not to run roughshod over others. Most of history is written by and about inflated egos who assumed they were, or aspired to be, the center of the universe! The inflated ego (hubris) is the root cause of many personal and societal ills.

The opposite of an inflated ego is a deflated or depressed one. Most egos, especially ones that have been excessively inflated for long periods of time, go through periods of being humbled. For an ego that tends to inflation, depression can be a necessary corrective, like the opposite swing of a pendulum. This sort of depression often occurs during crises that remind the ego of its vulnerability. This is usually a temporary condition that can lead to more balance if the ego consciously deals with its suffering and finds creative outlets for it, instead of wallowing in self-pity or trying to ignore it or escape.

Another form of ego depression (and here I'm not discussing clinical depressions caused by genetic inheritance or chemical imbalances) can be seen in an immature or weak ego with little sense of its rights or power and little hope of getting what it needs. This ego feels anxious, inferior, unentitled, and undeserving of the same rights and courtesies it readily extends to others. It lacks self-esteem and a healthy sense of its worth. Often it avoids confrontations to the point of allowing itself to be victimized, because it has difficulty asserting itself or acting on its own behalf when opposed. Like a starving kitten, this kind of ego could benefit from a prolonged feast at inflation's table!

Neither inflation nor depression is necessarily bad in itself. It all depends on context and degree. Many Epoch II egos are so stable that they rarely experience swings to either extreme, and when they do they are relatively minor. But an immature ego that depends on the external world for its sense of well-being is so buffeted about by the changing winds of circumstance that it is vulnerable to frequent and excessive inflation and/or depression. When good things happen such an ego tends to claim the credit and become inflated. When bad things happen it takes it personally, moves into depression, and feels resentful, misunderstood, and sorry for itself. The immature Epoch II ego is the primary cause of our conflicts and crises:

An overly depressed ego can become self-destructive, an overly inflated one can be destructive to others.

Whether inflated or depressed, every ego needs strength and balance. Above all it needs to become aware of itself and its relationship to the whole psyche. An ego training itself to look within is on the way to becoming more conscious. Aware that unknown forces influence it without its knowledge, it neither claims credit for its successes nor blames others for its problems. Because it sees its tendencies to be overly sensitive or insensitive, critical or accommodating, assertive or retiring, superior or inferior, it can more easily contain them and is no longer at the complete mercy of mood swings into inflation or depression. Because it has more awareness and objectivity it is less reactive.

Someone who is accomplishing this is on the way to becoming a spirit person, whether or not s/he espouses traditional beliefs (remember, there was nothing traditional about the beliefs of Abraham, Buddha, Jesus, or Mohammed in their own times), whether or not anyone else notices. In opening to the inner otherness with which it shares the psyche, a maturing ego brings the light of our feminine side into consciousness.

Integrating Inflation and Depression

- The next time you feel inflated or full of yourself, ask yourself what ego-need was just gratified. Then pay attention to how you are behaving toward others and how they are responding to you. Do you like what you see? If not, come up with a better way to act.

- The next time you feel depressed, ask yourself what immediately preceded your mood change. Was it something that happened to you, or something you were thinking?

- If it was something that happened, find a healthy way to express your discomfort.

- If it was something you were thinking, question the reality of your thoughts by talking them over with someone who has your best interest at heart and will be honest with you.

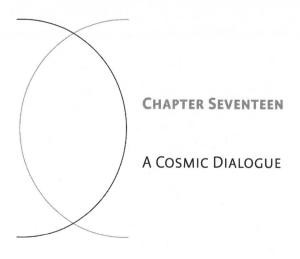

CHAPTER SEVENTEEN

A COSMIC DIALOGUE

God and Goddess are taking a twilight walk. God is feeling pretty good about himself and starts to tell Goddess about his day. "You won't believe everything I did today. This morning I inspired a televangelist to such heights that he raised $100,000 for his new church in one show. Isn't that awesome?"

Goddess nods and smiles.

"Then in that country over there," (he points his chin at a spot on the planet) "I got the board of a major corporation to donate a million dollars to establish a library that will house documents from every major religion."

Goddess nods and smiles.

God continues, "This afternoon a businesswoman was so inspired in her daily devotions that she created a brilliant new plan for an ecumenical community coalition that will study the problem of diminishing memberships in organized religion. How neat is that?"

Goddess nods and smiles.

"Then just before we started our walk I heard from a woman who wanted to thank me for helping her get a new job that will raise their family income by 38 percent! Now they can buy that new four-bedroom, three-bathroom house they've wanted. She kept saying, 'You are so good. You are so good. You are so good.' That was really nice."

Goddess nods and smiles.

God turns to Goddess. "Tell me about your day."

"Well, this morning I stood by the bed of a child dying of leukemia. Just before he took his last breath he looked up and smiled as he pointed at me and said, 'Look at that pretty light, Mommy.' I think it made his parents feel a little better."

God nods and smiles.

"After my hospital visits," Goddess continues, "I went to that rainforest over there where they're cutting down all those ancient trees. I fanned the flame in the foreman's heart until he stopped, took off his hat, and told his crew that what they were doing was wrong and he was quitting his job. Then he gave the crew the rest of the day off and went home to make love to his wife."

God nods and smiles.

"Then I saw a very weak light coming from a woman who was running along a dark road, sobbing because her husband had just hit her again. I stayed with her and kept whispering, 'Call that therapist whose number you wrote down last year,' until she took out her phone and made the call. She has an appointment tomorrow."

God nods, slows his step, then stops. He turns to Goddess, looks into her eyes, and says, "That's it? That's what you did today?"

Goddess nods. With a look of infinite tenderness God says to Goddess, "Your day was better than mine."

They embrace and continue their walk.

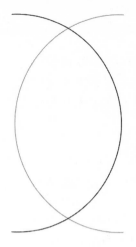

CHAPTER EIGHTEEN

The Divine Feminine as Holy Spirit

WHEREAS traditionally God the Father is seen as hard, dynamic, and assertive, God the Mother is soft, magnetic, and nurturing. God orders; Goddess suggests. God thunders; Goddess whispers. God is in your head and face; Goddess is in your body and heart. In these respects, Goddess is suspiciously like Christianity's Holy Spirit!

In Christianity the Holy Spirit was symbolized by a dove because of its beauty, gentleness, and ability to fly, which makes it an excellent mediator between heaven and Earth. In Islam, Alborak, a milk-white winged (dove-like?) horse with a woman's face and a peacock's tail mediated for the prophet Mohammed, transporting him from Earth to heaven. These spiritually *comforting* and decidedly maternal qualities—beauty, gentleness, milk, mediation between heaven and Earth—are almost universally ascribed to the feminine principle.

We're told that when Jesus's disciples gathered together after his crucifixion, the Comforter (another name for the Holy Spirit) manifested in a mighty wind and tongues of flame. Before the Church appropriated wind (or breath) and light for the male God, they were originally associated with Goddess.

Why? Because both breath and light *enable* life, just as every mother does. (Enabler is also a name for the Holy Spirit and a quality of the Divine Feminine in both its maternal and its transformative aspects.) A mother contains a growing child, then gives it the breath of life at birth. In Judaism, the Shechinah, the feminine aspect of God, is described as the *luminous* presence of the Divine in the world. During the forty years Jews wandered in the wilderness, she appeared as a cloud by day and a pillar of fire by night to comfort them with her presence and help them find their way.

Likewise, Gnostic Christians saw Sophia (whose name means wisdom) as a woman of light who filled nature and human beings with a spark of divine light that waits to be fanned into action. This spark is a metaphor for our evolutionary drive toward consciousness and completion! Whether we ignore her or honor her as Holy Spirit, Mary, Queen of Heaven, Sophia, Sapienta, Great Mother, Goddess, Shechinah, Hokmah, the Beloved, or the Divine Feminine, God our Mother is every bit as sacred, wise, and involved in our spirituality as the more familiar masculine aspects of Deity.

The Divine Feminine's light is embedded in every living being at its inception. As long as we are alive she is within us: suggesting, soothing, prodding, nurturing, hinting, questioning, befuddling, attracting, teaching, guiding, inspiring, affirming, contradicting, comforting, encouraging, enabling, enlightening. In fact, we embody the Divine Feminine, and the only way we can become separated from her is to die. Then her light departs—literally as well as figuratively—and our bodies become lumps of meat. If you've seen a dead body, you know what her absence looks like: The eyes are clouded because her light is gone.

As life is sacred, so is Divine Mother sacred. As life is about being and becoming, so is Mother. Because of her we enter the world with a compulsion to grow. We can't help it. It's simply how we're made. Physically, our destiny is to survive and thrive and adapt and change and procreate with increasing efficiency and grace, improving ourselves and our species. Spiritually, our destiny is to evolve into wise, consciously integrated beings who recognize the sacredness of all life and work to preserve it at every opportunity.

How do we honor the Holy Spirit's imperative to grow spiritually? By making the unconscious conscious. I've suggested meditation as a valuable practice that can help us be mindful of gut instincts, intuitions, meaningful quickenings, subtle energetic movements and emotions, and so on. But while identifying these signals from the unconscious *when they occur* is essential, it is not enough. Once we recognize them we need to know how to interpret them so we can find their deeper messages without being misled.

Historically, religions and governments have tried to solve this problem by devising commandments, rules, and laws as guides for behavior. If you have a strong urge to kill someone you hate, you know not to act on it because killing is against the law and you will be punished. But laws and rules can only control the big social taboos. They can't help someone undergoing a spiritual transformation know which internal messages (that arise in ordinary situations) to heed and which to refuse.

It's therefore up to us to become aware of the messages we get and test them for where they come from. Here are four tests we can apply to any compelling internal event. All contribute to greater consciousness.

Test 1: Listen to Your Conscience

An obvious test is, "Let your conscience be your guide." Someone in the latter phases of Epoch/Level II has already acquired a healthy conscience as well as a strong sense of duty and responsibility. Having experienced the satisfaction of operating from standards that go beyond self-interest, such people can't betray their evolving ethos without terrible guilt.

But guilt alone is not a reliable guide. If you're feeling guilty about the temptation to act on an inner prodding, more information is always needed. Are you feeling guilty because this might have truly harmful consequences? Or do you always feel guilty whenever you want to climb down from the tree, defy convention, and make an original choice for yourself? If it's the latter, know that it's normal to feel guilty when you're opening up to new ideas and ways of thinking.

In the early years of my inner work I had many dreams of trying to evade police or other authorities who wanted to punish me for breaking society's rules. An ego that is transferring its allegiance to the Self is indeed breaking the conventional rules of Epoch and Level II, and it is a very rare person who doesn't occasionally feel guilty about this.

Test 2: Question Your True Motivation

Some of us experience guilt when we eat a cookie, have a critical thought, or swat a fly. A more reliable test is to ask ourselves: What is my true motivation? Does my desire to critique this other person's behavior express my ego's need to feel smart? Important? Superior? Does it come from a compulsion to retaliate? To wound? To make him/her feel as small as I feel? Or do I truly want to clarify an important issue in the interest of helping this person or creating a more honest relationship with him or her? Does my desire to befriend someone come from a self-centered or ignoble motive like wanting to use them to further my own ambitions and ego needs? Or does it come from a strong sense that this is someone I really like who has the potential to become a treasured friend?

Questioning your true motivation is a crucial step in becoming more conscious of your unconscious. Think about it: It takes greater ego consciousness than normal to even think of asking yourself such questions, let alone to actually ask and then probe for answers. The key is to keep noticing your discomfort and try to understand the hidden part of you that is bringing it on. When you come up with an answer that resonates in a strong "Aha!" you know you've been in touch with the Divine Feminine. And there's another payoff: After enough practice, you get better at understanding other people too.

Test 3: Recognize Your Feelings

Some internal messages come in the form of compelling and recurring thoughts or ideas we believe to be true and positively motivated, perhaps even motivated by the Holy Spirit, when in fact they are not. The ego is very good at fooling itself. So another important test is to pay attention to the *feeling* that accompanies the thought. I can tell myself I want to improve my relationship with a loved one or enhance the functioning of a committee I'm working with, and I can believe myself when I say it; but if I'm feeling annoyed, superior, self-righteous, impatient, hurt, disappointed, angry, needy for validation or retaliation, or some other "negative" emotion in relation to this belief, I need to back off and regroup. When thoughts are at odds with feelings, trust the feelings. Feelings *never* lie about what's really going on in the unconscious.

Test 4: Question Your Moral Reasoning

A final test is to ask if the internal message is in accord with the guiding principles of Level III moral reasoning. Again, these are

- to serve equality and justice for all with nonviolence,

- to feel and be guided by love and caring, and

- to cause the least possible amount of pain and harm.

If acting on our "messages" would violate these principles, we can be sure they are not from the Sacred Feminine/Holy Spirit/Higher Self, but from our immature egos or negative forces in our unconscious.

Before we take a look at some of these negative forces, I'd like to share my experience of a not-so-subtle message from the Divine Feminine that features her gift of transforming light. At the time, I had absolutely no idea what it might mean or what, if any, guidance it might be trying to offer. But now I think it was all about comforting me, reassuring me that I was loved, and enabling my growth into increased consciousness.

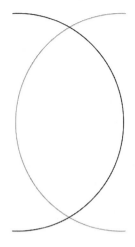

CHAPTER NINETEEN

A Manifestation of the Woman of Light

FOR TEN YEARS the lingering effects of my forest experience satisfied my spiritual needs. Then in 1970 a disturbing new obstacle arose. My husband and I had left graduate school and moved to a new town. Just before my twenty-seventh birthday, I gave birth to my first child. Shortly after Julie was born we joined an Episcopal church, where she was baptized. A few weeks later I auditioned for a religious play written by one of the parishioners. I was pleased to get the lead role of Stella (from the Latin, meaning *light*-bringing star), and started the rehearsals enthusiastically. Soon I began to feel estranged from God.

Another dramatic production, another spiritual crisis, another initiation from Sophia: Only now as I write do I see the pattern. For the second time, circumstances had come together in such a way that participating in a religious narrative featuring the symbolism of light reflected the mythic drama taking place within me—my quest for the Divine Feminine and her gift of spiritual en*light*enment.

During this time the charismatic movement was sweeping the country. I knew nothing about it before coming to this church; but as I worked closely with the director and other cast members, I became aware of a very different, more emotional and spontaneous way of experiencing God. I believed I had experienced the Holy Spirit ten years before, when my mind quickened to the meaning of scripture; but these people were talking about a baptism in the Holy Spirit that caused people to speak in tongues, utter prophecies, and lay healing hands on one another!

Part of me was attracted to these phenomena and part was repelled.

Before rehearsals we would gather in a circle and pray. One woman in particular exuded a strong and confident spirituality. While others prayed with recognizable words, Pat Nicolle would whisper strange sounds. I soon realized she was speaking in tongues. I also learned that she belonged to the Order of St. Luke, an Episcopal healing order. As such, she was often called upon to pray for people during healing services. What was this all about? Were these "gifts" of the Holy Spirit real? Or were they psychological phenomena made up by inflated, needy, and overly emotional egos?

I didn't know, and these questions threw me into spiritual turmoil. I had thought I had a good relationship to God. I believed I knew as much as most people about him, and more than some. It seemed to me I'd been a faithful student and was somewhat spiritually mature. But now I was seeing things I hadn't experienced and meeting people who seemed more advanced. This was a blow to my baby bear ego, and I began to feel depressed and estranged from God.

Soon I began to question God's very existence. I'm a serious-minded perfectionist with a nose for insincerity. I knew there are charlatans in every walk of life. I'd heard about delusional behavior and mass hypnotism. I understood that people are easily brainwashed into believing things they want to believe for emotional reasons, or to satisfy their ego needs. I'd read about Marx and others who considered religion an opiate of the masses, a sop for weak and fearful sheep.

I wanted the real thing, not some contrived spiritual experience concocted to assuage my fears. Had I been fooling myself all along? Was I just as susceptible to being duped as the next person? Was the Holy Spirit just a convenient idea?

One day, out of a deep sense of alienation from God, I approached Pat after a rehearsal. I was having problems with my faith, I told her. Did she know of anything that might help? At the next rehearsal she brought me two books. One was *A Reporter Finds God through Spiritual Healing*, about a scientifically minded skeptic who found faith after a long personal search.[2] The other was *The Healing Light* by Agnes Sanford, a gifted spiritual healer and the mother of Jungian analyst John Sanford.[3] (*There's the symbolism of light again. Why have I not noticed this before?*) I devoured both books. They alleviated my mental reservations somewhat, but something was still wrong. Why couldn't I *feel* anything? Where was the God who had felt so close for so long?

One Sunday soon afterwards I went up to the altar rail after the service, where the priests and a few lay persons were waiting to pray for people. Tentatively, I approached one of the priests and told him about my problem: I was attracted to the charismatic gifts and was experiencing some peer pressure to acquire them, but I had several reservations. What if they were fake, just mental delusions? I didn't want any part of them if they weren't authentic. I said I definitely didn't want to speak in tongues just because it was fashionable. And I seemed to have lost my faith. "I feel like I wouldn't feel a thing if Jesus himself walked up to me," I told him.

He said I had an overly strong conscience. I should relax my standards a little, be easier on myself. Also, I seemed to be dwelling on negatives. I'd probably feel better if I would just "accentuate the positive" and "eliminate the negative."

I left the altar feeling guilty. The priest must be right—after all, he was a priest. It must be my fault I had lost my faith. I was too scrupulous about spiritual matters, too negative. Maybe there were other, even worse, things wrong with me. Otherwise, why couldn't I believe like everyone else? But deep within, part of me felt cheated by his response, which seemed far too simplistic.

I had asked for help twice: once from Pat and once from a priest. Nothing had helped much, and yet I couldn't let it go. I was lost in a desert. My spiritual thirst was intense and I could no more ignore the longing in my soul than a starving bear cub can ignore the emptiness in her belly. My only recourse was to try again, so I made a third request.

I didn't know it then but have since learned that Buddhist masters often refuse to answer a student's question if they feel the time is not right, or if the question is inappropriate or unanswerable in words. Masters can be very intimidating, and few students have the nerve to ask a second time. Yet some do, and are again rebuffed. A student who is sincere and desperate enough to dare to ask a third time is given an answer. So it was with me. Three is the magic number in myths and fairy tales: The hero/ine is given three tasks, three wishes, three opportunities to solve the problem, three magical gifts, and so on. Three is also the magic number on the spiritual journey. There's something archetypal about trinity. Perhaps because it transcends duality?

I approached Pat again and made an appointment to meet her in the tiny old chapel where we would talk and she would pray for me. I remember little of what either of us said there, but what happened next is as vivid in my mind as the words on this page.

After we talked I knelt at the altar rail and she stood behind me with her hands on my head. The gist of her prayer, which was comforting and sincere, was a plea for faith. I felt embarrassed, self-conscious, bold, hopeful, confused, vulnerable, miserable. But in terms of spiritual sensibility, I felt absolutely nothing.

When her prayer was over I opened my eyes and became aware of a strange phenomenon. Midway between me and the altar I saw a tall—about six feet—thin, oval-shaped pillar of softly glowing bluish-white light hovering a few feet above the floor. It was not a clear, still ray of light, nor was it like the thin blanket of illumination a light ray sheds on the surface of an object or wall. It was three-dimensional, dense, and alive—a vibrant mass of pulsating energy that stood alone, unconnected to anything around it.

I blinked. Something was wrong with my vision. I must have closed my eyes too tightly, I thought. I closed them gently, opened them again and looked up tentatively, half fearfully. What if it were gone? It was still there. I blinked again and looked around the chapel. If it was in my eyes, I would see it everywhere I looked. It was nowhere else in the room, but when I looked back at the altar, *there it was,* still glowing in that odd pulsing way.

This couldn't be. It didn't make sense. It must be some strange phenomenon caused by the sunlight coming at an odd angle through one of the stained glass windows. "Do you see that blue light up there, Pat?" I asked.

"No," she said. "What does it look like?"

I described it as I looked at it, but Pat could see nothing. "Praise God," she said. "It's a manifestation."

What was a manifestation? I had no idea. This was too weird. Still, I felt *nothing.* I watched it for a moment longer. Then, as we prepared to leave, I took a few steps toward the door at the far end of the aisle and glanced back a final time. The light was gone. Okay. Sure. It was what I had expected. I had just imagined it, or else it was a trick of the light that only worked when I stood in a certain spot.

Seconds later, Pat joined me. As we walked down the aisle I looked at the large silver cross hanging from a chain around her neck. It was surrounded by a halo of the same pulsating mass of light, this time only slightly bigger than the cross.

Manifestation number two. Okay. So it was coming from inside my head; I was conjuring it up myself. Somehow I must be unconsciously creating this illusion because my need to believe is so strong. I was embarrassed at my weakness, confused. I felt no other emotion.

Outside the chapel Pat and I separated. I pondered this perplexing puzzle as I walked toward the church office to make a phone call; my friend Ginger was taking care of my baby at her house and I wanted to let her know I'd be there soon. What on earth was wrong with me? Either I was losing my mind and experiencing delusions, or what I'd seen was real and I was a hopeless skeptic who wouldn't believe in Jesus if he showed me the holes in his hands. If it was real, why didn't I *feel* anything?

Inside the office I looked around as I made my call. No strange lights anywhere. Then, as I was hanging up the phone, Pat walked in. There, on her chest, hovering around the cross as before, was the blue light. Again, the third time was the charm. Something hard inside me cracked, crumbled, began to dissolve.

As I walked out of the office my heart was pounding and I took several deep astonished breaths to calm it down. In my car I wept wrenching sobs of awe and gratitude. God was real.

Maybe God wasn't anything like the God of my childhood or the God of my church, and maybe the truth about who and what Jesus was had little relation to my church's ideas about him; but suddenly these things didn't matter. I knew beyond a doubt that the Mystery we refer to when we use the words *God* and *Jesus* is real.

Previously, my spirituality was tangled up with the conviction that religion was a *head* thing to figure out and get right. But now I was in a state of feeling-realization involving every cell in my body—a body celebrating the wonder of an extraordinary mystery with profound emotion and tears of joy. It no longer mattered if the blue light came from without or within. Wherever it came from, no matter what it meant, it had been there, and it was there for me! I felt more alive and loved than ever in my life.

If I die now, it will have been enough, I thought: *Does this mean I've finally arrived? Looking back, I can only smile at my naivety.*

Two awakenings had convinced me that something mysterious and sacred knew me, loved me, and dwelled in me. This knowing was enormously gratifying. For a time I felt an abundance of joy, gratitude, and compassion. But these feelings ebbed over the next several years, and I grew increasingly aware of flaws and dissatisfactions I hadn't noticed before. This was bothersome and discouraging. Where were these unworthy thoughts coming from? Why wasn't I becoming a better person? Why wasn't I happy?

I didn't realize then that these uncomfortable moments of self-examination were a very positive step forward. They marked my ego's first serious foray into my unconscious. Looking more closely at myself was very likely the whole point of this manifestation. The Woman of Light's message was not, "*You are so special and spiritual that I have decided to bless you with my magnificent presence!*" It was, "*You are a very unconscious, if well-meaning, soul who lives in a dense fog of repression and denial! My light dwells within you, but it is up to you to find it and make it grow. Hopefully this vision of your light will motivate you to bring more of it into consciousness.*"

As yet I had no clue of how unconscious I was, so I had no conception of consciousness. Nor did I know anything about wholeness and how it's necessarily composed of darkness as well as light. So even though I was beginning to desire self-knowledge, I didn't know how to acquire it; and I was plenty worried about what I might discover.

Soon after this experience my husband and I started attending a weekly prayer group and I noticed that our discussions would often elicit probing personal questions—for example, "Why am I feeling critical of that woman who gives every appearance of being so kind and loving?" or "Why did I just say that when deep in my heart I know it isn't true? Is impressing these people really more important to me than being honest?"

From then on, noticing my thoughts and feelings and questioning my true motives became commonplace; but my growing family and new home, church, and friends took up most of my energy, and I was happy to leave it at that. Actually, I think that's probably how it should be when one is only twenty-seven. Finding your way in the outer world is hard enough at that age. At any rate, progress in my inner archaeology was slow. It was another ten years before I was ready to receive Mother's third gift: the ability to see and accept my shadow.

But you won't have to wait that long. I think you're ready to hear about the shadow right now.

Notes

1. Eckhart Tolle, *A New Earth: Awakening to Your Life's Purpose* (New York, NY: Plume/Penguin, 2005), 201.

2. Emily Gardiner Neal, *A Reporter Finds God Through Spiritual Healing* (New York: Morehouse-Gorham Co. 1956).

3. Agnes Sanford, *The Healing Light* (St. Paul, Macalester Park Pub. Co., 1957).

THE THIRD GIFT
ACCEPTANCE OF THE SHADOW

Taken together, our complex of repressed energy is known as our *shadow*. Whereas the unconscious is everything we don't know about ourselves, the shadow is everything we don't *want* to know about ourselves.

CHAPTER TWENTY

Mining for Gold

SINCE experiencing the blue light, I've learned that others have similar manifestations. Like me, they rarely have a name for this energy at first. After searching for explanations, many of them, especially Jews, attribute it to the Sacred Feminine. Rabbi Leah Novick tells this of Shechinah's manifestations:

> The most common experiences are of light and radiance, which is consistent with the writings of many Jewish scholars who described her as a great light which shines upon all God's creatures. Many writers considered her the light of creation itself or the place of the primordial light.[1]

Christian Gnostics created myths about a woman of light who fell from heaven to be the co-redemptrix of Jesus, his partner in the work of salvation.[2] Because of her, each of us contains a spiritual spark that awaits "the breath of the emissaries of the fullness to be fanned into effective action. This spirit is of Sophia . . ."[3]

The contemporary sage Huston Smith refers to light as "the very foundation of matter, the underlying processes of nature, spirit, and consciousness."[4] He goes on to say that light is also

> a universal metaphor for consciousness. It is all over our vocabulary—for instance, we say "the light dawned" when we see a point. We are not talking about ocular light in this case, but it is the same word, which is part of the exciting way that the word "light" provides a bridge. In its highly technical, frontier-science usage, light

is absolutely fundamental to the scientific explanation of nature. The same word, universally and cross-culturally, is the word that we use for "understanding." This is a tremendous invitation to grasp the total nature of reality, and of our lives within it.[5]

It feels synchronistic to me that of the four Bible verses that sparked my spirituality at age seventeen, three were about light. They said I was the light of the world and should let my light shine so people could see God. At the time I thought that meant I should go around converting people to the God I'd learned about in church, perhaps as a minister or missionary. I never suspected these verses could be referring to something as far-fetched as unveiling the God within.

That puts an entirely different twist on these verses. They weren't saying I could be a better Christian by spreading the word about the Christian God and his Son. And they weren't saying I should "make nice" or wear a "happy face" all the time, putting on an act of perfection and goodness. To hide your light under a bushel is to repress the truths of your soul. To let your light shine is to be true to yourself: authentic, congruent, without covering up, pretending, or denying. To share your light is to allow your true self to shine through in everything you say and do. These verses tell us to acquire self-knowledge, to bring light to the darkness of our souls, to aspire to consciousness.

It took me years to understand this. When I finally began to get it, wearing a mask had become an ingrained habit that was difficult to break. Like most people, I found my unconscious self about as inviting as a dungeon because I associated it with badness and unworthiness. To open the door to it felt counterproductive to everything I'd learned from my family and religion.

So far I've treated *conscious* and *unconscious* as a rather clear-cut pair of opposites more or less synonymous with light and dark, but they are actually more complex. Let's explore some finer distinctions now.

Our *conscious* self is every part of us to which our ego has access. We're all aware of having certain feelings, ideas, beliefs, attitudes, opinions, personality traits, habitual responses, memories, knowledge, dreams, and so on. We don't hold all these things in our awareness all the time, but when our egos want access to this information, we can find it. The conscious realm is like our house. We might forget all about a certain pair of pants or shoes for a while, but when we remember them and want to wear them, we know where to look for them.

The unconscious contains everything we *do not know* about ourselves. For Jungians there are two levels of unconsciousness.

We can compare the first to a secret storeroom under the basement, whose existence and contents are unknown to us: This is called our *personal unconscious*. The personal unconscious is unique to each of us. Nobody else has the exact same family history, genetic inheritance, experiences, environmental influences, unexamined assumptions, or unacknowledged emotions as we do.

The second level lies even deeper than our personal unconscious. It is an inheritance shared by all humanity. Jung called this deeper layer the *collective unconscious*. Like a vast subterranean ocean of life-energy far beneath our house at the core of the earth, all humanity shares it; but very few of us know of its existence. It contains the most basic and primitive emotions, needs, and urges of our instincts and their psychological representatives, the archetypes.

I'll say more about instincts and archetypes later. For now it's enough to know that the instincts and archetypes are bipolar, by which I mean they have both masculine and feminine, and positive and negative potential. At their most civilized they feel like benevolent angels or gods. At their most uncivilized they feel like witches and demons that are as powerful, dangerous, autonomous, irresponsible, and amoral as Nature herself.

Much of our unconscious potential is perfectly benign, and some of it is extremely valuable, like buried treasure. Nonetheless most of us don't want to go there because we suspect it might contain something unworthy, unlikeable, and maybe even bad. So every time we catch a whiff of something we don't like (even though it might actually be good for us) we repress it. Having nowhere to go, the newly repressed material simply merges with everything else we've repressed. Taken together, our complex of repressed energy is known as our *shadow*. Whereas the unconscious is everything we don't know about ourselves, the shadow is everything we don't *want* to know about ourselves.

Everybody has a shadow. It is a non-negotiable given of the human condition. If you have an ego and a conscious self, you have a shadow and an unconscious self.

Just as your personal unconscious contains your personal shadow, the collective unconscious contains a collective shadow. The collective shadow is also bipolar. The positive aspects of this more primitive, uncivilized energy comprise our greatest potential for godliness. The negative aspects make up the archetype of evil, which is far more malevolent than the personal shadows of most people.

Your shadow, both personal and collective, is the other side of the coin of your psyche. If you aspire to psycho-spiritual maturity, you need to come to terms with it. You don't need to destroy the shadow any more than you need to destroy your ego; you need to acknowledge it and overcome your fear of it. This drains it of its toxic energy and brings you closer to the Self.

As Carl Jung said:

One cannot avoid the shadow unless one remains neurotic, and as long as one is neurotic one has omitted the shadow. The shadow is the block which separates us most effectively from the divine voice.[6]

So how do we recognize our shadow? Essentially, by turning our attention toward the things we don't want to admit about ourselves. Some are related to feared or disliked qualities we associate with masculinity or femininity. Others include instinctual needs we suspect but don't want to acknowledge. Still others are interests or qualities we've repressed because our families consider them unacceptable. For example, some people repress their creativity, sensitivity, empathy, intelligence, interests, talents, moral sensibility, spirituality, new ideas, strong ideals, enthusiasm for certain activities, or desire to achieve because these things are laughed at or criticized by others important to them.

Likewise, most of us find certain emotions so abhorrent that we don't want to admit to having them—things like hurt feelings, sadness, self-pity, resentment, anxiety, rage, jealousy, selfishness, criticism or judgment of others, hostility, pride, prejudice, disloyalty, envy, greed, self-righteousness, aggressiveness, lust, fear, and so on. Yet there are times when in our secret, innermost selves we all feel these things. Everyone does because these emotions are instinctual. Nevertheless, as long as we repress them, they belong to our shadows and influence us without our knowledge.

As a spiritual neophyte I believed (like everyone else I knew) that repressing my honest emotions, denying my disliked qualities, and generally pretending to be something I was not would make me more spiritual. I started trying to be spiritual after my encounter with the Mistress of the Forest. Flooded with a dizzying new awareness, I believed I had been touched by God. It left me so hungry for more that I began to devour the Bible. In Galatians I was thrilled to discover Paul's descriptions of the fruits of the spirit: love, joy, peace, patience, kindness, goodness, faithfulness, gentleness, and self-control. *This is it,* I thought. *This is what I've been looking for. These will be my spiritual goals.*

I memorized the list, reflected on the qualities, prayed for them every day, and tried to emulate them. *I'm on my way,* I thought naively. I believed that developing spirituality was simply a matter of knowing how God wanted me to behave, and then using my will to act that way. Anything I felt or thought that did not conform to "his will" (according to my understanding of these qualities and the biases of my family and religion, of course) I would just control with self-discipline. For my immature ego, the proof that I was on the right track was that the more strongly I identified with my ideals, the more "spiritual" I felt and the less aware I was of my shadow.

For people like me, being "spiritual" helps alleviate anxiety, preserve the status quo, and strengthen our sense of being safe and in control. Dreaming about future glory in a radiant heaven gets us through present suffering. By ignoring our shadow and acting humble and loving, we can keep feeling good about ourselves. By finding the answers to our spiritual questions in conventional beliefs, we never have to experience the loneliness of being an outsider or the terrifying responsibility of free choice.

Perfecting our personas to please the Father God we imagine as living in the light while shunning the darkness from which we are emerging–this is how immature Epoch II egos begin the spiritual journey. A young Epoch II ego doesn't know it's afraid or that it's constructing a mask. It's convinced it's free to do anything it wants. But the truth is, *we are not free to make original choices until the unconscious is made conscious.* If we are unaware of the limiting assumptions and other inner forces that control our behavior, we can't see the full range of our choices. And if we can't see our choices, it's impossible to change our behavior, no matter how much self-control or willpower we have.

The shadow is why we, like St. Paul, keep doing things we don't want to do and don't do things we think we should. Unfortunately, St. Paul didn't have access to the psychological understanding we have acquired since his time. Now we know that until we integrate our shadows into our conscious awareness we'll continue to despise ourselves, alienate others, act in baffling ways, fall short of our spiritual ideals, and wonder why.

Exploring our unconscious and getting acquainted with our shadows brings spiritual maturity. Mature spirit persons learn to *admit* to their "dark sides" so they can defuse them. Admitting doesn't imply making a public confession, broadcasting, complaining, excusing, wallowing, or surrendering. It just means being honest with ourselves. Other people can see our shadows anyway, and it's enormously frustrating to them when we deny something that's patently obvious to them. It's amazing how much conflict we can avoid by simply seeing and accepting responsibility for our part in it.

An unimaginable treasure awaits us in the unconscious, and we can find it by digging deep into our subterranean world. A recurring dream I had for many years clearly demonstrated the truth of this psychological principle to me. In it I was always outdoors following a path, usually at night, when my attention would be attracted to a sparkle of light in the dark earth beside the path. When I bent down to look, I would see that the light was reflecting off the rounded ridge of a half-buried coin. Pulling the coin out of the earth always revealed another one behind it, then another and another until I was delighted to discover an apparently bottomless stash of densely packed coins. The interesting thing is that once I became fully committed to inner work, I stopped having the dream. I no longer needed the reminder.

With practice our egos get better at seeing and restraining what's harmful. In doing so, we gain access to what is helpful. The reward of that first brilliant nugget—the rediscovery of a repressed childhood passion or the relief of accepting a formerly rejected quality—is so affirming that we are emboldened to continue our search. Then, energy previously expended on curbing our anxiety, maintaining our defenses, and perfecting our masks is made available to move in more personally enriching directions.

Integrating Light and Dark

The next time you have a nightmare or dream with a scary or disagreeable person,

- Write down everything you can remember about the dream, including your dream ego's emotional response to all that happened.

- If there is a frightening character, give it a name that fits its behavior, for example, Chaser, Stalker, Invader, Robber, Abuser, Killer, Poisoner, etc. Think of this character as something in you that is being wildly exaggerated to get your ego's attention.

- Have an imaginary dialogue with this character: Talk to it, ask it who it is, why it's acting the way it is, what it wants of you, what you can do to make it leave you alone, and so on.

- Look for signs of its presence in your waking life.

- If there is a frightening natural occurrence like an erupting volcano, hurricane, or flood, ask yourself what strong feeling is "erupting" into your consciousness, threatening to blow you away, or flooding you with emotion. Record your insights.

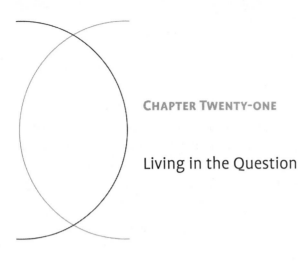

CHAPTER TWENTY-ONE

Living in the Question

YOU'RE WALKING along a busy street in your town. It's a lovely spring day—cool, slightly breezy. You've done this a hundred times: You pass familiar shops, see people you know, remember other times spent here. It's as good a place to be as any, you think.

Then . . . Wait! Who was that? A shadowy figure just stepped into a doorway up ahead. Wasn't it . . . ? No, it couldn't be. That was so long ago. High school. Didn't someone tell you that . . . ? A sudden stab of yearning surprises you with its intensity. Yes, that's how you used to feel. Sometimes you still . . . Then the guilt. You shouldn't be thinking like this. You have a great life.

You reach the doorway. Funny, you don't remember seeing this before. Has it always been here? You pause, stop. A piece of paper is tacked to the door. Something is written on it in a strange and unfamiliar script. Then you see your name at the top. Your heart starts to pound as you move closer to read the brief message:

Yes. This is what you've been looking for.

You catch your breath in confusion. Or is it excitement? Fear, maybe? Your stomach tightens. Your temples begin to throb. Your fingers tremble as you reach for the note. It crumbles in your hand and powders your shoes with ashes. There's a keening in your ears, a fuzziness in your head. Your vision blurs. Sirens sound.

Warning! Warning!

You grasp a handle that feels like a twisted, knotty root and the door swings open.

Total darkness. Then soft patches of muted light flicker on a wall. That smell; what is it? It reminds you of your grandmother's basement. Or was it Grandpa's workshop? Behind that, a faint pleasant sweetness. Isn't that the perfume Mom used to wear? It fades into muskier odors of mushrooms, humus, fur. Are there animals in here? There's a coppery taste in your mouth. What does that remind you of? You jerk your head. A rustling noise, a slither. Is that music? No, it sounds like a faint trickle of water in some deep cavern below.

Then, far in the distance, you see it. The tiny glimmer draws you like a magnet.

Is that where . . . ?

You are so still you can feel your pulse and hear your breath.

Is this when your real life finally begins?

Despite the warnings screaming in your head you tentatively step across the threshold and search for purchase. A stepping stone appears beneath your shoe. Odd, didn't you have sandals like that as a child? You lift the other foot. A different remembered shoe, another mossy stone. Very gently the door closes behind you.

What *is* this place?

This is the place of Mystery. You came here often as a child. Remember? It's where you were born. You stopped coming here many years ago, when some of it began to disturb you. There are some very wild and scary things here.

Sometimes a secret yearning for this place fills you like an ache. Remember when adulthood beckoned like a circus tent? When your favorite holiday was light years away and every cell of your being yearned for it? When did the boredom set in? When did life start stretching out before you like a vast, barren desert? Sometimes you've wondered, *This can't be all there is, can it? Do I really want to live the rest of my life this way?*

More questions. Now you're starting to feel bad. This hurts. You don't want to go there. Maybe you'll put the book down and go find something to eat.

What part of you is hurting? What part feels guilty?

What part wants to escape?

What part wants to eat? Or drink? Or turn on the TV? Or call a friend? Or go to bed?

What part is afraid?

What is it afraid of?

Where is the yearning coming from? Why won't it go away?

What part of you is asking these questions?

Do you want to listen to this voice?

Or would you rather keep listening to the voices that got you where you are today?

How would it be if you just agreed to live in the questions for a while?

Integrating Clarity and Mystery

- Choose the most interesting of the questions above, or think of a more compelling question of your own, and live with it for a week. Drink your coffee with it in the morning. Drive with it. Cook with it. Go to bed with it. Reflect on it.

- Write down or otherwise record important insights so you won't forget them.

- Then start over with another question.

- After a few weeks of this ask yourself one more question: Am I ready for the Mystery yet?

- If the answer is yes, then all you have to do is keep living in the questions. The answers will come when you're ready.

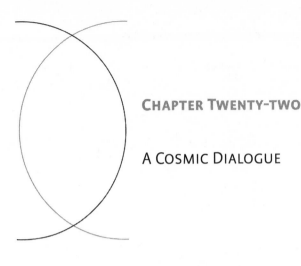

CHAPTER TWENTY-TWO

A COSMIC DIALOGUE

It's evening and God is in the heavenly kitchen, washing up after dinner. He and Goddess made a lovely Asian meal together: Korean Kim Chee and a Chinese stir fry. They like diversity. They had nectar to drink and ambrosia for dessert. They also like tradition.

They made a mess. Usually they share the clean-up, but tonight Goddess had an emergency call on Earth. God has had a long day. He's tired and annoyed. He doesn't *want* to feel annoyed, and Goddess might return at any moment. He is trying hard not to *look* annoyed because he doesn't want to annoy *her* with *his* annoyance.

Sure enough, Goddess walks in. God is scrubbing the wok. She comes closer. He keeps scrubbing. She peers closely at his face. He keeps scrubbing.

"What's wrong?" she asks?

God throws down the washrag, and soapy water splatters the heavenly white marble countertops. "I *knew* you were going to be annoyed at me. Did I say anything? Am I complaining? No. I'm just trying to clean up here so I can go to bed."

Goddess takes a backward step. "Um," she says. "You *look* like something's wrong. You *sound* like something's wrong. Are you *sure* nothing's wrong? Like maybe you're just a little bit irritated that I left you alone with the dishes? Here's how you looked just now." She bends over the sink, grabs the dishrag, tenses her shoulders, pulls her eyebrows together, and furiously attacks the wok.

God chuckles despite himself. "Okay, you're right. I was irritated because you left me alone with the dishes. But I didn't *want* to be irritated because I know you worked as hard as I did today, and sometimes you clean up alone when I'm really busy. I didn't want to act irritated because I know that annoys you. But I'm tired tonight. I'm sorry I snapped at you. I didn't want to do that."

Goddess wraps her arms around God and lays her head on his chest. "I know, honey. Sometimes you get cranky when you're tired."

"It's true," he admits. "I do. And sometimes my crankiness makes you cranky. But it didn't tonight. You were great. Thanks for being so accepting of me. It helped me accept myself."

"I love your honesty," she says. "And you're cute when you're trying not to be annoyed. I'm sorry I left, but it was an emergency. They're starting another war. I've done what I can for now, so I'm back. Why don't you let me finish this?"

"Why don't we do it together?" God says. "I'll clean up the sink and you can put the wok away. Then we can both retire sooner."

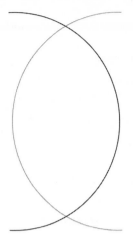

CHAPTER TWENTY-THREE

The Divine Feminine as Dream Mother and Shadow Projector

IN THE previous story, God was feeling annoyed. Instead of admitting it, he tried to cover it up. But his annoyance had to go somewhere, so some of it went into his body and some got projected onto Goddess. He was thinking, "I have to act like everything's fine or she'll get annoyed at me. She's so *sensitive* about the least little thing! Why can't I just feel the way I feel without having to worry about how she'll take it?" If he weren't feeling the least bit annoyed, it never would have occurred to him to expect *her* to feel it.

Most of us believe that our unwanted emotions and attitudes make us unworthy of being loved by God or anyone else. So we shroud them in darkness where we won't have to think about them and others can't see them. But we're fooling no one but ourselves. Our repressed material is always obvious to others, and it's a wise person who can see and admit to his/her shadow when someone points it out.

If we're ready to face our shadow, we don't have to wait for someone to tell us about it. We can learn to spot it ourselves. Without reading any further, for example, take a piece of paper and make a list of the five people you dislike the most and what you don't like about them. Humor me. No fair peeking at the next paragraph.

No fair looking ahead!

Don't look . . .

You better not be looking . . .

Okay, if you're done, ask yourself: What part of me is like that? If you're really honest with yourself, you'll discover a part of your shadow.

This doesn't mean you're just like that controlling woman or blowhard man who drives you nuts in waking life and keeps showing up in your dreams. It just means there's a little part of you that's like a little part of them. There's nothing horrible about that—you're human, remember? Everyone has faults.

To reward yourself for doing the tough work of clear-seeing, now make a list of the five people you most like and admire in the world and what you like best about them. Then ask: What part of me is like that? This time if you're honest you'll discover the hidden treasure in your shadow. It's true. You're not exactly like these people, but there's a part of you that's just like the parts of them you so admire.

How do I know this? Because I've experienced it for myself. And because others far wiser than me, Carl Jung among them, have studied it carefully. They've discovered that everyone's psyche performs a very curious and little-known phenomenon: It's called "projection," and it shows us our shadows all the time. Like characters in a film or dream, these images of our dark sides are always right in front of us. But to know what we're actually seeing, we have to direct our focus inward.

Since we associate unconsciousness with the undeveloped feminine principle, I like to think that the Divine Feminine is what projects our shadow outward so our egos can see it. I consider this one of her most valuable contributions to our spirituality. She does this in two specific ways. When we're asleep, she is our Dream Mother who shows us frightening or unlikeable people, animals, or events in our dreams. When we're awake, she projects our shadow onto people or events to which we have strong emotional reactions. In either case, the tipoff is our emotions. Anything to which we have a strong emotional reaction, positive or negative, is a projection of something in us of which we're unconscious. If we can tolerate the messages we get from Dream Mother or Shadow Projector, eventually some of us dare to dip a toe in shadow's dark pool. The full significance of such moments often goes by unappreciated, but having the courage to investigate even the tiniest piece of our dark side deserves fireworks and a gold medal for valor! This is true heroism and a gigantic stride forward in spiritual growth.

The next heroic step is to allow our shadow to have its say. As Edward

Edinger notes that if the psyche is to be transformed, "all thoughts, deeds, and memories that carry shame, guilt, or anxiety need to be given full expression."7 Giving these things an outlet doesn't mean giving in to them. It's simply a way of liberating trapped energy and turning it into a fire that can purify and transform the unhealthy aspects of shadow.

Appropriate practices we can adopt to express shadow material include art, writing and journaling, dreamwork, therapy, role play, dance, and active imagination.8 The goal and gift of this kind of work is compassion. Being freed from fear is being freed to love—free to love our real selves even though they may contain some unlovable parts. Free to love others.

Why does the Divine Feminine show us our shadows in our dreams and projections? Because this is how she teaches us compassion. In accepting ourselves, we learn to accept others. In forgiving ourselves we forgive others. In loving ourselves we love others.

Our spiritual Mother is like a good human mother who always loves her children even though she's fully aware of their faults. Even though she knows they can be bad sometimes. Everyone has a shadow. Everyone thinks and does bad things sometimes. But this doesn't mean we're bad through and through. We're just humans, for heaven's sake, and we still have a lot of growing to do.

There ought to be a label on everyone's forehead that says Incomplete R Us! Then maybe we'd realize it's normal to be imperfect. Then maybe we'd forgive ourselves for having ordinary human failings, and get on with the loving.

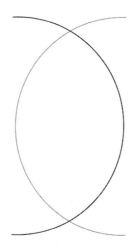

CHAPTER TWENTY-FOUR

A Shadow Dream about Projection

PROJECTION isn't easy to understand. The process is so deeply unconscious that our egos find it almost impossible to believe we do it. Early in the twentieth century, C. G. Jung was among the first psychologists to see and explain it; but the knowledge still hasn't mainstreamed in a big way. This is a terrible shame, because if you understand projection and use your understanding wisely, you have one of the most powerful tools for self-knowledge there is.

To explain it, I'd like to share a dream that came up while I was working on this section.

Pictures of the Property

I am in a church parish hall with a group of people in the town where we have a summer home. Bob and Charlie are here. [Not the real names of two talented and kindly contractors who in waking life have helped remodel and landscape our home.] Bob says he's looking forward to seeing my pictures of the property, especially the pond. As he says this, I see an image of the pond: There's a big, dark, blurry, circular blob in the center of it, below the surface.

Charlie says he wants to see my pictures of the fish in the pond. I see an image of the fish swimming around: They're blue and fuzzy with beautiful sparkly white outlines. There are lots of white sparkles in the water around them.

I realize everyone here is expecting me to make a presentation of my pictures that show the changes to our property, but I haven't brought them. I step to the front of the audience and face them. A film projector is on a tall tripod to my left and a little behind me. A line of film runs from the reel backwards and disappears beneath the wall behind me. A man appears to be trying to rewind it. A slide projector and one other piece of video equipment are also slightly behind my left side.

I tell the man I won't be needing these things and then say to the audience, "I'm so very sorry, but I completely forgot about this. I didn't bring my pictures with me." Then I joke about how forgetful I'm getting in my old age and am gratified to hear a warm chuckle coming from Charlie in the audience. I can't see his face because it's covered by a shadow, but I'm relieved to know he isn't annoyed at me. I feel awful about letting these people down, especially Bob and Charlie. I hope I can bring my pictures another time.

Knowing the context for this amazing dream will help you understand what it reveals. For several days I'd been writing this book from six to ten hours a day. Whenever I'm this intensely focused on work in waking life, Dream Mother often gives me dreams at night that show things about my writing that I haven't figured out yet. She can do this because, unlike my ego, she sees the big picture of my conscious and unconscious selves.

The two nights before I'd also had dreams about builders and construction workers. In the above dream, Bob and Charlie represent aspects of my unconscious masculine side that are helping me build this book. Their message is that they want to see pictures of what we've been working on. Bob wants to see the picture of the pond with the mysterious dark blurry shadow in it. Charlie would like to see a picture of the fish.

My personal associations to these images are crucial to the meaning of this dream. For me, the pond (we have one in waking life) represents the watery depths of my personal unconscious. (An ocean, being so vast, would represent the collective unconscious.) The dark shadowy blob in the pond represents—guess what?—my shadow!

Because they're in the pond, the fish also represent aspects of my shadow. That they have lots of sparkly lights in and around them makes me think they symbolize positive unconscious spiritual potential. Fish were once a secret symbol of Jesus, and for me the sparkly lights suggest Sophia's sacred sparks.

When I consider my associations to these symbols, the workmen's comments, and what's going on in my waking life (work on this book), I realize that my unconscious masculine helpers are telling me something very important. They want me to show images of the shadow here—in this book, because they think it would be spiritually beneficial to readers! How neat is that? But wait, there's more.

The next part of the dream features projectors set up by another unrecognized masculine helper to my left and a little behind me. But there's something odd about this: In waking life projectors are behind the *audience*, not behind the *speaker*. This unusual detail tells me that Dream Mother is trying to make an important point.

The ego looks out at the world just as my dream ego looks out at its audience in this dream. But the dream says that *behind* my ego there is a projector, waiting to project images out onto the faces of the audience. In other words, the audience is like a *screen*. And what do I project onto them? Images of my shadow.

The parish hall wall behind me symbolizes the boundary between my conscious and unconscious selves. My dream ego has no idea what's on the other side of that wall, just as my waking ego has no idea what's in my unconscious. However, the film is coming from beyond the wall, which means that the images that will be projected out onto the audience come from my unconscious! Sure enough. When I look to the audience in my dream, I cannot see Charlie's (real) face because of the *dark shadow* on it.

The shadow on Charlie's face tells me he carries a projection of my shadow. Something about him is like a part of my own unconscious masculine side! And the puzzling placement of the projector shows exactly how Goddess's trick of projection works: She shows me my shadow by projecting images of it onto others!

So how is Charlie like my shadow? Well, I have mixed feelings. There are things I like about him—he's attractive and gentle and very polite and non-assuming. What I don't like is that he procrastinates and can be neglectful of things we ask him to do. Sometimes after several months of looking at a half-finished project I get very annoyed at him.

Aha! (Here's where the light bulb switches on.) In the dream, *I* was the one who had forgotten to do something important. Charlie's appearance there suggests that there's a part of me that's just as forgetful or neglectful! In other words, the annoyance I feel toward him in waking life is a sign that I have a Shadow Procrastinator and Forgetter in myself that I don't like! Ouch. My ego doesn't like to admit this, but there it is.

Why do I put up with this behavior in Charlie in waking life? Why don't I just find somebody else to do the job? Because I still haven't come to terms with the part of my shadow he resembles to some extent. If I knew how to handle the parts of myself that are like him, I'd be better at handling the situation with him in my waking life.

But the "bad" news—and it's not really so bad is it? I'm human, right?—comes with good news also. Charlie's chuckle about my forgetfulness was very comforting. Why? Because it says there is a positive part of my shadow which, like Charlie and the sparkly fish I associate with him, understands and forgives me for this flaw.

Despite these faults, Charlie's not a bad person. He has a passion for pulling fish out of the water just as I'm passionate about fishing for insights in the depths of the unconscious. (He's also a professional fisherman and often fails to show on his construction jobs because of it.) And, to be truthful, my search for self-knowledge is sometimes so obsessive that I neglect other important tasks. In this respect, Charlie and I are exactly alike! Understanding that we share the same trait is humbling. It makes me far less judgmental of him and more forgiving of us both.

Finally, in the dream I feel terrible about forgetting to bring my pictures for people who have come specifically to see them. This strong emotion my dream ego is feeling is important because it relates to something in my waking life. It tells me I would feel awful if I let readers down by forgetting to provide some helpful images about the shadow and projection that would help clarify these difficult concepts for them.

At the end of the dream I hoped I would have another opportunity to make my presentation. And I have. By describing the images of this dream and what it means to me, I've just done it!

What blows my mind when something like this happens is seeing that when I attend to my dreams, Dream Mother attends to me. This dream was an amazing gift from her. Not only did it provide important knowledge about my shadow, but it made a valuable contribution to my work.

It's enormously comforting to have this kind of help coming from within.

I love it.

What did you dream about last night?

Notes

1. Leah Novick, "Encountering the Schechinah, the Jewish Goddess," in *The Goddess Re-Awakening*, Shirley Nicholson, ed. (Wheaton, IL: Quest Books, 1989), 211.

2. Stephan A. Hoeller, *Jung and the Lost Gospels: Insights into the Dead Sea Scrolls and the Nag Hammadi Library* (Wheaton, IL: Theosophical Publishing House, 1989), 76.

3. Ibid., 110.

4. Huston Smith, "The Initial Glimpse of Spirit," *Parabola*, 26, no. 2 (May 2001), 84.

5. Ibid., 86.

6. C.G. Jung, *C.G. Jung Letters*, vol. 2, ed. G. Adler and A. Jaffe (Princeton: NJ: Princeton University Press, 1973), 545.

7. Edward F. Edinger, *Anatomy of the Psyche: Alchemical Symbolism in Psychotherapy* (LaSalle, IL: Open Court Publishing Company, 1985), 42.

8. For an excellent discussion of dreamwork and active imagination, try Robert Johnson's *Inner Work: Using Dreams and Active Imagination for Personal Growth* (San Francisco: HarperOne, 1989).

THE FOURTH GIFT
EMOTIONAL INTEGRITY

There is no such thing as spiritual integrity without emotional integrity. Like it or not, we need to own up to our honest feelings and figure out what to do with them.

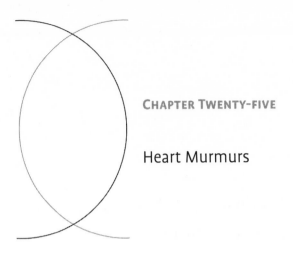

CHAPTER TWENTY-FIVE

Heart Murmurs

MOST of us think we know everything we're feeling, but the truth is we don't. Our egos are skilled deceivers. They believe exactly what they want to believe. Luckily we can count on Dream Mother to show us the truth.

Years ago I dreamed I was responsible for a baby that had a huge head and bright, intelligent eyes. Her head was connected to a limp, lifeless, doll-like body by a thin spinal cord—which made picking her up or moving her around extremely problematic. I puzzled over that image for months. I just couldn't see what that fragile baby had to do with me.

Several life lessons later, I get it. Most of our dreams are about us. This one said a large part of me was living in my head, just like that baby. My decisions were based on mental thoughts and ideals that had little to do with how I felt or what I was passionate about. The fact that the baby's body was inanimate meant that the organ that would normally animate it—my heart—was barely functioning (metaphorically, of course). Dreams often exaggerate to get our attention.

Why would a person live this way? In my case I think there were two reasons.

The most obvious is that I was still unconsciously trying to protect myself from feeling the long-buried pain of my parents' divorce and my father's death. But why, as a child, did I choose to shut down my heart as a response to them? Why didn't I let myself feel my pain? Why didn't I grieve openly and freely, as many children would?

I think it was for the second reason: Self-control, idealism, and dignity were among the most important values of my religious, well-meaning family. Cerebral to a fault and dutiful to the point of exhaustion, my Dutch and English relatives prided themselves in modeling reason and stoicism. Nobody I knew, save my handsome unfortunate father with his aberrant streak of romanticism, exhibited a taste for drama or the instinctual life. When reason is your rule, following your heart seems like a fatal flaw. It was, in fact, fatal for my father, and I learned my lesson well.

Perhaps there were memorable instances in my lineage when restraining strong feelings saved someone's life, just as there are instances in other families when being angry and fiercely aggressive is equally effective. Preferences like these are part of every family's unconscious heritage, and they can persist long after their usefulness is outlived. Much of our social learning is so deeply embedded in our psyches that we can be oblivious to negative aspects of "correct" attitudes that ensured our ancestors' survival.

The mindset that values head over heart is characteristic of Epoch II egos that feel compelled to repress and control frightening aspects of the feminine. The head and mind are strongholds where egos feel comfortable and safe. But hearts and bodies? Many of us just don't want to go there. There lie vulnerability, pain, suffering, mortification, death.

Hearts are associated with the capacity to feel, to fully experience pain and pleasure, sadness and joy. Feeling and emotion are almost universally accorded to the feminine principle. This explains the Catholic Church's extensive use of Immaculate Heart symbolism for Mary, and why Sophia's wisdom is called the wisdom of the understanding heart.

One emotion in particular—compassion—is the core value of religion. Composed of the prefix *com* (Latin for "with") and passion, it means that true spirituality is about living *with passion*. This does *not* mean being passionate about your beliefs while criticizing or disliking people with differing beliefs! This is the consummate lie of dualistic thinking and obsessive masculinity. When it's about words and ideas and not tender feeling, so-called compassion is an act of will that comes from the head and not the heart. This is fake compassion. When you worship God in a way that makes no difference in how you live or relate to others, it's empty worship. Fake compassion and empty worship do not make a person spiritual, and they will never heal a soul or make a lasting difference in the world.

Living with compassion means *feeling* passion: passion for yourself, for others, for life. Following your passion means doing what you truly love, what feels good and right to your Self. This is not a license to be selfish or irresponsible, but a spiritual path that releases your creativity and empowers you to make the difference that only you, with your particular form of genius, can make.

Here's the bottom line. When we repress the life in our hearts—our ability to suffer, care, and empathize, to need and feel and be afraid—we close the door to the most positive aspects of the feminine. When this happens, we're also in danger of opening another door to the worst excesses of the negative masculine: hatred, prejudice, slavery, religious intolerance, ethnic cleansing, repression of women, destruction of the environment, terrorism, war, September 11. Fortunately, most of us with underdeveloped or broken hearts don't manifest these extremes, but live relatively harmless lives.

Let there be no misunderstanding. I am *not* arguing that the masculine principle is inherently more negative than the feminine, or that feeling is superior to thinking, or that the masculine-oriented Epoch II ego is somehow inferior to the mostly unconscious ego of Epoch I. The development of our masculine emphasis on reason, logic, and clear discrimination has been absolutely crucial to the ego's evolution. Without these and the positive aspects of other masculine qualities, there would be no such thing as consciousness at all!

My point is this: Just as unconscious immersion in the feminine becomes a fetter when it is outgrown by the strengthening ego, so does the obsessive masculine eventually become a liability to continued growth and expanding consciousness. If we keep growing, at some point, undue repression—whether of the masculine or the feminine, thinking or feeling—robs us of the chance to discover our genius and develop our fullest potential.

For many people, awareness of our head's tendency to repress our heart's realities emerges in a big way during midlife, though for many others it comes much earlier. Whenever it happens it's because what we've repressed has gained so much power that it can no longer be contained and erupts into the outer world. This is very traumatic to the ego because it seriously challenges our self-image causing all sorts of symptoms like fear, unstable relationships, depression, heightened anxiety, and so on.

The good news is that these symptoms are actually positive signs. The intense conflict forces us to *feel* instead of just intellectualizing, and when we actually *feel* our pain, we're more open to growth. Feeling our pain opens the door to feeling our vulnerability and tenderness. These, in turn, prepare the way for an authentic feeling *relationship*. And here lies our true salvation, for in a feeling relationship the intelligence of the discriminating head is humanized by Sophia's wisdom of the understanding heart. This fuller, unified wisdom leads to authentic passion and compassion.

Jung said, ". . . emotion is the chief source of consciousness. There is no change from darkness to light or from inertia to movement without emotion."[1] He believed that only in the advanced stages of the individuation process (what I'm calling Epoch III) does the ego have contact with the Self in its feminine aspect. This means that our ego's acceptance of our honest feelings and emotions, combined with its union with the Self, walks us down the aisle to the sacred marriage of integrated consciousness. And because spiritual growth accompanies psychological growth, as we deepen the Sacred Marriage within ourselves, we also create a new, unified God-image for a new world.

Integrating Head and Heart

- Make a list of all the things you are passionate about; things you loved or loved to do as a child; things you love or would love to do now.

- Which passion(s) are you neglecting? Why? Do you want them in your life now? What would have to happen before you could follow the neglected passion or passions?

- Select the passion that calls to you most strongly and create a plan for how you can bring more of it into your life. (Of course you must not pick a "passion" that is morally, psychologically, physically, or spiritually destructive. If you're struggling with something like that, seek immediate help from a professional.)

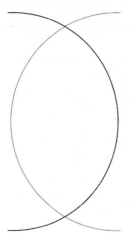

CHAPTER TWENTY-SIX

Cultivating Emotional Intelligence

ESSENTIALLY, head and heart symbolize logic and emotion. These are the bases of two different ways of making decisions: with reason and analytical thought, or with personal values, feelings, and passions. Conventional thinking tends to polarize this pair: The head is the golden-haired prince and the heart the poor stepsister. Those of us who are conditioned by this bias can be brilliant when it comes to mental I.Q., but as dim as burned-out bulbs when it comes to emotional intelligence. Others are the opposite: emotionally savvy but oblivious to reason and logic. Our goal is to develop and balance both so we can stop stumbling and start dancing.

In the history of Western philosophy, Epoch II consciousness eventually produced the brilliant thinkers Socrates, Plato, and Aristotle. Socrates advocated questioning as a more effective way of teaching than authoritative telling because his pupils' answers showed him the bases of their thinking. He wanted to strengthen their ability to think logically while eliminating irrational influences. His student Plato, and Plato's student Aristotle, advanced this ideal further. Westerners have valued logic over emotion ever since.

A young ego that aspires to goodness knows how dangerous ungovernable emotions can be, but it rarely understands that polarization creates problems too. Those who work the hardest to repress their emotions are the most susceptible to being overwhelmed by them. This is the symbolic meaning of dreams about floods, tidal waves, tornadoes, volcanic eruptions, and earthquakes. For example, if we don't like anger, believing it to be an ugly emotion that is beneath us, our egos will ignore all evidence of it. We could be gritting our teeth, clenching our fists, and shaking with rage and our ego will believe itself when it prompts us to say, "No, I'm not angry. I'm fine!"

Even if we grow conscious enough to admit to our anger, this still isn't the whole emotional story. Think about the last time you were angry. Anger is such a powerful emotion that many of us can recognize it right away. But ask yourself: What were you feeling just before you got angry? Anger is almost always a reaction to a more subtle and uncomfortable emotion. This could be almost anything you don't want to feel or admit to: fear, hurt, self-pity, embarrassment, apprehension, confusion, frustration, ignorance, jealousy, selfishness, intimidation, vulnerability, loneliness, guilt, envy, rejection, or feeling weak, powerless, misunderstood, victimized, betrayed, unloved, and so on.

Did you realize you were feeling something else before you got angry? If you didn't, you're not alone. Emotional ignorance is rampant. It is a severe liability in our efforts to attain consciousness and intimacy—let alone in our struggle for global peace! In today's world we desperately need the wisdom that emotional integrity brings.

Most of us know about rip tides, which are powerful and dangerous undercurrents in the ocean. We have a lot of them along the east coast of Florida. It can be a beautiful sunny day with the waves only a bit stronger than usual, and then you wade in and, wham! Your legs are pulled out from under you and you get carried away. If you're not a strong swimmer or if you try to fight the current you can drown.

Our unconscious emotions are like that. They run beneath our habitual behavior all the time and rarely capture our ego's attention unless we're looking for them. Unfortunately, if we don't break the cycle of stepping into them, they will just keep dragging us down without our ever knowing what hit us. We not only will keep wounding the people around us, but will unwittingly pass the same currents on to the next generation.

I'm embarrassed to say that I was not fully aware of our family's unwritten emotional code until I was in my early *fifties*! Before that I had no idea how limited my ability to recognize and express certain emotions was. Prime among these were anger, hurt, sadness, embarrassment, loneliness, and wounded pride. I was pretty sure I knew exactly how I felt in every situation—so much so that when an acquaintance told me she always carried a list of emotions to refer to so she could recognize her feelings, I was incredulous. I couldn't imagine being that unconscious. And yet, I was.

Having no idea of how emotionally clueless I really was, whenever I had a problem in a relationship I assumed it was the other person's fault. How could they *possibly* find fault with me? After all, I was so *spiritual* and *nice*. (Ouch!) This is just one example of how unconscious a well-meaning Epoch II ego can be about the hidden emotional life.

We all repress emotions in certain situations. Sometimes this is just good manners; at other times it's a normal coping mechanism that helps us survive overwhelming difficulties. Likewise, most of us have expressed an emotion in a way for which we were sorry later. Again, this is normal. Consciousness of our emotional behavior at every moment is an ideal, rarely a reality. But we are headed for trouble when we can no longer feel our pain or compassion, or when our emotional excesses hurt others on a regular basis, or when we won't even try to restrain negative emotions or deal with uncomfortable feelings to create more understanding and intimacy with loved ones.

Most of us believe we're in touch with our emotions if we feel the basic ones like love, anger, fear, happiness, and sadness. But it is possible to feel and recognize some emotions and not others. It's also possible to feel a certain emotion in one situation yet be totally unaware of the same emotion in a different circumstance. Moreover, knowing you're feeling an emotion doesn't necessarily translate into the ability to contain it or use it wisely. Consider the following symptoms of emotional ignorance. Which of these have you experienced?

25 Common Symptoms of Emotional Ignorance

1. Feeling angry, happy, sad, anxious, afraid, guilty, ashamed, rebellious, hurt, or sorry for yourself, etc., without knowing why or being able to control it.

2. Acting scornful, superior, patronizing, fearful, seductive, resentful, manipulative, critical, etc., without realizing it.

3. Not recognizing, understanding, or being able to admit to having

a certain emotion, even when you experience it in a dream or someone points it out to you in waking life.

4. Recognizing and responding from your anger while ignoring the hurt, sadness, fear, self-pity, self-doubt, guilt, or other less-obvious emotion that gave rise to it.

5. Being swamped by a strong emotion—for example, grief, jealousy, fear, or anger—and allowing it to escalate to the point that it hurts you, another person, or a relationship.

6. Becoming infatuated or falling in love with someone you barely know.

7. Acting on your attraction to someone without being able to control yourself when it would be hurtful to you, him/her, or other innocent people.

8. Having obsessive and/or intrusive fears, thoughts, anxieties, or worries you can't control that are unrelated to chemical imbalances or mental illness.

9. Trying to alleviate anxiety or other uncomfortable emotions with excessive use of cigarettes, alcohol, drugs, or compulsive/addictive behaviors.

10. Feeling stressed out, overwhelmed, or drained of energy on a regular basis without knowing why (except for the last, which could, of course, have a physical cause).

11. Expecting others to make you happy and blaming them for your unhappiness instead of taking responsibility for (which requires admitting to) your own feelings and the unsatisfactory life situations that give rise to them.

12. Feeling guilty or critical of yourself for having certain normal human emotions such as anger, fear, or self-pity; or, at the opposite extreme, pleasure, happiness, or joy.

13. Habitually expressing only the emotions you think you *should* express based on your family's emotional personality.

14. Feeling justified or not caring when you do or say something that hurts someone else.

15. Feeling no compassion for people who are hurting. This includes yourself.

16. Holding grudges without wanting or trying to resolve them.

17. Hating/despising others who are different from you; and/or hating/despising yourself for being different from others.

18. Being caught in a repetitive cycle of abuse, remorse, and over-compensation toward another person; or allowing another person to act that way toward you.

19. Expecting others to meet your emotional and/or physical needs without noticing or appreciating how they meet yours; or believing you have to meet another person's emotional and/or physical needs whether or not they notice or appreciate your efforts.

20. Avoiding apologizing or talking with someone you have hurt because you don't want to feel the guilt or admit to having said or done something hurtful.

21. Being unwilling or unable to cry or grieve over your pain or losses.

22. Being unable to enjoy your successes.

23. Feeling a strong internal pressure to habitually act cheerful and put on a happy face regardless of how you really feel.

24. Habitually withholding your true emotions from your partner, family, or friends.

25. Moodiness.

If you see any of these symptoms in yourself, welcome to the human race. If you are ready to deal with them, welcome to the threshold of consciousness: Your ego is beginning to acknowledge the power of your unconscious. You are getting it that sometimes you are not emotionally aware, and that because of that you are victimized by repressed emotions that prevent you from living with the fullness and harmony for which you yearn.

Logic needs the balance of emotional intelligence. It's not enough to be able to debate theological concepts, quote scriptures from memory, pray without ceasing, or walk on our knees to our favorite shrine. There is no such thing as spiritual integrity without emotional integrity. Like it or not, we need to own up to our honest feelings and figure out what to do with them.

Integrating Logic and Emotion

- Keep a journal of your emotions for a week. Every time you feel a different emotion, no matter how fleeting, write it down at the top of a new page. Below, briefly describe the situation that gave rise to that emotion and how you responded. The next time you feel the same emotion, write another brief description below the previous one.

- At the end of a week, see which emotions occur most often and look for patterns. Focus on the most bothersome ones and plan a new response that seems more open and healthy.

- Record your insights and follow through on your intentions.

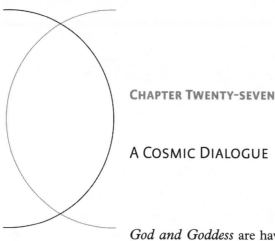

CHAPTER TWENTY-SEVEN

A COSMIC DIALOGUE

God and Goddess are having their weekly chat. They do this on Saturday mornings to air unexpressed emotions and deal with unresolved issues. They have three commandments:

1. Thou shalt speak the truth.

2. Thou shalt not speak with anger, blame, or hostility.

3. Thou shalt listen without interrupting when thy partner is speaking.

It has taken God eons to be comfortable with this kind of intimacy. He used to think it was sissy, but he's beginning to believe what he's said about love for the last couple of millennia, and he's getting pretty good at practicing what he preaches. So this morning God says, "Is there something wrong? You've seemed a little distant lately."

"Yes," Goddess replies. "It's about what happened Thursday before our evening walk. You were cleaning out the Angelarium, trying to organize all those stacks of used harps, trumpets, scrolls, and flaming swords."

God nods. "Yes, I . . . oops, sorry. I didn't mean to interrupt. Go on."

Goddess continues, "Thank you. When I came in to get you I noticed that the aisle to my Dovery in the back was still so narrow and cramped that I would have to turn sideways to get past your things. It's been that way for months now, and I keep bumping into things."

God nods, keeping his mouth firmly shut.

"So, knowing that you wouldn't finish cleaning up that night and probably wouldn't get back to it for some time, I asked if you could just move some things aside so I could walk through more easily. And you immediately became defensive. First you said, 'Well I have my own way of working and right now I have things where I want them to be.' And when I said, 'Yes, but I can hardly get through. Couldn't you just scoot a few things out of the way for now?' you got all huffy and responded in that critical way you have, 'I've been working hard here and I'm tired! You want me to do it right this minute?'"

God nods gravely.

Goddess continues. "Your hostility hurt my feelings, and if you remember I said, 'Well you don't have to be mean about it. It's just been such an inconvenience and seems so little to ask.' By then you were shoving things around angrily and I was angry too, and then you got that emergency call and had to leave and we haven't had a chance to clear this up. The truth is, my feelings are still hurt that your automatic response to me was hostile and defensive instead of loving and under- standing. I would have helped you move the things, and I didn't need it to be done that moment. But you acted all put upon. You deliberately misunderstood my request and made me the bad guy."

God sighs. He thinks about what Goddess has said and considers his response. Goddess waits for him quietly.

Finally God says, "I understand what you're saying. I had a system going there with those stacks and it seemed important to keep them that way. Plus, I was tired and maybe feeling a little sorry for myself because you hadn't been helping me and then you came in and wanted me to change what I'd spent all that time doing. It felt wrong to me then and I couldn't see your point of view. But I see it now. I'm very sorry I responded to you that way. I should have told you how I was feeling in a kind way so we could work it out together instead of behaving in a way that hurt your feelings and separated us."

Goddess sighs. She's quiet for a moment. Then she smiles, "Thank you for understanding. I feel much better now. I'm still a little hurt, but I realize I'm easily wounded by your impatience and aggressiveness and I probably take these things too personally. Tell you what: I'll try to be less sensitive if you'll try to remember how painful your 'attack mode' is for me."

"That's a deal," God says, as they embrace.

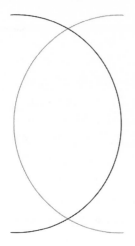

CHAPTER TWENTY-EIGHT

The Divine Feminine as Dragon Lady

REPRESSION is a normal way of coping with uncomfortable contents of our psyches and getting along with others. Everyone does it. Like every other human quality, it has positive and negative aspects. For example, as putting a lid over a fire extinguishes the flame, repression quiets feelings and urges that threaten to escalate to a danger point. Likewise, choosing to repress an emotion or opinion that could be hurtful to another if honestly expressed is sometimes the kindest and most socially responsible thing to do. And sometimes it keeps us safe.

But repressed feelings, even if quieted rather than intensified, can return to haunt us. They can become downright problematic when they no longer serve the best interests of our growth or relationships. The longer, harder, and more habitually we repress a strong and persistent emotion that is a true expression of our fullest selves, the more energy we give it—and eventually it starts leaking out into our behavior in disagreeable ways beyond our control.

Uncomfortable feelings are like baby dragons that start out innocently enough. If we love them and pay attention to them and allow them to come out and play they will grow up to become our pets and friends. But if we fail to tame them, if we ignore them and starve them and keep them cooped up in dark and cramped cages, they can grow bigger and more malevolent every day.

Some myths that emerged in the Middle East around 2000 B.C. featured a storm god of fire and lightning who conquered a dragon of darkness and evil. According to Merlin Stone, "the plot and the underlying symbolic theme of the story is so similar in each myth that, judging from the stories that do use the name of the female deity, we may surmise that the allegorical identity of the dragon or serpent is that of the Goddess religion."[2]

People today still call a powerful, assertive woman a Dragon Lady. To many men—especially ones with difficult, domineering mothers—their own feminine sides and some women seem extremely dragon-like, something terrible and threatening that needs to be overcome. Jung agreed and considered the dragon to be "a mother-image (that is, a mirror of the maternal principle or of the unconscious) . . . "[3]

The Dragon Lady is a mystifying paradox. In one meaning she represents powerful repressed emotions. In another she symbolizes the regressive powers of the preconscious, personal unconscious, and collective unconscious. Consider this from Carl Jung:

> The threat to one's inmost self from dragons and serpents points
> to the danger of the newly acquired consciousness being swallowed
> up again. . . . The hero's main feat is to overcome the monster of
> darkness: it is the long-hoped-for and expected triumph of con-
> sciousness over the unconscious.[4]

This mythic theme is universal because the struggle to become conscious enough to overcome evil is universal. There really is a negative, powerful, emotionally charged pattern of feminine energy in the collective unconscious that prefers the dark, and it can be so seductive that it requires heroic effort to free ourselves from its grasp. For some people it might feel like a vampire that saps our life-blood, leaving us too melancholy to strive for the light. For others it seems more like a dangerous siren that pulls our Epoch II ego back into the comforting cradle of childish passivity and dependency, thus preventing us from attaining our selfhood. Or it could feel like demons or monsters that terrify us, carrying the potential for so much suffering that we just want to escape in compulsions and addictions.

The masculine aspects of evil are invasive and other-destructive; the feminine are devouring and self-destructive. To succumb to the negative shadow of the god is to cast off the positive feminine, in which case one wreaks havoc, death, and destruction everywhere one goes. To succumb to the devouring nature of the goddess is to cast off the positive masculine and return to the preconscious realm of childhood where, losing all self-awareness, nobility, or sense of moral responsibility, we float, passive and uncaring, in a blissful, death-like ennui.

This is a great tragedy, for it is only by relinquishing childhood and developing our masculine qualities that we discover our individuality. We are meant to face our fear of the feminine and fight our way out of our mother complexes, so that we can grow detached enough to have healthy relationships with women and the feminine principle. We are meant to become the heroes of our own myths, the creators of our own meaning, the discoverers of our own treasure. Every ego needs the adventure of the unfolding spirit to fulfill its destiny. This is the symbolic meaning of the dragon-slaying hero myths from every culture and religion that emerged during humanity's early transition into Epoch II.

But there is a positive side to the dragon, too. Hindus and Taoists honor the wisdom of Epoch III integration in their representations of dragons as powerful spiritual beings, masters of the waters and guardians of treasures, especially the pearl of perfection that symbolizes enlightenment and bestows immortality. In China and Japan the dragon grants fertility "because it is closely associated with the powers of water and hence with the yin [feminine] principle.[5]

Thus, another meaning of this complex symbol is this: To attain psycho-spiritual maturity we need to confront the lure of the feminine unconscious, both personal and collective, and face the feared contents we either had repressed or been unaware of until they erupted unexpectedly. It is this terrifying descent that earns the authentic hero the ultimate prize. This is the journey of integration that Carl Jung recorded so fearlessly and vividly in *The Red Book,* the story of his confrontation with the terrors of the collective unconscious.

Heinrich Zimmer wrote,

To see the twofold, embracing and devouring, nature of the god-dess, to see repose in catastrophe, security in decay, is to know her and to be *saved* [emphasis mine]. . . . She is the perfect figuration of life's joyous lures and pitiless destruction: the two poles charged with extremest tension, yet forever merging.[6]

Our journey to the salvation Zimmer writes about begins when we acknowledge our pain and fear and decide to face it. An ego that doesn't seek emotional integrity won't begin this work, and one that doesn't find it won't finish. The only way to neutralize Devil and Dragon Lady is to have conscious dialogues with them.

Each of us has everything we need to develop emotional integrity. Two venues in particular provide more than enough material to work with on a daily basis, and both are associated with the feminine. I've already discussed the first one: dreams. Dreams are the mother lode of emotions: The deeper you dig, the richer you get. Any emotion highlighted in a dream, whether expressed by our dream ego or another character, belongs to us. Likewise, any emotion that is not expressed in a dream situation when we would normally expect it to be—for example, not caring when someone is suffering and needs our help—tells us something about ourselves.

When I was confronted with a very large dinosaur-like dragon in one dream, for example, I knew it had something to do with my emotional life. Although it wasn't exactly menacing, I was nevertheless afraid as it lumbered toward me. As I stood there trying to decide what to do, I realized in a lucid moment that I was dreaming. *Wait a minute,* I thought. *If I'm dreaming I have nothing to be afraid of. I can handle this.* So I looked around and saw a long green hose lying on the ground. I picked it up, formed it into a lasso, and roped the dragon which merely stood there placidly, no threat to anyone at all. I knew it was a dream, but nevertheless I felt as proud as any hero.

For me, this dream suggested I was coming to terms with two emotions. I associate dinosaurs with a desire to return to a prehistoric past of unconscious instinct. In other words, part of me didn't want to assume the responsibility of psychological maturity that comes with increased consciousness. The dragon with its fiery breath feels like the strong repressed anger that occasionally erupted despite my ego's best efforts at self-control. Hopefully it would no longer be an ungovernable force with the potential to create problems for me in waking life. This wasn't because I had killed it or escaped from it, but because I was overcoming my fear of it. I had less need to repress it and it seemed less menacing.

The other invaluable source of instructive emotional material is a couple relationship. Because relationships, like emotions, are almost universally associated with the feminine, and because they are equally problematic in today's world, this will be our next topic.

But first, I'd like to round off my discussion of emotions with the next installment of my own story.

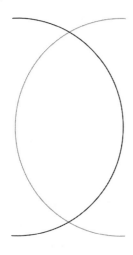

CHAPTER TWENTY-NINE

Dragon Lady Breaks Through

AS A CHILD I was vaguely aware of emotional discomfort from time to time—sadness, fear, hurt, worry, self-pity, loneliness. My habitual response was to ignore it, toughen up, and get on with life. I had absorbed my family's belief that only weak people have problems and only shameless people share them. To me, the strongest, most admirable people were proud and stoic. They used their will to banish undesirable feelings. If they should ever have a real problem that wouldn't go away, they kept it to themselves, far from prying eyes and judgmental minds. I identified totally with people like this and was proud of my ability to be "just fine" no matter what. Secretly, I thought people unlike me in this respect were weak.

What I didn't know then was that always needing to be "just fine" is a facade, a wall we put up to hide the normal fear and pain of being human. Nobody is perfectly okay all the time. The more we need to believe we are, the more hidden discomfort we're probably covering up. Wearing a mask like this takes a lot of energy. Even the toughest of us have to take it off sometimes, if only at 2:00 A.M. when no one can see us. This may be the only time some of us ever suspect that there's more to us than meets the eye.

Sometimes, the very fear and pride that cause us to create our masks are the only things strong enough to get us to take them off. At seventeen I asked for help from Mrs. Walstrom because I was afraid of looking like a fool in front of the whole camp. At twenty-seven I took my spiritual numbness seriously because spiritual meaning had become profoundly necessary to me. In both cases, admitting to my discomfort, asking for help, and experiencing a numinous breakthrough released a great surge of energy that propelled me forward for many years. But nothing lasts forever, and the only thing we can really count on in a spiritual odyssey is change: Our inner feminine is always beckoning us toward expanding consciousness, deeper meaning, and greater intimacy.

I never lost my religious outlook, but I did gradually lose some of the comfort, confidence, and good feelings it had originally brought. I had assumed that a strong faith would satisfy me spiritually, that spiritual fulfillment would bring fulfillment to every other sector of my life, and that this condition would be permanent. It became clear over time, however, that something was still missing. More was needed. In my mid-thirties I found myself at another crossroads.

One morning I was home alone and put Kris Kristofferson's album *Jesus Was a Capricorn* on the stereo. As I listened carefully to the words, tears began to roll down my cheeks. I had occasionally cried for no apparent reason before, but until this day I had refused to give in to my body's embarrassing betrayal. This day, instead of automatically brushing away my tears I let myself cry. With some surprise I thought there must be a reason I was crying. I must be sad or unhappy about something. What could it be?

For the first time, my fear that there might be something wrong with me that I didn't want to know about was less compelling than my need to understand myself. I listened carefully to these soulful, spiritual songs and struggled to understand. Over the next months as I played them again and again, I began to glimpse some reasons for my tears. It seemed as if practically every song was written especially for me.

"Jesus Was a Capricorn" is about the intolerance people have for people and things they don't understand. What struck me most was that it was written by someone who had acquired enough strength to take the criticism he got for daring to be true to himself. Why did that make me cry? Shame? Self-pity? Envy? Longing? All of them, maybe, for I knew beyond any doubt that I didn't have that strength.

"Sugar Man" is about a woman who sells her soul to a pimp for drugs that help her escape the pain in her life. She isn't strong enough to face it without them. Why did I cry? I think it was shame over a shocking new awareness: For the first time in my life I considered that maybe I, too, was trying to escape secret pain.

"Help Me" is a heartfelt cry for spiritual help from someone who has finally given up trying to struggle all alone through the darkness. It's a recognition that the ego is simply not enough, a confession of human limitations, and a painful plea for consciousness. My tears told me that I was tired and flawed, there was so much I didn't understand about myself. I needed help.

"Jesse Younger" is about someone who loses his family's love and support when he dares to make choices that seem wrong to them, even though they're right for him. This helped me recognize my own fear that the same thing would happen to me. I was experiencing a classic conflict between my desire to be true to myself and my need to keep my personality, habits, lifestyle, and relationships just as they were so as not to rock a familiar, comfortable boat.

"Enough for You" is about a man's sadness because the woman he loves is in pain over her unfulfilled life. Why did that make me cry? Because like that woman I felt unfulfilled, although I had no idea why. Was it because of talents I had failed to develop, interests I had never pursued? I didn't know. I just knew I was unhappy. Worse, I knew that if I fully faced my unhappiness I might eventually have to act on it. I might have to change my life, which would impact my relationships. Then my husband might have to suffer the same sadness as the man in the song, and his suffering would be all my fault.

"Why Me" is about repentance for wasted life, gratitude for the gift of another chance, awe at God's love for flawed humanity, and the desire to help others who have the same struggles. These were my thoughts, feelings, experiences, and needs, and they were so terribly beautiful and so dreadfully sad. No wonder I cried.

To some people, letting yourself cry over a bunch of songs might not seem like a big deal; but to me it was. I didn't even cry when my father died, for heaven's sake. This really threw me. What was it all about? I had been so good. I had gone to college, married a wonderful man, created a secure loving healthy family and a comfortable lifestyle. We attended church, tithed, went on spiritual retreats. We were in an adult prayer group and hosted a weekly college prayer group in our home. What did I have to cry about? How could I be unhappy? What in the world was wrong with me?

At the time I truly had no idea what was going on. The very idea of wanting more made me cringe inside. I thought I must be a selfish, ungrateful wretch. What I really was, was unconscious. I had been so busy intellectualizing everything that I'd given no time, attention, or credibility to my honest feelings. Why hadn't being religious satisfied me? Because there is no such thing as spiritual maturity without psychological maturity. I had been living in my head and ignoring my heart. What was missing from my life was the real living, breathing, *feeling* human being! What I really wanted was to know my shadow, feel and express my hidden emotions, live with integrity, be my true Self.

What I didn't understand was that Spirit and Psyche need each other for completion. Both are essential components of the sacred marriage. Neither can create it alone, and neither can enter into it until sufficiently mature. My religion filled my intellectual needs, but it simply wasn't equipped to help me handle the human, subjective part of the equation.

This was about eight years after my experience with the blue light. I had been asking myself some probing questions, but I was still putting more energy into ignoring my unconscious than exploring it. I was afraid of my real feelings. They were dragons that lurked around the edges of my awareness. No way could I let them in, not even if I knew how—probably not even if I'd known that was the only way to find what I was looking for. The stakes were too high for my baby bear ego; the risks too great.

So for a while I did nothing. But Sophia was not about to give up on me. She knew who I really was because she was the spiritual spark burning in me. She understood my fears and saw my value. She knew I was worth the work she was putting into awakening my ego so I could start the holy work of fanning that light into full flame. My tears had broken down a little more of my resistance to her, and that was all she needed. It would be only a few more years before I would see the full force of her power.

Notes

1. C.G. Jung, "Psychological Aspects of the Mother Archetype,"in *The Archetypes and the Collective Unconscious*, 2nd ed., *Collected Works*, vol. 9.1 (Princeton, NJ: Princeton University Press, 1959), 96.

2. Merlin Stone, *When God Was a Woman*. (New York: Harcourt Brace Jovanovich, 1976), 67.

3. J.E. Cirlot, *A Dictionary of Symbols* (New York: Philosophical Library, 1971), 88.

4. C.G. Jung, "The Concept of the Collective Unconscious," *The Archetypes and the Collective Unconscious*, 2nd ed, *Collected Works*, vol. 9.1 (Princeton, NJ: Princeton University Press, 1959), 166, 167.

5. Boris Matthews, trans., *The Herder Symbol Dictionary* (Wilmette, IL: Chiron Publications, 1978), 61.

6. Heinrich Zimmer, "The Indian World Mother," in *The Mystic Vision: Papers from the Eranos Yearbooks*, Joseph Campbell, ed. (Princeton, N.J.: Princeton University Press, 1968), 96.

The Fifth Gift
Partnership

We are made to yearn for union with otherness. Relationships form the core of human experience and determine
the direction and outcome of the spiritual journey.

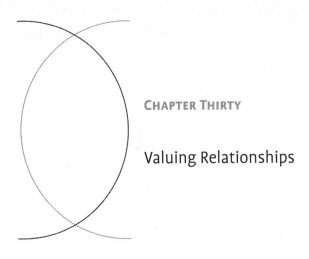

CHAPTER THIRTY

Valuing Relationships

THE BIOLOGICAL differences of our earliest ances-tors brought about role specialization. Males were usually bigger and stronger, didn't give birth to babies, and couldn't nurse them. It wasn't imperative that they stay close to home, though many might have preferred to. The physical ability and social freedom to go hunting gave rise to the male standard of leaving home to pursue and conquer prey. To succeed, a man had to focus on one task and shut out distracting feelings that might interfere with the dangerous work of hunting. Success brought security to the tribe and status to the best hunters.

Many females were excellent strategists and huntresses. But if they had children, whatever they did or wanted to do had to be accommodated to the new life they were to nurture. Most began to specialize in gather-ing—shopping in the neighborhood for roots, berries, herbs, and other things that would be useful around the cave—honing relationship skills, and multitasking. They were able to be aware of their feelings and express them in helpful ways while feeding the baby and stirring the pot. Women who were most adept at these skills were likewise admired by their peers.

Neurosurgeon Leonard Shlain tells us that over time, their brains evolved in subtle ways to reflect these specializations. When the male God rose in power, cultures began to impose stereotypical roles on men and women. In some religious sects it is still considered against God's will to vary from these ancient standards. Yet, in Shlain's words,

Each man has a gatherer/nurturer aspect to his personality, psyche, and mind, just as each woman has hunter/killer aspects to hers. Every individual has encased in his or her skull both a feminine brain and a masculine one. Any particular society can accentuate one or the other of these two ways of interacting with the world, depending on the demands of the environment or the shaping influences of its inventions.[1]

Technology and growing psychological awareness have freed many of us from the compulsion to force people into roles for which they are not psychologically or temperamentally suited. Stereotypes and barriers are crumbling all around us, and that's a good thing. But neither the human brain nor most societies have had enough time to fully adapt to our rapidly changing world.

Having meaningful work makes us feel powerful, successful, and fulfilled. It's a universal need. Nourishing and sustaining intimate relationships is also a universal need that brings great satisfaction, love, and pleasure. The best case scenario is to develop our own unique combination of the two—finding great meaning in work, paid or unpaid, that helps us cultivate mutually nourishing relationships.

Our relationships, like our dreams, are natural teachers with much to say about us: who we really are, how we're living our lives, what we really feel inside, what we know and don't know about ourselves, how the image we present to the world differs from our inner reality, how our moral beliefs stack up with our actual behavior, what we have the courage to face and what we're afraid of, how open to otherness we are, how compassionate, how tolerant of differences, how emotionally mature, how giving. Intimate relationships are especially good at showing us our shadows. All we have to do is listen to the complaints of our significant others! But most of us are too fragile and defensive to see and accept the truth in what they say.

Vitriolic partisan politics, continuing international conflicts, and escalating divorce rates are a few of many signs that most of us still lack knowledge or skill to create lasting relationships that are fair and healthy for all concerned—let alone to distill self-knowledge from them! This is especially true of love relationships, for which most of us tend to have self-centered motivations and unrealistic expectations.

Why are our relationships so problematic?

How can we improve them?

What can they teach us about psycho-spiritual maturity?

You might be surprised that we can find answers to these three important questions in myths that address the ego's journey through life. Although some of them are quite old, their psychological truths are relevant today.

By "myth," I don't mean untruth. I mean Myth as the literary genre of stories that explore humanity's relationship to great powers, with absolutely no disrespect to the beliefs of any religion. Some aspects of some myths can be based on historical facts, but it is pointless to try to literalize them. They are intended as metaphors for the life of the soul and our relationship to what's sacred. Myths don't have to be true on the outside to be true on the inside.

For example, the myth of White Buffalo Woman taught the Lakota people that Earth was their grandmother *and* their mother. All living things were the children of Mother Earth and therefore part of their own family. Every aspect of nature was sacred. Being overly attached to the senses and things of the world was ignorant, as was treating Earth or any living thing with disrespect. Having a proper relationship with Earth and the spirit world would "keep the soul" and help the people increase and prosper. We may not believe that at a specific time in history a powerful maiden goddess emerged from the spirit world, taught the people, and then changed into a white buffalo before disappearing; but can we deny the value of her message?

Because myths express cultural beliefs, they are important guides for behavior. Different categories of myths address different psycho-spiritual challenges. Hero myths are metaphors for the ego's heroic struggles to become conscious. Their primary emphasis is on how an individual ascends to new empowering heights. Through hard work the hero meets difficult challenges, develops special skills, makes glorious accomplishments, achieves great acclaim, and receives wonderful rewards. Emulating our heroes through noteworthy accomplishments in the father's world of work thus becomes the major life goal of the average person in Epoch II, exactly as it should.

The same emphasis pervades Epoch II religions. The ego's need to rise above the darkness of unconsciousness and prove its heroic potential explains why so many Epoch II-ers stress the miraculous deeds, character traits, charisma, and rewards of Moses, Buddha, Jesus, and other spirit persons. With the emphasis on heroic ascent, people often miss the psychological and spiritual meanings that underlie their day-to-day relationships. This leads us to our first question.

Why Are Our Relationships So Problematic?

No one achieves his or her goals, worldly or otherwise, in a vacuum! Every hero develops important relationships. The Lone Ranger isn't really alone. He has Silver and the two of them always ride with Tonto and Scout, usually escaping grave danger because of them. But few of us notice this motif. We worship the individual hero, the leading star whom we reward with the most prestigious Oscar. Our undervaluing of relationships, and the crucial roles they play in our spiritual journeys, makes it easy for Epoch II egos to discount the contributions others make to our successes.

The Epoch II ego tends to believe that success and happiness in relationships and life are just a function of how clever, determined, and self-disciplined it can be in the external world. *If I can go to the right schools, learn the right theories, find the right job, make enough money, say the right words, wear the right clothes, impress the right people, give my partner whatever s/he needs from me to be happy, act as if I care, and, if necessary, bluff, fight, or spin my way to the top, then I'll live happily ever after.* To many immature Epoch II egos, this is pretty much what hero myths—and life—are about.

This conventional mind-set has very little connection to reality because it focuses on outer appearances and accomplishments, and completely overlooks the potent and often disastrous influences of the unconscious on our behavior. We blunder through one terrible relationship after another making the exact same mistakes. Yet when one relationship is over we tell ourselves it will be different next time. We take jobs we don't enjoy because of the promise of money, security, and status, then wonder why we aren't happy. We heed advice, follow rules, marry good people, attend places of worship, and wonder why our lives feel so meaningless. We shake our heads over the failures of people we know as if we're way too smart to let things like that happen to us. Meanwhile we give no mind to the problems we cause in our own relationships or the sadness and emptiness of our own unlived lives.

So, to answer our first question about relationships: Our relationships are problematic because the Epoch II ego can't see or learn from its own everyday reality as long as it's caught up in an obsessive need to develop and preserve its identity through heroic deeds in the world. If we want to resolve relationship problems we need a new approach. We need to value improving our relationships as much as we value developing our individuality. To learn how to do this, we need to balance outer work with inner work.

Integrating Individuality and Relationships

- Reflect on how much time and attention you give yourself: your outer work, your inner work, and your personal interests and passions. Estimate how many minutes and hours per day and week you spend on these pursuits.

- Reflect on how much time and attention you give your partner or others with whom you are in primary love relationships.

- If there is an imbalance that makes you or your loved ones uncomfortable, think about concessions you can make or ask for to achieve more parity.

- Discuss this matter openly and honestly with those involved.

- Together, create a plan for how you can each create more balance between your need to serve your individuality and your need to serve your relationship. Then act on it.

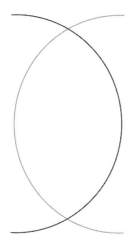

CHAPTER THIRTY-ONE

The Soul's Yearning for Union

DIFFICULTIES in relationships bring up powerful emotions and irrational actions. Both are opportunities to notice what's really going on in our unconscious. This is why relationships, like dreams, are such good spiritual teachers. For them to work, we have to stop our knee-jerk reactions of defending, retaliating, and getting one-up and start watching and listening to ourselves.

This is extremely difficult when we're swamped by strong emotions. In very emotional situations, the Epoch II ego is usually clueless, and the shadow is in charge. We don't listen to what others are trying to tell us. The ego finds it nearly impossible to believe that the criticisms of others are justified, but there is almost always a grain of truth in them. This doesn't mean we're bad to the bone or that every accusation is completely true, only that a part of our shadow sometimes shows up in disagreeable ways. Our partners know this better than anyone!

I believe that anyone—no matter how accomplished, religious, well-intentioned, or enlightened—who has difficult ongoing relationships with co-workers, clients, family, and friends is out of balance because s/he is out of touch with important parts of his/her feminine side. (Indeed, the ability to nurture loving relationships with otherness is one of three measures of mature spirituality! I'll have more to say about the other two later on.) People who isolate themselves from others and don't cultivate intimate relationships are usually a bit off-kilter for this very reason: They have no one to bounce back the truth to them, no mirror to reflect their shadows.

We are made to yearn for union with otherness. Relationships form the core of human experience and determine the direction and outcome of the spiritual journey. As American Buddhist master Jack Kornfield says,

> All of spiritual practice is a matter of relationship: to ourselves, to others, to life's situations. We can relate with a spirit of wisdom, compassion, and flexibility, or we can meet life with fear, aggression, and delusion. Whether we like it or not, we are always in relationship, always interconnected.[2]

If being able to nurture loving relationships is a measure of mature spirituality and all of spiritual practice is a matter of relationship, then improving our relationships is essential to the spiritual journey. This leads to the second question.

How Can We Improve Our Relationships?

Although hero myths neglect the theme of relationship, there are older myths that depict the maturing ego's compassion and sense of responsibility for others. In contrast to hero myths, the motif of these stories is descent. Many of them feature females—for example, Isis, Psyche, and Inanna—who go willingly into the underworld to face the God or Goddess of Death for the sake of their relationships.

In one of these the Canaanite virgin goddess Anath, daughter of the sky god El, descends into Sheol to confront Maveth, the lord of the underworld, who has stolen the beautiful light of the sun and moon. Anath challenges the god of sterility to a game of chance, and over a period of eight days wins back the full light of the sun and moon as well as her own freedom. When she returns to the land of the living she travels through Canaan, leaving light behind her everywhere she goes so that her people might prosper.

A similar myth dating back to 2000 B.C.E. features the Sumerian Goddess Inanna, Queen of Heaven and Earth (called Ishtar by the Semites).[3] The first half of her story is upbeat. As an adolescent, Inanna gently tends a tree in her garden and fantasizes about having a throne (representing her queenship) and a bed (representing her womanhood) made from it. When a snake, a bird, and the dark maid Lilith make their homes in it and will not leave, she weeps all night to no avail. At dawn she asks the sun god for help, but he refuses her. So she brings her request to her brother Gilgamesh. He heroically cuts down the tree and carries it into the city, where it is fashioned into a throne and a bed.

Now it is Inanna's turn for heroism. Having established her queenship, she journeys to visit Enki, the god of wisdom. Gaily they challenge each other and toast each other with beer. After a while Enki is swaying with drink and the over-effusive host offers the treasures of his kingdom to his guest: the attributes of civilization. Inanna loads them in the Boat of Heaven and sets off for home. When Enki sobers up, he wants his treasures back and sends a servant with six monsters to rescue them. Inanna refuses to return what is rightfully hers and asks for help from her priestess, who utters an earth-shattering cry that sends them back to Enki. When Inanna gets home she gives her gifts to the people.

Having proven herself worthy of queenship, she starts looking for a husband. After a loving, sensual courtship she marries the shepherd Dumuzi and settles down to raise two sons. This is where most hero myths and fairy tales end. But in Inanna's case, we find out what happens *after* happily ever after.

After a season Dumuzi undergoes a classic mid-life crisis. He tires of Inanna and wants his freedom to pursue other women. This sets off a corresponding crisis in Inanna. Instead of retaliating in affairs of her own, she journeys to the underworld to attend the funeral of her brother-in-law. Her sister Erishkegal, Queen of the Underworld, who is jealous of Inanna's life and vitality, strips Inanna of all her accomplishments and possessions and hangs her on a meat hook to die.

After three days, with the help of her priestess who has been waiting for her, Inanna is rescued by Enki, the god of wisdom. Upon her return she discovers that Dumuzi never tried to save her or even missed her. Enraged, she condemns her terrified husband to take her place and spend half the year in the Underworld. Feeling compassion for Dumuzi, his sister, Deshtinanna, offers to share his death by replacing him for the other half-year.

What can we learn about improving relationships from these stories? The story of Anath contains these messages:

- Bringing the light of consciousness to others is so important that we need to face our fears, even if it means suffering and facing the unknown.

- Confronting others with injustice, asking for what we need, having a playful attitude, daring to take chances, and persevering for as long as it takes are excellent ways to gain light and win our freedom.

- Those who obtain light from the underground journey need to share it with others.

Inanna's myth offers some of the same lessons about relationships, plus the following:

- You can't get everything you want or do everything by yourself.

- Wishing, fantasizing, drama, and venting your emotions only get you so far; at some point you have to stop crying, take matters into your own hands, and ask for help.

- If the Sky God doesn't respond to your requests for help, try asking your family and friends.

- You don't get to be queen by sitting around on your throne all day; you have to earn your sovereignty through work that helps others and gains their respect.

- Females want to do heroic deeds just as much as males do, and must be given chances to.

- There is wisdom in accepting the hospitality and generosity of others.

- Relaxing and having fun can bring great benefits.

- When confronted with a threat to your possessions, war is not the only answer; feminine wisdom knows ways that don't require fighting and killing.

- The feminine principle is a civilizing influence that brings enormous benefits to humanity.

- Sometimes the people you love stop loving you and it's not your fault.

- A fearless exploration of the depths of depression and the unconscious can be very painful, but it can elicit wisdom and result in empowering rebirth.

- Going out of your way to meet the needs of mean-spirited and bitter people can get you in serious trouble.

- When people you love are in trouble, do everything you can to help.

- When people you love desert or betray you, you will feel anger and will be justified in expressing it.

- Showing compassion to cowards and villains lightens their burden and takes nothing away from anybody.

Some descent myths feature males (Hermes, Adonis, Osiris, Orpheus) who take the death journey either to rescue a beloved woman or to complete the Great Mother's birth/death/rebirth cycle *for the benefit of their communities.* Whoever the character and whatever the details, the descent is always in service to the feminine principle of species-preservation and relationship.

Descent myths teach values of the feminine principle that are mystifyingly obtuse to the average Epoch II ego. Usually they present a "darker, less glorious image of the process of development [*than do the hero myths*]. . . . In the concrete imagery of mythos, the metaphors are shocking indeed: Violence, rape, death, and dismemberment . . . "[4] Descent is a metaphor for the latter phases of the ego's journey, during which it must surrender to forces beyond its control before it can move to Epoch/Level III.

Descent myths are about the phase when our maturing ego becomes more interested in working for others than proving ourselves. Here we become willing to endure the pain of sacrifice, relinquish worldly power, and die to the world's notice and acclaim. We are content not just to enjoy the pleasures of winning, but also to suffer what appears to the uninitiated as loss. These are all matters of relationship, too, except here they are about the soul's yearning for a relationship with the Sacred.

Descending to the Self

Suffering and descent prepare us to meet the Great Mother's most mysterious and terrifying persona—the Mistress of the Dead. Facing our mortality and overcoming our fear of death provides us with the feminine wisdom needed not only to improve our human relationships, but also to establish a conscious partnership with Divine Unity. In myth after myth, the one who consents to the descent transcends the conflicts of the physical world to attain immortality and union with the gods. This is not about having correct beliefs, it's about uniting opposites. It's about the ego's struggle to create a meaningful relationship, indeed, a partnership, with both polarities of the Sacred—inner as well as outer, feminine as well as masculine. The ancients knew this, but with the advent of the Sky God their wisdom was gradually lost, hence the widespread ignorance about the true nature of the spiritual journey.

Only one descent myth retains authentic transforming spiritual power for a large portion of humanity in today's world. In the Gospel of Matthew we read that at the moment of Jesus's death, the curtain in the temple that had kept worshipers separate from the Holiest Place is torn apart. The symbolic message is that the human ego is ready to experience sacred union for itself without the need for priestly intercession. If Jesus could do it, so can we. However, to have any hope of attaining the spiritual wholeness we seek, we need to be willing to suffer temptation, die to the world, and *establish an intimate partnership with the unconscious* (underworld) just as he did.

Unfortunately, by the time of Jesus's historical appearance, many powerful Epoch II egos were trying to discredit Goddess. The underlying truth of the psyche's potential for integration and partnership with the Self *in both its feminine and masculine aspects* was already being watered down. Since that time, most Christians have interpreted his death and rebirth as the heroic feat of a supernatural being solely in service to Sky God.

The fact that hero myths have surpassed descent myths in popularity over the past two thousand years (with the exception of the Jesus story) is a testament to the Epoch II ego's resistance to the trauma of being forced to defer to the Self. Indeed, the ego initially perceives its "step down" from center stage as a tragedy and not the triumph it truly is. This explains the rapid distortion of Jesus's true message and the misunderstanding of it that still persists in the minds of many.

Because the ideals of individualism and male supremacy that are inevitable by-products of the Sky God still persist, masculine theologies offer little practical guidance about how to establish intimacy with others. Our continuing ignorance in this area is a serious obstacle. The Epoch II ego needs to learn that the only accomplishment that brings lasting success, meaning, and happiness to the human soul is the heroic rending of the veil that separates us from God. The only way to do that is to befriend the Self, the indwelling union of our masculine and feminine life energies and our connection to the Sacred.

Integrating Ascent and Descent

- Jot down the major, most important and meaningful events of your life, both positive and negative.

- Who or what were you having a relationship with at the peaks? What was the status of your spirituality at those times?

- Who or what were you having a relationship with, or trying to have a relationship with, at the valleys? How did that influence your spirituality at the time?

- Look for trends or patterns. Of what value were the peak times? The valley times?

- Summarize your spiritual journey so far in terms of how your relationships have influenced your spiritual development.

- In what ways are your relationships improving?

- Make note of important insights that have implications for future spiritual growth.

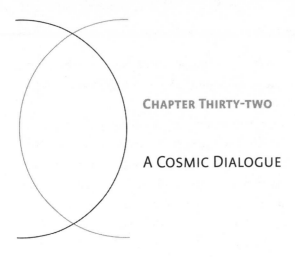

CHAPTER THIRTY-TWO

A COSMIC DIALOGUE

Goddess is tending to lilies and roses in her garden. She planted them just far enough apart that the thorns of the roses won't tear the tender lilies when the winds of heaven blow through. Various other plants grow between and around her favorite flowers in an artful blend that leaves enough space for each to grow.

God needs a break from work and goes looking for Goddess. He finds her there and stands quietly watching. He notices how graceful and harmonious the garden is, even with so many different plants of different sizes, shapes, and colors.

"How beautiful your garden looks," he says after a while. "You have a green thumb. What's your secret?"

"It's all about relationships," Goddess answers.

"What do you mean?" God asks. "Flowers have relationships?"

"Yes, they're connected to each other and to everything in their environment. If you want them to thrive, you have to know what kind of soil each plant likes, how much food, water, sunlight, and space to give each one, and which plants get along better with which companion plants."

"I've never thought about plants needing companions," God muses.

"Yes. For example, this eon I've planted sweet cicely, cosmos, feverfew, poppies, epimedium, nicotiana, and marigolds around the lilies." Goddess points to each one as she names them.

"The companion plants for my roses are coreopsis, delphiniums, daisies, salvia, morning glories, alyssum, lavender, and garlic."

"Garlic?" says God in surprise. "What's that about? Roses and garlic seem like such opposites."

"I guess they are, but they really love each other," she replies. "They both thrive in neutral soil—not too much acid or alkaline. These lilies over here like alkaline soil and those over there prefer acid, so garlic has problems with both of them, but it gets along perfectly with roses. When each plant gets exactly what it needs, they can all live very happily together in the same bed."

"Sort of like us," he says with a mischievous smile.

"We're getting pretty good at that, aren't we?" she agrees.

They sit on the garden bench and God tells her about a particularly knotty problem in his work. Goddess shares her opinions, which God finds enormously helpful. After a time, they both return to work they love. Each feels appreciated by the other and refreshed and ready for whatever may come next.

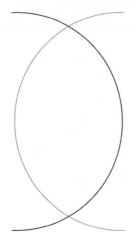

CHAPTER THIRTY-THREE

The Divine Feminine as Partner Maker

PARTNERSHIP is a paradigm of equal and mutually respectful relationships between opposites. This ideal is incidental to many myths. For example, sometimes union with a beloved other is a reward for heroic behavior after which the story ends. But until Apuleius included the story of Psyche and Eros in his classic novel, *The Golden Ass*, written between 160 and 180 C.E., few seriously addressed the difficulties of achieving and preserving this most desirable union. An allegory about the struggles of the mortal soul (Psyche) to unite with divinity (the god Eros), this myth also teaches how two individuals can nurture a healthy relationship. Both meanings are relevant to our theme of the sacred marriage. *As above, so below.*

When the beautiful mortal maiden Psyche failed to attract a suitor, her parents abandoned her on a mountain. A gentle breeze wafted her to a home in the valley where her every need was met by servants of the home's mysterious owner, Eros. He was a god and forbade her to look upon his face, so they could only be together in the dark of night. One night when she could no longer endure the temptation she shone a light on him after he fell asleep. A drop of hot oil from her lamp woke him up and the god abandoned the human woman for seeking to know him.

Psyche suffered deep depression and self-doubt and was forced to endure many difficult trials. Losing heart and hope and admitting her utter helplessness, she succeeded in her tasks only by listening to mysterious voices (Eros) and accepting help from willing creatures. For her last trial, Psyche descended into Hell where she met Persephone who gave her a box of magic makeup. Despite the urgent advice of a voice not to open the box, Psyche succumbed to the temptation. Opening it, she found nothing but utter darkness, which put her into a deep sleep. But because she had persevered Eros rescued her and took her to Mount Olympus. Zeus made her immortal and Psyche and Eros entered into the sacred marriage. The story ends with the birth of a daughter named Joy or Pleasure, depending on the translation.

An unusual feature of this beautiful myth is that, like the Jesus story, it features motifs of ascent *and* descent. As a story within a novel, it was not intended to promote the beliefs of a specific religion, although Apuleius appears to have been a devotee of the Egyptian goddess Isis. But as the product of an evolving ego that understands the wisdom of descending for the sake of creating the sacred marriage, it speaks to my third question about relationships.

What Can Our Relationships Teach Us about Psycho-spiritual Maturity?

Here are some timeless messages from the myth of Psyche and Eros:

- Seek intimacy with your beloved no matter how strong his or her resistance to being seen and known might be.

- Tolerate the tension between self and other and every pair of opposites without giving up.

- Endure the temptation, loss, pain, and fear of the unknown that a committed struggle for intimacy inevitably brings.

- Heed inner guidance from your honest emotions and the highest meaning of love without betraying your conscience, compromising your integrity, or causing unnecessary harm to another.

- Notice the natural world and accept help from its creatures.

- Learn new skills to develop your individuality.

- Take risks for the sake of valuable relationships.

- Care enough about meaningful relationships to die to the world and make the underworld journey.

- Your willingness to connect with the Goddess of the Underworld has spiritually transforming power.

- Trust that even though you may succumb to temptation and make mistakes along the way, your commitment to love makes you worthy of being loved.

- The sacred marriage is your spiritual destiny, your greatest pleasure, and your gift to the world.

- The sacred marriage will usher you into the eternal company of the gods and bring lasting joy.

The Couple

Many today recognize the spiritual significance of intimate relationships. Jungian analyst Dr. Martin Odermatt of the C.G. Jung Institut in Zurich has discovered that the symbol of The Couple carries profound spiritual meaning for a growing number of us.[5] Again, I'm not talking about gender, but about the masculine and feminine principles that subsume all opposites and inform all relationships.

In essence, Dr. Odermatt believes that the couple relationship has become a new symbol for the Self that is gradually replacing the Epoch II ideas about God. In his extensive work with couples, he has discovered that whereas people used to look to religion for relaxation, regeneration, peace, harmony, and emotional security, they now expect to find these qualities of life in relationships with their partners.

People also look to the couple relationship to stimulate their creativity and intellectual growth. They want their partnerships to confirm their individuality and uniqueness. And they look to the couple relationship for deep, ecstatic religious experiences, particularly of a sexual nature. These societal trends reflect our emerging awareness of our need for honest, intimate relationships, a need that is rooted in a growing hunger for the Sacred Feminine.

In his books that deal with the soul, Gary Zukav has moved toward many of the same conclusions. One book, *Soul Stories*, is an insightful study of the differences in relationships between the *old* man and woman—those who still function from stereotypical ideas about gendered roles in traditional marriages—and the *new* man and woman who are in the process of developing the relational self through what he calls spiritual partnerships.[6] In spiritual partnerships, both partners are as involved in becoming empowered individuals as they are in wanting to be intimately related to one another. Both act in accord with their true Selves, and both fully honor each other's individuality and spiritual growth.

There have always been couples, but never before have we invested the symbol of The Couple with so much spiritual meaning and saving power. In the past we looked to individual heroes to save us. Now something momentous is happening. We are discovering deeper levels of meaning in the ancient myths, and we're generating new myths about creating real intimacy between the opposites. I believe this is happening because the Epoch II ego is evolving on a large scale into Epoch III, and to serve that end the sacred aspects of femininity are entering collective consciousness. The signs are everywhere.

For example, psychology no longer limits itself to the analysis of the individual, but has expanded to encompass in-depth assessments of the tangled relationships between couples and within family systems. Relationships are the focus of popular music, and relationship skills are candidly discussed in books, magazines, newspapers, and television. Likewise, it's increasingly common to find premarital counseling and classes on marriage and relationship skills in secular venues and many places of worship.

Other signs are unisex clothing and hairstyles, the sexual revolution which has significantly weakened the sexual double standard, growing respect for inner-directed spiritual disciplines, the collapse of dictatorships and spread of democracy throughout the world, the Green movement, chaos theory, systems theory, an unprecedented respect for diversity, increasing equality between the genders in the home and workplace, and so on.

A person in whom The Couple is emerging asks scary questions and risks new behaviors. For most of us this means accepting our repressed feminine sides. In practical terms this entails expressing our true feelings honestly and kindly to reveal the tenderness behind our toughness, the fear behind our anger, the vulnerability beneath our strength.

Can we imagine accepting the Divine Feminine's gift of partnership? Can we imagine a spiritual entity like The Couple living in us, transcending the opposites of maleness or femaleness? Can we imagine what it would look like if we could experience this kind of partnership in our personal relationships and religions? Can we imagine what the world would be like if nations lived together in this kind of partnership?

The work of integrating the Divine Feminine begins with us, but we don't always choose it. As the following story shows, sometimes it chooses us.

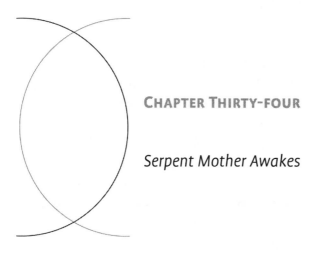

Chapter Thirty-four

Serpent Mother Awakes

EARLIER I quoted Jack Kornfield: "All of spiritual practice is a matter of relationship." People who tend to live in their heads need to develop a living relationship with their own physical and psychological realities before their spiritual lives can develop fully. This is the path the Mother chose for me.

The East has long known about the power and effects of evolutionary energy. Few Westerners know that such a thing even exists, let alone that it profoundly affects our spirituality. Yet, through the ages, committed seekers have experienced the disconcerting effects of its awakening. Each has interpreted it in keeping with the prevailing doctrines of his or her culture. In India it is called *kundalini* and equated with the feminine goddess, Shakti; in China it is Chi; in Christianity it is associated with the Holy Spirit; in Freudian psychology it is encompassed in the term "libido." Regardless of what we call this energy, the effect it has on us as it undulates through our lives is profound.

No one can predict when or how Serpent Mother will awaken or what impact she will have. One thing we can say with certainty is that we have absolutely no authority over her. She has a logic all her own and stirs when she deems us ready. Unfortunately, the fact that our spirits may be ready for a mega-dose of evolutionary energy does not necessarily mean that our psyches are. Most people suffer mightily when she is aroused; for the *kundalini* serpent is, above all, an agent for growth and change, and few egos welcome change.

One effect of *kundalini* energy is that as the "serpent" (as it has traditionally been envisioned) moves up the spinal cord she removes energy blocks that tense our bodies and hamper our psycho-spiritual development. Because our resistance to change is so powerful, these blocks can be deeply entrenched in our bodies. Our inability to relax and yield to this evolutionary energy can create extremely uncomfortable physical symptoms.

For others, the discomfort is primarily psycho-spiritual. Genevieve Lewis Paulson, in *Kundalini and the Chakras*, tells us that many Christian mystics experienced the symptoms of *kundalini* release and called them "sufferings," which they accepted as necessary for their spiritual growth.[7] The medieval mystic St. John of the Cross called a difficult period of his spiritual development the Dark Night of the Soul. He described it as "a time of blankness, misery, a stagnation unlit by any of the voices, visions, and raptures that defined and made glorious the earlier stages of this joyous inward journey toward self-discovery."[8]

Less spiritually oriented individuals might see the depressions, dry spells, temptations, self-hatred, moral lapses, religious doubts, and other painful mental and emotional symptoms these people endured as signs of character flaws or mental illness. What they don't know is that this experience is real and life-serving. The *kundalini* serpent wakes us up from our half-lived lives so that we can love our true selves, find deep pleasure in living, and fulfill the potential of our souls.

In 1980, the idea of the *kundalini* serpent probably would have seemed heretical to me. My church didn't teach about Christian mysticism or mystics from other religions. The only mystic I knew of was Jesus. But after the blue light I began to understand scripture in ways I didn't before. For example, Jesus told his disciples they could do the same things he did and more. Did he know about the latent potential dormant in the human body waiting to be activated? Had he experienced the real but hidden forces of nature that scientists are just beginning to comprehend? Did he associate these with feminine aspects of Deity?

The book of Acts tells us that many people received unusual powers on the day of Pentecost, after they heard a sound like a mighty rushing wind and saw strange flickering lights they called "tongues of fire." Saint Paul believed ordinary people can acquire what he called gifts of the spirit:

prophecy, teaching, wisdom, knowledge, faith, healing, miracles, discerning spirits, speaking in tongues, and the interpretation of tongues.[9] But as far as we know, he never associated these gifts with the serpent, let alone the Divine Feminine.

When I had my own experience with the serpent, I finally understood why this particular symbol is featured in the Old Testament creation story. The serpent has a role as the catalyst responsible for Adam and Eve's change from ignorant creatures to conscious human beings who understand the difference between good and evil. As such, it represents a feminine evolutionary energy force that has always been, and still is, at the root of awakening consciousness. The Divine Feminine is all about initiation and transformation.

My introduction to Serpent Mother was so frightening that for many years I didn't tell even my husband. It can be unwise to reveal our most intimate spiritual experiences. Not only do you open yourself to scorn and judgment, which set the stage for self-doubt and depression, but talking about them can contribute to ego inflation. Only during the last few years have I trusted myself to speak of this, and then only to a very few carefully chosen people. I share it now because I believe it may be of help to some readers.

In my late thirties, despite being a relatively mature and reasonably intelligent person, I wasn't very conscious psychologically. I had an idealistic, naïve, everything-will-be-okay-if-I-just-ignore-the bad-and-stay-spiritual-and-good outlook toward life. The major step of going back to college for a doctorate in the fall of 1979 constellated many repressed and unresolved issues. I became increasingly aware of my dragons, without knowing this was a positive development. In my growing discomfort I prayed often for help and guidance.

The stage was set for what happened in the spring of 1980, around the time of my thirty-seventh birthday. One night I awoke from sound sleep with the strangest sensations I had ever experienced. What awakened me was a terrible roaring in my ears. It was as loud as if I were in the middle of a tornado or standing directly beneath Niagara Falls. For a moment I lay there stunned, uncomprehending. Then, as the strangeness of the phenomenon began to dawn on me, the only thing I could imagine was that a major blood vessel had burst in my head and that what I was hearing was a deadly, unchecked flow of blood racing past my inner ears.

Soon I realized I was feeling something. There was a warm and powerful tingling sensation throughout my body. It felt as if every cell was being injected, not unpleasantly, with tiny pricks of energy.

The third thing had to do with my vision. It seemed as if the bed, in fact, the entire room, was somehow vibrating and flickering in an odd sort of way. I think this was what frightened me the most. If the room and bed were truly shaking and this was something like a hurricane or earthquake, then why wasn't my husband awake and terrified too? But he lay still, peacefully asleep beside me, totally unaware of any of these phenomena that were so real to me. How could this be?

I was terrified. Was I possessed by the devil (this was the era of *The Exorcist*)? Was I having a stroke? Was I dying? I didn't want any of these possibilities. I didn't even want to wake up my husband. What if he didn't believe me? Would he think I was crazy? What could he do anyway? Would he want to rush me to the emergency room? We'd have to wake up the children and dress them and pile them in the car—I didn't want to put them through that. And what if *they* began to worry that I was crazy? I couldn't bear the thought. If we did go to the hospital, what would I tell the doctors? I was in no pain. How would I explain these bizarre symptoms? I couldn't even put what was happening to me into words. They'd probably think I was crazy too.

I decided I would rather have my husband find me dead beside him in the morning than make a big deal of this in the middle of the night and have him think me demented. If I lived through this, what would his belief that I was seriously mental do to our relationship? Finally I became too frightened to think about it any longer. Convinced that the only thing to do was go back to sleep and wait for death, I closed my eyes, trying to ignore the roaring in my head and strange sensations in my body.

When I awoke the next morning (somewhat to my surprise and relief), the events of the night were too weird to comprehend. I had never heard of such a thing happening to anyone (it didn't occur to me to associate this with Pentecost) and I was certain no one, not even a doctor or my priest, would believe me. What if they tried to commit me?

I couldn't let that happen. My children needed me. I was still alive and that was all that mattered. And I was pretty sure I was relatively sane. So true to my lifelong habit of ignoring discomfort and pressing on with stoic resolve, I resolved to tell no one and never think of it again. I didn't completely forget it, of course; but I managed to push it so far away that I rarely thought about it.

If the Sacred Feminine had a head, she would surely have been shaking it in dismay. Or maybe she was merely chuckling at me. The ego is a hard nut to crack. Not even the threat of death was powerful enough to budge my rock-solid belief in mind over matter! But a process had been set into motion, and my will could no more stop it than a tree can run from lightning.

The name of that process was Change.

Notes

1. Leonard Shlain, *The Alphabet Versus the Goddess* (New York: Penguin/Compass, 1998), 27.

2. Jack Kornfield, *A Path with Heart* (New York: Bantam Books, 1993), 287.

3. This story is summarized from Diane Wolkstein and Samuel Noah Kramer, *Inanna Queen of Heaven and Earth: Her Stories and Hymns from Sumer* (New York: Harper & Row Publishers, 1983).

4. Gisela Labouvie-Vief, *Psyche and Eros: Mind and Gender in the Life Course* (New York: Cambridge University Press, 1994), 10.

5. Martin Odermatt, "The Symbol of the Couple." From notes taken at a two-part lecture at the C.G. Jung Institute, Kusnacht, Switzerland, January 18–19, 1996.

6. Gary Zukav, *Soul Stories* (New York: Simon and Schuster, 2000).

7. 7. Genevieve Lewis Paulson, *Kundalini and the Chakras: A Practical Manual* (St. Paul: Llewellyn Publications, 1992).

8. Sophy Burnham, *The Ecstatic Journey* (New York: Ballantine Books, 1997), 42.

9. *Holy Bible*, King James version, I Corinthians, 12: 8–10.

The Sixth Gift
Balance

Many Warriors in today's world have grown beyond their youthful obsessions with surviving, proving themselves, conquering otherness, and fighting change. The key to their empowerment is their partnership with their feminine selves.

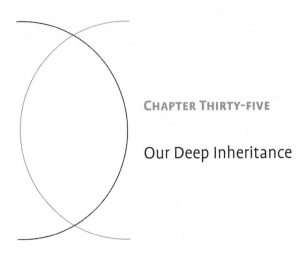

CHAPTER THIRTY-FIVE

Our Deep Inheritance

THE BIZARRE phenomena experienced by Jesus's followers on the day of Pentecost were a prelude to profound personality changes. Timid and fearful women and men hiding from the Roman authorities in deep discouragement were suddenly emboldened to teach openly. On fire with faith, passion, and love, they stepped up. The dramatic empowerment and spread of Christianity that began from there was attributed to the work of the Holy Spirit.

Over time, the Holy Spirit came to be seen as a third masculine expression of the Sky Father and his Son, and as the exclusive property of the new Christian religion. Scholarly research into the history of religions, however, has found this mysterious entity everywhere and in every age. From shaman to priest, guru to rabbi, yogi to Sufi, anchorite to Mennonite, medicine man to mendicant, mentor to mystic, one thing these individuals have always had in common is a personally empowering experience of sacred energies.

Does it matter what we call it or to what we attribute it? To those who experience it, not at all. But for the sake of people whose spiritual growth is inhibited by lack of information and a one-sided God-image, and in the interest of uniting the world's religions in understanding and peace, it's time to give the Divine Feminine her due.

Remember the Gnostic description of Sophia

- as the archetype of the entirety of life, growth, and development?

- as the part of Deity associated with individuation and union with spirit?

- as the co-redemptrix of Jesus, his partner in the work of salvation?

- as a woman of light who fills nature and human beings with a spark of divine light that waits to be fanned into effective action?

All these qualities are associated with spiritual change. All express maternal and transformational aspects of the feminine drive for species-preservation. All were instrumental in the strange events of Pentecost. Whether we call it Sophia, Holy Spirit, Shakti, *kundalini*, *chi*, libido, the energy of life, sufferings, evolutionary energy, or any number of other names, this energy is real. It is feminine, personally empowering, and spiritually vivifying. And it largely has been ignored by Western and Middle Eastern mainstream religions.

The physical origins and dynamics of *kundalini* power are still a mystery, but we're getting a better understanding of its psycho-spiritual elements. My thesis is that the goddess's activation is associated with our drive for species-preservation and the four primary feminine archetypes that express it: Queen, Mother, Wisewoman, and Beloved.

Nobody has ever seen the archetypes, but we all have felt the awesome mystery of their power in overwhelming instincts and emotions. The five instincts—nurturance, activity, reflection, sex, and creativity—are patterns of *physical* energy. The archetypes are *psychological* patterns of these energies, clusters of emotions and images we associate with each instinct.

We know about the archetypes because we feel their tremendous power over us. They seize us with powerful emotion, causing us to fall violently in love, be overwhelmed with jealousy, sink to the depths of depression, seethe with aggression or blind ambition, tremble in fear and awe, or respond to another's plight with profound compassion.

Jungian analyst Janet O. Dallett writes:

"Archetype" is Jung's word for the psychological image of a god, and when an archetype is activated, we speak of its impact as numinous. In other words, numinosity is the charge of energy in whatever we experience as divine or demonic. If you want to know what is numinous to you, consider what you find fascinating, compelling, thrilling, mysterious, horrifying, gripping, tremendous,

terrifying, dreadful, or awesome. Think about the things with
which you are preoccupied in spite of yourself.[1]

The Greeks personified these numinous experiences in gods and goddesses. Eros, Aphrodite, and Dionysus represented the instinct for sex
and the ecstasies of love. Persephone, Hermes, and Athena stood for the
instinct for reflection which sometimes causes depressions that plunge us
into the dark abyss of suffering and sometimes leads to wisdom and victory over the dark forces of the unconscious. Zeus, Hera, and Apollo were
social leaders who personified the varieties of cultural accomplishments
and emotions, both noble and ignoble, that can accompany the instinct for
nurturance in the social arena. Ares, Artemis, and Demeter were associated
with the instinct for activity which is sometimes aggressive and warlike, and
sometimes life-serving. Hephaestus represented the instinct for creativity
. . . and so on.

These images provided the Golden Age with something concrete to
help people understand the mysteries of their unknown selves a little better. The Hindu pantheon of gods and goddesses provides the same service
for much of the East today. Whether we think of the archetypes as Greek
deities on Mount Olympus, Indian divinities on the Himalayan Mount
Sumeru, God in Heaven, or basic patterns in the collective unconscious,
they are genuine forces that influence and transcend the life of an individual. Because they have been with us from the beginning, they are, in a
very real sense, immortal.

Nobody knows the exact number of archetypes that comprise the
psyche. My own classification differs in at least one respect from others I've
seen: From when I first began to see them as psychological representations
of physical instincts, I've wanted to identify the fundamental masculine and
feminine archetypes that best represent each instinct.

Guided in part by Jung's typology of personality traits, in part by the
Indian doctrine of the four ends for which humans live and strive, and
by the research of noted psychologists such as Toni Wolff, Robert Moore,
Douglas Gillette, Jean Shinoda Bolen, Carol S. Pierson, and Jennifer and
Roger Woolger, I determined that four archetype pairs govern four differ-
ent domains of instinctual human functioning—social, physical, mental,

and emotional. To be fully functioning spirit persons, we need to awaken, activate, and heal our fullest potential—masculine and feminine—in each of these four areas.

The Instincts and Archetypes

The Social Domain

Goals: Lawful Order and Moral Virtue

The Instinct for Nurturance

King ⟵——————————————————⟶ *Queen*

The Physical Domain

Goals: Power and Success

The Instinct for Activity

Warrior ⟵——————————————————⟶ *Mother*

The Mental Domain

Goals: Release from Delusion

The Instinct for Reflection

Scholar ⟵——————————————————⟶ *Wisewoman*

The Emotional Domain

Goals: Love and Pleasure

The Instinct for Sex

Lover ⟵——————————————————⟶ *Beloved*

The Spiritual Domain

Goals: Perfection and Completion

The Instinct for Creativity

⟵——————— *The Couple* ———————⟶

I represent the fifth instinct, creativity, with the archetype of The Couple. I see The Couple as integrating the other four archetype pairs in a sacred marriage of fully individuated and fully related opposites. This union fully activates the creative instinct and brings us into the spiritual domain and Epoch III integrated consciousness.[2]

As the chart shows, the masculine archetypes comprise the half of our psyche's potential that is devoted to self-preservation. Deriving a God-image from these archetypes alone not only limits our ideas about what is sacred, but also severely confines our perceptions about the meaning of our life and how to live it. Attaching all our hopes to this one-sided way of thinking practically assures that we will not achieve wholeness or salvation.

A particular archetype's status in us depends on our physical inheritance, personality, environmental influences, and ego's evolutionary stage. Some people have highly developed Warriors but unawakened Mothers, for example, whereas for others the opposite is true. When an archetype is activated it gives rise to certain predictable attitudes and behaviors. Since we are all quite familiar with the masculine archetypes, I will deal primarily with the feminine.

The activation of our Queen might cause us to sponsor an artist or support a social cause we had previously ignored. Developing Mother energy might motivate us to nurture relationships and new life, feel a close kinship with nature, and accept difficult changes. A growing Wisewoman might enable us to truly listen to ourselves, reflect on our personal realities, and accommodate the differing viewpoints of others. A new respect for our Beloved might cause us to acknowledge our true beauty and worth and help us express painful repressed emotions with honesty and courage for the sake of love and intimacy.

Recent research is showing that the brains of males and females are hard-wired with subtle differences at birth. The psyche, however—by which I mean the sum total of our psychological potential—is androgynous. Every one of us can develop every quality we associate with masculinity and femininity at that level.

We see proof everywhere. For example, there are many instances of female warriors: the Amazons, the sword-wielding Hebrew Judith, the Celtic Queen Boadicia, and others like them. Likewise, there are many males whose distinguishing characteristic is their passion for nature and the maternal desire to preserve the many species that live here. Examples are oceanographer Jacques Cousteau, naturalist John Muir who inspired America's national park system, James Lovelock who developed the Gaia theory, and so on.

Every archetype has positive and negative potential. Heinrich Zimmer said,

> Every being has a twofold aspect, reveals a friendly and a menacing face. All gods have a charming and a hideous form, according to how one approaches them . . .3

Zimmer was a professor of Sanskrit and Indology at Heidelberg in the 1930s and one of Joseph Campbell's professors at Columbia University in the early 1940s. Along with Carl Jung, he was one of the first contemporary philosophers in the West to see the harmony beneath this apparent dualism. Like the Indian philosophy and Hindu mythology he studied, he attributed this harmony to the feminine principle:

> . . . but the Great Goddess is the energy of the world, taking form in all things. All friendly and menacing faces are facets of her essence. What seems a duality in the individual god, is an infinite multiplicity in her total being.4

When we don't acknowledge the Great Goddess's multiplicity but limit our worship to an incomplete god, we contribute to disharmony. Disharmony arises from obsessing over one archetype and repressing its opposite. For example, many male-oriented institutions where the Warrior's toughness and hardness are the ideal—the military, law enforcement, men's pro sports, some corporations, etc.—have strong biases against gentleness and softness, which are usually seen as fatal weaknesses. "Don't be a girl." "Act like a man." "Only sissies cry." "Get tough!" "When the going gets tough, the tough get going." "You're getting soft." And who can forget soft in the head, lily-livered (lilies being symbols of femininity and purity), having a soft job, etc.

These biases don't reflect the true relative merits of the Warrior and Mother. They just express the Epoch II ego's preference for the Sky God and the masculine archetypes. Warrior and Mother each have specific ways of manifesting strength and courage and both have weaknesses. Being too hard is obviously as problematic as being too soft, and it is easy to find examples of both extremes in either gender.

Warrior and Mother symbolize the energies we use as we strive for

power and success in our outer and inner worlds. Of all the masculine archetypes, the Warrior is probably most closely associated with the
drive for self-preservation. Some of his special qualities are hardness,
toughness, stoicism, perseverance, doingness, physical strength, durabil-
ity, competition, self-discipline, emotional detachment, goal-orientation,
and achievement.

We all have an inner Warrior. As you probably realize from what I've
shared about my early life, his is the first form of energy my Epoch II
ego consciously activated. He's the part of us who gets up every morning and shows up at school, work, the gym, yoga studio, library, chapel,
or meditation room day after day, doing whatever it takes to succeed and
make our lives (and the lives of those we love) more comfortable, secure,
and fulfilling. What would we do without him? If there were no Warrior
energy in our psyche we wouldn't be alive today.

Fueled by the drive for species-preservation, Mother is the Warrior's
partner. She represents the polar opposite of his hard-driving, penetrating
aggressive energy. Her qualities include maternal nurturing, beingness,
softness, physical and emotional relatedness, receptivity, fertility, fecun-
dity, creativity, flexibility, caring, trusting, initiating, opening, evolving,
changing.

She too indwells every psyche. As the feminine energy of the instinct
for activity, she is the part of us that does whatever it takes to create new
life and to protect, nourish, and preserve it. She makes it strong and
healthy enough to ensure that our species will thrive from one generation
to the next, and honors each psychological, physical, and spiritual phase
it undergoes on its transforming journey from birth to death and beyond.
What would we do without her? If there were no Mother archetype in the
human psyche, we would not be alive today.

Can you see any reason why we might need more of one of these
drives than the other? Is one somehow better or more worthy? Is there
a good reason why both genders can't or shouldn't fully avail themselves
of both? This isn't either/or, it's both/and. Both work together for human
evolution. If you understand this, you understand balance, the sixth gift
of integrated wisdom.

Integrating Self-Preservation and Species-Preservation

- Make a list of everything you did in the last twenty-four hours, or usually do in a typical day.

- Beside each item note the approximate amount of time it took. Adjust until it adds up to twenty-four hours.

- Analyze what took more of your time and energy. Was it serving yourself and your passions? Was it serving your loved ones? The way you actually use your life's precious moments determines your dominant psychological orientation. If you honor both drives regularly, you're probably in a good place. But if you are strongly lacking in one area, you might want to start figuring out how to take this drive, and the archetypes that represent it, more seriously. It's your call.

- If you're ready for a change, choose an archetype that's undeveloped in you, and think of a way you can activate it that will be truly fulfilling to your inner self.

- Use your Warrior and Mother energy to follow through with your plan.

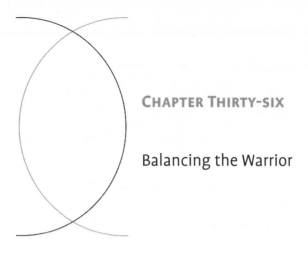

Chapter Thirty-six

Balancing the Warrior

CURRENTLY the Epoch II Warrior is out of hand and civilization is out of balance. To understand how this happened let's look at the differences between the Mother's creativity and the Warrior's ability to manifest it in the physical world.

The Warrior needs to produce things that help him gain power over his world—things like tools, boundaries, houses, palaces, books, boats, cars, telephones, airplanes, computers, money. There's nothing subtle about these things. Everyone can see them and almost all of us want them. They are visible signs of the Warrior's prowess. Making and owning them gratifies an Epoch II ego's need to be appreciated and admired. As our Warrior comes to depend on and identify with things he has made, it becomes crucial to protect them. Skills once used to protect his life are then used to preserve his power, status, possessions, social position, theories, passions, beliefs, and religious traditions.

Each archetype has its own specialties. The Warrior's genius is his willingness to fight to the death for what is precious to him. If this gift isn't used with discretion, his bravery can turn into an instrument of destruction. To an Epoch II ego that identifies obsessively with the Warrior, preserving what we have feels like a struggle for survival. All too often it's really only about protecting our power and status. If this becomes more important than human life, a Warrior, like Darth Vader, turns to the "dark side." His obsession destroys the delicate balance between self-preservation and species-preservation, and his shadow makes him reject otherness.

Empowering the feminine archetypes is the antidote to the Warrior's excesses. But the feminine qualities are so much softer and more subtle than the masculine that we find them more difficult to see and appreciate. We often neglect the invisible contributions of the Sacred Feminine: the Queen's social caring, cultural contributions, and shared authority; Mother's endless nurturing and species-preserving activity; Wisewoman's imagination, inner knowing, symbolic meaning, and intuition; and the Beloved's magnetism, emotional honesty, inspiration, and sacred beauty. So we squander Goddess's resources on this planet and sacrifice her contributions to the Warrior's more visible signs of successes. Is this ignorant or what?

If we have eyes to see her, one place where the Divine Feminine's activity is particularly obvious is in the realm of physical Nature. Mother Nature is about natural resources and the ongoing processes of life. Her activity is never-ending creativity. This is most apparent in Nature's birth/death/ rebirth cycle. All new life originates in her and all decaying life returns to her for recycling. The laws of physics are scientific explanations for her balancing and connecting forces that hold the universe together and maintain delicate relationships necessary for species-preservation. Mother Nature holds the keys to life's greatest mysteries. From where does the animating spark of life come when we are conceived? Where does this energy go when our bodies die?

Once Mother has created, incubated, and introduced new life into the world—whether in the form of mental insights and ideas or in various physical forms—our Warrior enjoys shaping it into useful things. Caught up in the thrill of producing, it's easy for an Epoch II Warrior to take all the credit for what he produces, while dismissing the complex processes and interrelationships that make his productions possible. An ego with this mind-set tends to forget that it can manifest nothing without Mother's resources, which include the life in our bodies and all over this planet.

One process in all feminine energies is change. To Mother change is natural and desirable. New life is produced to take over when the old dies off. But to an Epoch II Warrior, any change that could alter or destroy something he has manifested puts his hard-won sense of security at risk. Changes feel alien and dangerous, and he resists unwanted change with all his strength. This is simply what the drive for self-preservation does.

When it's not partnered with the drive for species-preservation, the results are conflict, war, destruction.

This is a crucial reason for pursuing the balance symbolized by the sacred marriage.

Integrating Manifestation and Creativity

- Toward which direction do you lean—actively accomplishing or passively ideating? A blend of both is healthy; too much of either is worrisome. Compulsive doers and idle dreamers set off red alerts. Something is missing at either extreme.

- If your Warrior is obsessively active, write down all the things he does to excess and how you can tell when he's in charge. Select one of his excessive behaviors that's most bothersome to you or your loved ones, and decide how best to divert his energy in a more positive or balanced way the next time it shows up. Then do it.

- If your Mother comes up with all sorts of creative ideas and plans but rarely follows through, choose the idea or plan you would most like to manifest. Outline the steps you need to take to make it happen. Take the first step.

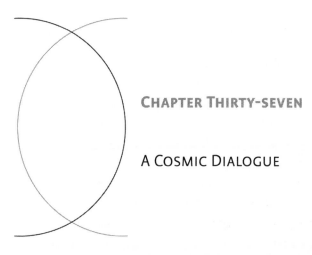

Chapter Thirty-Seven

A Cosmic Dialogue

God is on a tirade. Sort of like some TV evange-lists, but *really* amped up. Retribution time. Judgment hour. Separating the sheep from the goats. Hellfire and brimstone and all that stuff.

Goddess peeks in the doorway. "Hi, Honey. What's up?"

"The children again. I just heard from a tribe begging me to make another tribe stop invading their territory. Then I heard from the other one—with the same request. Both claim to be completely innocent. It's always the others who are the problem. I'm about ready to throw in the towel and write off this whole experiment as a bad idea! What were we thinking? This sibling rivalry is intolerable. My head hurts from all the complaints! Why can't they love each other? Why can't they be perfect like us?"

Goddess smiles. "Well, dear, I wouldn't quite call us perfect yet. It's taken us a long time to get where we are, and we're still learning."

"Well, that's true," God admits somewhat reluctantly, "but what about their sense of moral responsibility? Can't they disagree without having to kill each other off? We've been telling them for millennia."

"I guess that's not long enough. The first lesson they learned about morality was that bad was what would get them punished, and good was what got them rewarded. So the ones who got praise for destroying what their families considered bad figured that revenge and retribution are good. Most of them seem to have grown past that stage, but some are still stuck. It's disheartening, but I'm not willing to give up on them. We don't really want to go back to that old punishing mode do we? It will only reinforce their immature reasoning. Isn't there another way?"

"Well dear," he says, "I've tried everything I can think of and I'm fresh out of ideas. Why don't you see what you can do?"

Goddess returns to Earth. She finds a philosophy professor reeling from a recent article that viciously tears her latest theory to shreds. Her first instinct is to get revenge by writing an equally nasty response to the colleague who wrote it. Goddess blows on the scholar's flame while whispering to her heart, "Why don't you explore a new area? What about researching how people grow in moral reasoning?"

Next she finds a religious leader looking through books for ideas for a sermon. Goddess whispers, "You've been pointing fingers and preaching about keeping God's commandments for a long time. Yet you've broken many of them yourself. Why not share what you've learned about compassion? And do it from your heart; not your head."

A mother is putting her children to bed and trying to make up a new story for them, but she's distracted by the pain of her husband's betrayal and their recent divorce. "It would be very satisfying to make him the bad guy," Goddess whispers, "but let's tell a story about a man who learns that goodness is about caring and doing what one can to prevent hurting oneself or others."

A soldier on a battlefield finds one of his enemies lying wounded. He raises his rifle, and then hears a tiny voice in his head say, "Help him. He's another human being. He's your brother, and he wants to live too. Help him."

These people feel the conflicts between their need to stay safe and get revenge, and their sincere desire to ease their own pain and the pain of others. They hear Goddess and search their minds and hearts. Then each of them takes the risk of acting on their new insights. They don't know if they're making a real difference, but they feel very good about what they're doing.

However, God is watching, and he sees the future as well as the present. He knows that thousands of lives are changed for the better by these choices.

"Well done, my dear," He says when Goddess returns. "I couldn't have done it better myself." He feels a bit better about his wayward children. He feels better about himself, too.

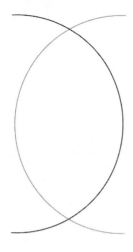

CHAPTER THIRTY-EIGHT

The Divine Feminine as Changing Woman and Warrior Tamer

MOTHER is the feminine archetype of evolutionary activity, the agent of growth, transformation, and change in every form of life. Like a good personal mother, this aspect of the Sacred Feminine wants us to become powerful, successful, healthy, and mature. She gives birth to us, nurtures and protects us, and continually promotes our development. Physically, she is the life in our bodies and all the growing, sustaining, and healing energies that keep us alive and kicking. Psychologically and spiritually, her energy propels us to surpass the limitations of our forebears to improve ourselves, our societies, and our species.

The one thing common to all the Mother's activity is change. Change is a really tricky thing. I've pondered it for years. What causes one person to change while another stays the same? It's definitely not easy to change ourselves. And many of us find it extremely difficult to accept changes in others or our outer lives.

I suspect our openness to change is a function of how attached we are to qualities we associate with masculine archetypes. Grounded in the drive for self-preservation, the masculine principle is associated with stability whereas the feminine is chaotic and unpredictable. To a young ego as to an obsessive Warrior, the unknown is a terrible threat to our sense of safety.

Change occurs in the physical world when something over which we have no control disrupts the status quo and forces us to find new ways to adapt. Hurricanes, floods, earthquakes, avalanches, fires, famines, plagues, accidents, territorial invasions, wars, shifting boundaries, the passing of old regimes and the rise of new ones, illness, loss of jobs, divorce, death—these invite us to seek creative solutions to suffering. A growing ego accepts the challenge; one bound by fear, pride, or repression denies its pain, scrambles to restore everything to its pre-crisis status, or tries to escape in increasingly unhealthy ways.

The same principle rules the universe within. Here, the catalyst is often an aspect of one's shadow that has been so forcibly repressed that it erupts like lava into the outer world, often creating equally disastrous effects. No wonder we've had so much resistance to the Divine Feminine for so long. No wonder so many people fight the scientific evidence of evolution. If God is the unwavering safety of tradition, Goddess is the chaotic abyss! But change is as necessary to psycho-spiritual growth as it is to the continuation of our species and the life on this planet. It's how life is. We can fight it like frightened, ignorant children or we can grow up and flow with the natural processes moving us toward balance and union.

In Navajo mythology, this concept is expressed in Changing Woman who represents two spiritual goals: our ability to achieve immortality by reproducing ourselves (self-preservation), and the peace and harmony needed to perpetuate all living things (species-preservation). Both goals require cooperation between masculinity and femininity. Changing Woman's message is that if there is no harmony between these opposites, there can be no harmony in the world.

Rising to Goddess's challenge to accept change will subdue our temporal, Epoch II Warriors and transform them into spiritual, Epoch III ones. A spiritual Warrior knows it's not enough to develop his skills to the utmost so he can make new stuff and protect it from change. In the big picture, what matters is what he is manifesting and why.

What is his highest goal? Is it to win an Olympic medal that will make his country proud? To sing with the Metropolitan Opera? To become rich and famous? To buy wonderful things that will make his and his family's life easier? These are all worthy ways of expressing our uniqueness. But if they are all our Warrior lives for—if he keeps his focus on himself and his success in the outer world without attending to his relationships or the world within—he won't attain his spiritual destiny.

There are many Warriors in today's world who have grown beyond their youthful obsessions with surviving, proving themselves, conquering otherness, and fighting change. These wise and accomplished spiritual Warriors see the big picture. They have established new goals and found new outlets for their changing priorities. The key to their empowerment is their partnership with their feminine selves.

Reverence for the feminine side of God will likewise help us channel the courage and self-discipline of our Warriors into manifesting healthy new changes instead of defending toxic traditions. The Sacred Feminine encourages Warriors to serve a nobler concept of morality that encompasses the protection and preservation of not just us, our families, businesses, social groups, beliefs, or even our nations. She inspires Warriors to protect the planet and everyone on it from more injustice and pain, and she challenges them to do this without shedding blood.

Helping Mother nurture the evolution of every form of life to its fullest potential is our Warrior's most sacred calling and the true test of his nobility. There have always been a few ready to answer this call. Examples from recent history include peace activists Mahatma Gandhi, Nelson Mandela, and Martin Luther King Jr., environmentalist Rachel Carson, feminist Gloria Steinem, primatologist Jane Goodall, and former American vice-president Al Gore with his work to avert a climate-change crisis.

I believe more spiritual Warriors live on the planet today than in any other era of our history. They give me hope. If more of them will listen to Mother, accept her gift of balance, and step forward with her messages, they can make a lasting difference.

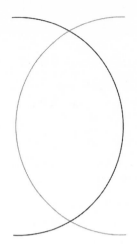

CHAPTER THIRTY-NINE

Dances with Changing Woman

TWELVE YEARS after my experience with Serpent Mother I read June Singer's book, *Androgyny: The Opposites Within*. When I got to her account of Gopi Krishna's encounter with *kundalini*, FLASH! On went a light bulb. Here was an explanation for what happened to me. Not only was his physical experience similar to mine, he also was beset by the soul-sickness that became my constant companion for the next several years. Until I read this book, I hadn't connected my terrifying experience that night with the extraordinary changes that began shortly afterwards.

Singer confirmed something my intuition had been signaling for quite some time: What happened was not evil, but good. I had experienced a powerful, very positive evolutionary energy surge that was as real and physical—if not as physically painful—as an electric shock. Without any conscious knowledge on my part of what this was or what effects it would have, this mega-dose of totally unexpected energy shifted my life into a new dimension.

The major changes were psychological. For the first two years my stomach ached almost daily and I lost twenty pounds. But the physical discomfort was nothing compared to the suffering in my psyche. It was as if the *kundalini* serpent had ripped a gaping hole in the boundary between my conscious and unconscious selves. An abyss filled with dragons opened beneath my feet, and I spiraled headlong into the darkness on an underworld journey.

During that time I managed to function normally in the external world. But inwardly I suffered the anguish of the young Persephone, a lost and lonely soul forced against her will to live half the year in the underworld. Never had I felt so alone, misunderstood, or alienated from everyone and everything. Often I felt depressed, hopeless, and sorry for myself. Sometimes I was filled with rage. Occasionally I was so miserable I entertained fantasies of suicide. For the first time I didn't have everything under control. There were times I felt so separated from my old self that I wondered if I were mentally ill.

Painful as this all was, my earlier experiences with the Mistress of the Forest and the Woman of Light had prepared me. I was open to the possibility that my suffering might be a gift with valuable meaning. I had no conception yet of the Divine Feminine, but intuited that God had something to teach me. I *knew* I was being invited to the dance. I also knew that the reasons for my discomfort and the answers for my life lay within me and not with other people or outer circumstances.

Led by a growing trust in my intuition, I began to read psychology and self-help books, write poetry, and keep a journal. I discovered Jungian psychology and dreamwork. In dreams I met shadow parts of my personality. In waking life I gave them names and had creative dialogues with them through writing, art, meditation, and private rituals. This creative work gave me a much-needed outlet, eased my discomfort, provided hope, and helped me see my dragons more clearly. As I faced them I discovered (to my great surprise) that they weren't nearly so terrible as I had feared. To paraphrase Joseph Campbell: Where I had thought to find an abomination, I found a god.[5] I was discovering what Christians call the Christ within and experiencing self-discovery as a spiritual path.

As my self-knowledge grew, I began to break away from habitual behavior and the expectations of others to make some original choices for myself. Every advance brought renewed energy and an increased sense of empowerment. In time I began to feel quite wonderful. Life was fresh with potential. I was filled with vitality and hope.

Spiritually, instead of thinking of God as far removed from Earth and human life, I was recognizing the sacredness of soulful, physical life. By withdrawing my attention from ideas and theories about God and taking myself seriously, by listening to my strongest feelings and deepest yearnings and putting an increased emphasis on self-knowledge, I was discovering the feminine aspect of God. I was seeing and feeling Divine Mother every-where: in my dreams, in my waking thoughts, in my body for which I was gaining a marvelous new appreciation, and in Nature to whose wonders I was once again happily awakening.

Nine years after my *kundalini* experience an unusual dream dramati-cally displayed the overall effect Serpent Mother's awakening was having. It used another image of energy closely related to the power of the serpent, the explosive zig-zag of electricity and lightning. Here's how I wrote it at the time.

Dream #269

Serpent Power

I am both observing and participating in this dream. It is night, and I am standing alone on a high piece of ground with nothing but earth below and sky above. My legs are spread apart, my feet are planted on the ground, and my arms reach up to the sky. Brilliant currents of power, like electricity or bolts of lighting, are coursing through my body in wave after jagged, undulating wave.

This power extends beyond my bare feet and is being mapped in the earth. It goes up through my hands into the sky. The source of this power is not known but it goes through me to others. Am I some kind of channel?

This is not something for which I should receive any credit or special attention. It simply is, and it applies especially to my children. It gives them perspective, wisdom, and meaning. Is it feminine (earth) power? Is it connectedness? I don't know. But I feel enormously blessed and extremely powerful.

Traditionally lightning has been associated with sky gods like Zeus, Thor, and YHWH. I believe this dream, though, illustrated two basic forms of energy—feminine and masculine, physical and spiritual—to show me that a combination of both is necessary. Why do I believe this?

For one thing, the dream contained images of both Earth Mother and Sky Father. For another, it was as if the power came from and headed toward both the earth and the sky at the same time, with my body as the conduit. And it wasn't lightning so much as powerful currents of energy which, because I couldn't conceive of any other kind, I could only associate with electricity.

Finally, the end of the dream revealed a feminine purpose when I understood that these energies were to be used in service to my children! In other words, at least some of this life-giving energy was from and for the Mother who was nourishing the growth of my soul and my relationships with loved ones. I was opening up to the powers of the universe and evolving spiritually, not only for the sake of my physical children but also for people who could benefit from insights I might be able to share.

I think my dream was saying, "Look. You are a spiritual being in a human body, poised between heaven and earth. You are being charged with the Father's and Mother's energies so that you might realize your soul's purpose. You are waking up and learning, and there are others who can benefit from what's going on here. Do what you were born to do. Believe in yourself. Assume your own authority. Share your own truths, tell your own stories to others who are interested."

I had this dream in June of 1989, a few days after leaving my last college teaching job. Since the *kundalini* experience, my life had become much more meaningful. I felt so confident that I decided to quit teaching to pursue a passion second only to my desire for self-knowledge: I wanted to write a book about psycho-spiritual growth. Four months later I began *The Bridge to Wholeness,* which describes this time in more detail.[6]

1990 brought long periods of "inspired" writing. I felt more creative than ever. Many times, after having a valuable insight and finding an immensely satisfying way to express it, I sat in front of my computer screen with chills surging through my body and tears streaming down my face. I was feeling, "Thank you, Mother. Thank you." Never had I experienced such joy, such a profound sense of connection with the Sacred. Masculine energies were responsible for the mental concentration and self-discipline it took to write, but something profoundly feminine was providing the inspiration, creative ideas, and trust in the process.

Following my passion in work was life-changing in that area. In other areas, change has been much slower and less dramatic. For instance, I know better than to aspire to perfection—not only because it's impossible, but also because it orients me toward the future and prevents me from living in the present. Nonetheless, there's still a part of my shadow that can be a painfully inhibiting perfectionist: *Oh no! I can't stand up and sing in this Karaoke bar! What if I make a fool of myself?* Maybe this will always be my basic inclination. Yet I'm more spontaneous, more aware of the present moment, and more open to change than ever before. Maybe just moving in that direction will be enough for me.

After all these years I still struggle to acknowledge the truths of my body and emotions. I have to remind myself it's okay if my energy changes from one day to the next; it's okay if what energizes my husband makes me tired, if sometimes I get so wrapped up in my thoughts that it takes a while for me to even know I'm tired. I'm getting it, and that in itself is heartening. Instead of simply serving as a vehicle for my ego's needs, my body and emotions are becoming my partners and guides.

Essentially, it feels as if a new form of awareness is growing in me. Before the *kundalini* experience, I was traveling through life with only one eye open. I saw almost everything through the lens of the drive for self-preservation and the masculine archetypes. But when Serpent Mother awakened the feminine side of my Self, I began to see through my second eye too.

My new binocular vision made a wider field of view available, with more precise depth perception and an enhanced ability to detect things that were previously indistinct. From this union a third way of seeing emerged. I think of it as an Observer whose expanded consciousness is my soul's connection to spirit and my ego's connection to Self. It's still young and erratic, but getting stronger.

This more conscious, objective way of perceiving life is a common experience for committed seekers in today's world. Quaker Tom Rothschild writes:

> Our society is in . . . a time of change, searching for a myth that will allow us to express eternal truths while viewing the world in a manner consonant with scientific theory.

> This change calls me to go deeper, to explore who I am as an

"observer" in the laboratory of my own life. A great deal of the time, I have virtually no inner awareness even of my own existence, much less of what I could be observing of the outer world. By stopping to give attention to my own existence, my awareness of it can grow and perhaps begin to include awareness of what surrounds me as well. And when I become very still and bring my attention to a deeply centered awareness of my whole self, including my thoughts, feelings, body, sensations, I can sometimes find moments of contact, even connection, with others and with all of the world around me. In these moments, the new understandings of science and mathematics are no longer paradoxes but the beginning of a new myth for the current age.[7]

Serpent Mother didn't eradicate my shadow, but with help from Observer I started seeing it more clearly. My painful emotions didn't disappear, but I was feeling, identifying, and accepting them more easily. My fears and anxieties didn't go away, but by noticing them and seeing how unfounded and unhelpful most of them are I could relax and let go of them. Relationship problems didn't disappear overnight, but my awareness of how I contribute to them and my ability to entertain opposing points of view improved dramatically.

I'm pretty sure this is what is meant by becoming more conscious. Notice I say *becoming*. One of the most comforting things I've learned is that consciousness isn't a destination, but a process. Knowing that takes the heat off, softens me, helps me forgive myself, just *be* myself.

Most comforting of all are the ongoing experiences of sacredness: in my body, in my emotions, in sudden insights, via dreams, imagination, intuition, synchronistic experiences, meaningful images, relationships with loved ones and friends, or just in simple moments of profound awareness of the beauty and miracle of life. Deity is so much more than abstract, remote masculine spirit! God is concrete. *With* us. *In* us! Serpent Mother instigates our spiritual transformation and Changing Woman dances in us, with us, and around us every moment of our existence, now pulling us this way, now bringing us closer to that.

I no longer have to wait ten years for another message from God. I can do the inner work that brings me in touch with the Sacred right now.

Now I know that *this* is how we find God: by finding ourselves.

This is how we honor God: by honoring ourselves.

This is how we listen to God: by listening to ourselves.

This is how we change the world: by balancing opposing energies and opening to change.

Notes

1. Janet O. Dallett, *The Not-Yet-Transformed God: Depth Psychology and the Individual Religious Experience* (York Beach, ME: Nicolas-Hays, Inc., 1998), 3.

2. The chart "The Instincts and Archetypes," illustrates these relationships.

3. Heinrich Zimmer, "The Indian World Mother," in *The Mystic Vision: Papers from the Eranos Yearbooks*, Joseph Campbell, ed. (Princeton, N.J.: Princeton University Press, 1968), 95.

4. Ibid.

5. Joseph Campbell. "The Hero's Adventure," Program One, *Joseph Campbell and the Power of Myth, with Bill Moyers* (New York: Mystic Fire Video, 1988).

6. Jean Benedict Raffa, *The Bridge to Wholeness: A Feminine Alternative to the Hero Myth.* (San Diego: LuraMedia, 1992).

7. Tom Rothschild, "A Finger Pointing at the Moon," *Parabola*, 33, no. 2 (summer 2008), 62.

THE SEVENTH GIFT
SOVEREIGNTY

Each of us is her worthy child, connected to her other children by our common mother. Because of that we are fully entitled to have sovereignty over our own bodies and souls and to be treated with equality, love, kindness, and care.

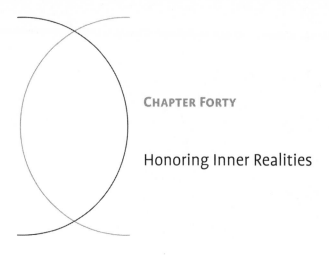

CHAPTER FORTY

Honoring Inner Realities

AN ANCIENT "great saying" is *As without, so within.* Essentially, this means that the processes of the physical world are metaphors for the life of the soul: The world is like a giant screen onto which our soul's dramas are projected. When we look at ourselves through the eyes of Goddess—by which I mean with awareness of our inner life, attention to feeling, and openness to symbolic meaning—we see these dramas everywhere. One of the best places to see them is in art.

Themes in the ego's heroic journey to consciousness appear not only in ancient rituals, scriptures, and myths, but in contemporary books, films, songs, and other works of art:

- *separation* (leaving the safety and comfort of the Epoch I maternal matrix to find your identity)

- *achievement* (developing your Epoch II ego's heroism by finding and proving your individuality)

- *sacrifice* (changing your Epoch II ego's attitude toward power)

- *suffering* (entering the dark abyss of the unconscious and confronting the shadow and archetypes)

- *surrender/death/descent* (losing the safety and comfort of familiar assumptions and conventional formulas; leaving Epoch II ego-consciousness behind and submitting to a greater authority)

- *receiving help from unexpected sources* (befriending the shadow and the feminine)

- *rebirth* (moving into Epoch III consciousness; acquiring self-knowledge; freedom from the prisons of rigid belief systems; empowerment to make original choices; establishing a relationship with the Self)

- *return* (re-entering the community on your own terms as a maturing individual)

- *reunion* (being reunited with the feminine and participating in the hierosgamos in which the opposites are united), and

- *blessing* (bringing healing new consciousness to your community).

These themes are deliberately developed in such literary works as Somerset Maugham's *The Razor's Edge*, J.R.R. Tolkein's *The Lord of the Rings*, John Fowles's *The Magus*, and even the humorous *Skinny Legs and All* by Tom Robbins. Films with the same intent include Alan Ball's *American Beauty*, M. Knight Shyamalan's *The Village* and *Lady in the Water*, and George Lucas's *Star Wars* series. The songs of Kris Kristofferson and other musicians likewise engage many of these issues.

Ultimately, the symbols, characters, issues, and motifs of a work of art emerge from the artist's compulsion to understand and express him/herself better, to unite his/her inner opposites, to evolve into greater maturity, and to share what s/he has found. Some artists know this; others don't have a clue. Yet every artist grapples with these themes in one way or another simply because they are core concerns of every soul.

Not only do the outer and inner universes reflect each other in art and everyday living, they also continually interact (another mystery symbolized in the mandorla). This interaction has been intuited by spirit persons for thousands of years. An Epoch II dualistic worldview prevents us from seeing how it works in everyday life. What an awakened soul sees as evidence of a deep connectedness is meaningless to one still asleep. This is the theme of two highly underrated films from the early 1990s: John Patrick Shanley's comedy *Joe Versus the Volcano*, and Lawrence and Meg Kasdan's drama, *Grand Canyon*. For some, these films are profound; for others, they're just entertaining diversions.

We humans are remarkable in our ability to tap into both universes at the same time and apply insights gained from one to the other. We're like alchemical vessels in which opposite elements interact to create something new: sovereignty over our own lives. As our awareness of both realms expands we begin to see ourselves and others objectively and can watch ourselves watching. We can be involved in an activity and hear what we're thinking while knowing that we're attending to our thoughts. We can see how we're behaving and recognize the impact our behavior has on others. We can know what we're feeling and decide whether to respond in a habitual way or create a new response.

The more conscious we become of our inner lives and outer behavior, the more creative we can be. The creativity consciousness confers is one of our most valuable gifts and greatest joys. We are all artists with a need to express our unique lights in totally original ways—to show the world something it hasn't seen before.

This gift isn't limited to outer things. Most of us will never study at expensive art schools or spend thousands of dollars on teachers and materials or starve in a musty garret for our art. But that doesn't mean we'll never create something of exquisite beauty and value. *As without, so within.* The most valuable thing we can do with our creativity is transform how we *live* into a work of art. We do this simply by *being who we are,* that is, behaving authentically—in complete accord with the uniqueness of our maturing souls. In this worthy effort the world is our school, intention and perseverance are our currency, and everything we need to learn is inside us. Like a blank canvas aching for the artist's brush, our true Self is a creative spark waiting for us to feed and tend it until it grows into an eternal flame.

Composed of the fully activated and consciously developed King and Queen and the masculine and feminine archetypes and energies they represent, the Self symbolizes the masculine ego's union with the feminine unconscious and the creative consciousness they release into the world. When the fog of our unknowing is dispelled we find inspiration everywhere: in art, in nature, in dreams, in the people we meet and the experiences we have. Above all, we find it in the processes of our own souls.

Thus do we embrace our sovereignty, the seventh gift of integrated wisdom.

Integrating the Outer and Inner Universes

- Have you experienced a crisis or received an intuition that stopped you in your tracks and made you ask yourself what your life is all about? If so, you've received an invitation to the inner dance. The important question is, did you accept or decline? If you declined, don't worry; it's not too late. As long as you can still think, reason, and read books like this one, you can begin the search for your true treasure.

- Start today by taking on a practice that will help you pay better attention to your inner life: reading, classes, meditation, dreamwork, body work, journaling, counseling, artistic expressions of every kind—whatever appeals most.

- Persist in your new practice for as long as feels necessary—at the very least until you receive a few valuable intuitions and insights—and don't hesitate to take on a different practice that calls powerfully to you. Since creating the sacred marriage is an ongoing process, persevering in a meaningful spiritual practice for the rest of your life will bring the greatest benefits.

- To cement an especially profound awareness in your consciousness, celebrate with an original ritual using meaningful symbols, objects, actions, music, poems, imaginative dialogues, food, etc. Use your imagination. Do it once or do it many times. Whatever feels right. Whenever something important happens that you don't want to forget, create a new ritual. Rituals, especially those you create for yourself, sacralize your most meaningful experiences.

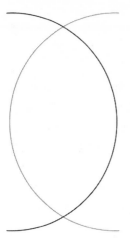

CHAPTER FORTY-ONE

Following Internal Guidance

WESTERN institutions place weighty emphasis on the physical world of measurable fact. It's often assumed that objective, historical, commonly agreed-upon truths are the only "real" truths. Our subjective truths—personal values and perceptions, ethics, ideologies, beliefs, passions, appreciations, intuitions, happiness, meaning, self-knowledge, and spiritual well-being—tend to be dismissed as irrelevant or inappropriate.

Here again we need to balance artificially polarized positions. The subjective reality of our inner universe, our personal *way* of being, is every bit as valid as the external, objective *facts* of our being. We can't manifest our unique authority until we learn to trust and honor it.

A young ego naturally begins its growth into consciousness with an outer-referential focus. Having no relationship with the Self, it must depend on others for guidance. It acquires its ideals, values, and virtues from external authority figures whom it idealizes as long as they satisfy, and abandons when they disappoint. If it is ambitious it might scramble for a leadership position without acquiring the self-knowledge, integrity, or moral maturity needed to be a truly beneficent leader. If it is spiritually oriented, it can get sucked into a questionable movement or follow a charismatic leader whose ethics and practices are unbalanced and self-serving.

The bias against subjectivity originates in the young ego's need to develop the masculine archetypes and earn society's rewards. We can see the preference for objectivity in the Scholar and his primary arena of influence, the educational system. But to quote Lyonpo Jigmi Y. Thinley,

Chairman of the Council of Ministers for the government of Bhutan,

> the academic community has not developed the tools we need
> to look at happiness, one of our primary human values. This has
> led to a paradoxical situation: the primary goal of development
> is happiness, but the subject of this very goal eludes our analysis
> because it has been regarded as subjective.[1]

Of society's institutions, the family and religion are most concerned about our subjective welfare. Yet they, too, can get sidetracked by the ego's focus on external authority and conformity. Too often, children are admonished to "Do as you're told. Mother and Father know best." Too often questioning seekers are advised to "have faith" or "put your trust in God" instead of being given the practical help they need to find spiritual meaning for themselves.

Fortunately, as our ego's consciousness expands, our masculine archetypes become stronger and healthier in many ways. We've already seen how an Epoch II Warrior initially channels its drive for power and success into highly visible achievements and how, with maturity, it broadens its sphere of influence to honor the feminine drive. Similarly, while an immature King might impose his personal authority on others, a maturing King seeks to create lawful order and moral virtue throughout society with clear thinking and hierarchical authority. Religion, business, education, the traditional family, and the branches of America's government—executive, legislative, and judicial—are all founded on the maturing King's values.

To the extent an institution cares about individuals and strives to honor their rights and freedoms and satisfy their differing needs, it demonstrates the growing respect for feminine archetypes that is characteristic of a maturing ego. The global movement toward democracy is a positive sign that humanity is evolving toward Epoch III. So is the increase in the number of female political leaders. This doesn't necessarily mean these women are listening to their internal guidance or acting from integrated wisdom, though. Many, in fact, are still influenced far more by masculine values and archetypal energies than feminine ones. But it does suggest that some of the old stereotypes and prejudices against women and the feminine are losing ground as our mainstream consciousness matures.

The good news is that with a willingness to change, commitment to inner work, and perseverance a maturing ego can grow more inner-referential. This is one characteristic of the Epoch III ego. It doesn't ignore outer realities or dismiss the guidance of others, but it also looks within. It weighs traditional methods against current realities, logical thought against caring feeling, and conventional morality against its own conscience and a maturing ethos based on understanding and compassion. In this way it creates original solutions that benefit everyone.

True wisdom and nobility cannot be conferred by the world. They are earned by a maturing ego that honors its own authority in combination with the authority of the integrated Self.

Integrating External and Internal Guidance

- The five institutions of society are family, business, government, education, and religion. In which domain do you rely on guidance from external authorities? In which do you act on your own authority? Which institution is currently most problematic for you? Why?

- Your five instincts are nurturance, activity, reflection, sex, and creativity. Which instincts do you tend to trust and express honestly and openly? Which feel less well developed and more inhibited or repressed? Which is currently most problematic? Why?

- Choose one of the problematic areas and create a strategy for healthy change.

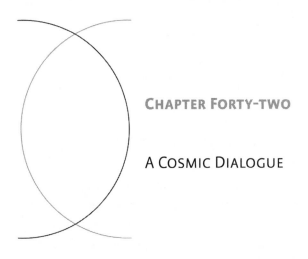

A Cosmic Dialogue

God is weeping. Another war is being waged on Earth and there is much suffering. So many of his children are hurting. So many are hurting others. He thinks of his myriad efforts to help them. He sees change, but it has been so slow. There is little hope and much despair.

Goddess enters the room. She sees his face, wraps her arms around him, and holds him, crooning gently, "There, there, darling. There, there."

After a while, his tears subside. "I love them so much," he says. "It feels as if my heart will break. I've done everything I can think of. Why don't they get it? Why do they keep doing this to themselves?"

Goddess composes her thoughts. After a moment she speaks. "I've wondered about this for a long time, and I think I know. We've never spoken about this because it's so painful for both of us, but I sense the time has come. I'm talking about our divorce. When was that? Around five thousand years ago? You banished me from our home, destroyed all my images, and forbade our children to ever mention my name again."

God looks at her sadly. "Yes, I remember too well," he says. "I was just coming into my strength and I was cruel to you. I was afraid of your power then. I wanted it all for myself. I was young and foolish and full of myself. I forgot how essential you are to our creation and wasn't thinking about the effect your absence would have on our children."

"Yes, that's exactly what I'm getting at. Our divorce wasn't just about us. It created huge separations in our children, too. The more you told them I was evil, the more they hated their women and the more the women hated themselves. So many stopped listening to me that for a while I thought my light would go out completely on Earth. But it hasn't. It's still there."

"Yes," God says. "And it's been growing brighter since we got back together, and they've started remembering you."

"We've got to find a way to heal that separation," Goddess says. "They need to know you've changed and want me back. They need to feel my love. They need names for me and images of me so they'll understand what they're feeling. This is already happening to some of them. But if there's to be any hope for their survival, more of their leaders will need to acknowledge me too."

"I agree," says God. "Maybe it's time for both of us to step up our activity. Why don't you see what you can do down there? I'll keep working from here."

Goddess returns to Earth and looks for those of her children whose hearts are ripe for opening. She knows their hearts intimately. She always has, because that has always been her primary home.

A soldier is hungry but too exhausted after a day in the field to get up and go to the food tent for dinner; just then a sister soldier brings dinner to her. Another is sitting on the ground with his rifle by his side writing a poem about fireflies when one lands on his hand and remains there pulsing with light.

A mother is agonizing over what to say to her young son about a terrorist attack that killed his older brother. She picks up an unread book sitting beside her bed and it opens to a page that has a beautiful dialogue between a parent and child about death.

An angry teenage boy is getting ready to join his friends on the streets for what promises to be a brutal gang war. As his hand reaches for the doorknob he hears a woman's voice shout, "Tim! Stop! Don't go out there." He freezes, confused because his mother is at work. Then he realizes the words came from the TV program he was watching. His name is Tim. He doesn't go out that night.

Each of these people feels touched by something vast and mysterious. Their hearts unfold to a strange new light that fills them with wonder and awe. They feel known and loved. Each feels a bit more worthy on this day, a bit less afraid to trust their own intuition.

God sees what Goddess is doing, and is very pleased. But he knows the separations are far from over. He's listening to the prayers of their leaders and answering them, but many don't hear, and many who hear don't really understand. Others understand but refuse to act on his message of sacred union and he knows why. They're still terrified of Goddess and still hungry for power, just as he was those many years ago. They still want to be King, and they want to reign alone.

God sinks his head in his hands. "What have I done?" he moans. "What have I done?"

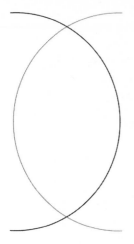

CHAPTER FORTY-THREE

The Divine Feminine as Personal Social Sovereign

THE MATURE Queen is our social, moral, and spiritual authority. She's the part of us that wants to mother society, culture, and the inner life. In the outer world, she is activated in social leaders who rule with benevolent feeling, moral virtue, and respect for individuality and diversity. Her values are the basis for democracy, the Bill of Rights, communes, kibbutzim, and all communities and organizations that promote equal rights, personal authority, and shared responsibility. We see evidence of her in activists who work in the trenches for social justice, in philanthropists who endow the arts and humanities, in community volunteers. Every form of social activism rooted in an understanding and caring heart originates in our Queen.

Other aspects of her influence aren't as easily observable, yet are of equal value. For instance, she is well-developed in people who trust their own opinions, take personal responsibility for their own behavior, treat others with kindness and compassion, and behave in thoughtful, ethical ways. The world may never notice or reward the maturity that prevents a person from acting on antisocial impulses—things like gossiping, lying, breaking promises, blaming, demanding special treatment, or lashing out in anger. Nevertheless, the self-awareness and self-restraint that are characteristic of the Queen's nobility have a positive influence on every situation.

These and other qualities of the Queen shape us into the very best kinds of leaders—the ones who follow their internal guidance and nurture the strengths of others, the ones who know what's truly important and really care. Three examples of social leaders with mature Queens are Abraham Lincoln, Mahatma Gandhi, and Mother Teresa.

An Epoch II ego can be completely unaware of the Queen. Or it might honor its growing awareness of her by becoming obsessively self-sacrificial until it burns out and self-destructs. But a person with a fully developed Queen knows his/her value and the value of every soul. Such people apply their empathy and integrity equally to the universe without and the universe within. Their assessments of situations are founded on carefully wrought internal value systems. They base their decisions on what's truly important in the big picture and the long run. They listen to their internal guidance and know when and how to act on it. They use their authority and power to alleviate the suffering of others, but won't sacrifice themselves unduly out of unconscious compulsions or a false sense of martyrdom.

After the ancient Queen of Heaven and Earth was banished by the Sky God religions, many of us believed what we were told—that she was a heretical, dangerous superstition fabricated by ignorant minds. Maybe we even thought she was an abomination, and that anyone who honored her would go straight to hell!

In fact, the opposite is true. Our disdain for the Divine Feminine has thwarted the healthy progress of civilizations and stymied the spiritual growth of individuals. As a physical force of nature and a psychological reality, she is essential to the movement of individuals, institutions, and societies into Epoch III. Each of us is her worthy child, connected to her other children by our common mother. Because of that we are fully entitled to have sovereignty over our own bodies and souls and to be treated with equality, love, kindness and care.

Who do you suppose has the most to lose if we all understood our true worth and heeded the internal guidance of our Queens? Think people who demand unquestioning obedience because they are in thrall to immature and obsessive Epoch II Kings, Warriors, Scholars, or Lovers. Think Hitler, Stalin, Saddam Hussein, Idi Amin. Think Pharaoh who wouldn't free the Jews. Think Tomas Torquemada who led the Spanish Inquisition. Think slave traders. Think men who dominate or abuse their wives or women who obsessively dominate and control their children.

Think the Roman empire that had absolute control over Jerusalem at the time of Jesus and to whom he was a dangerous subversive. Eminent Bible scholar Dominic Crossan and co-author Richard G. Watts tell us what the real issue was when Jesus entered Jerusalem and created a disturbance in the temple:

> His vision of open table and free healing clashed wildly with what he saw in the Temple . . . [which] was in the hands of high priests who . . . were hired and fired like servants by the Romans and Herodians, whose puppets they had become. Jesus' symbolic act of destruction. . . . was like going into a draft office during the Vietnam War and pouring blood over drawers of file cards, or like climbing a fence at a missile site and hammering on the nosecone of an ICBM. It was a symbolic negation of everything the institution stood for.[2]

Whatever else he might have been, Jesus was a religious revolutionary who had discovered and empowered the Queen's authority. We each have that same authority, the same right to speak out against domination and injustice, the same prerogative to act on our truths—not only in the family, education, business, and government, but in religious matters as well. Despite what we might have been told, we are not born bad and unworthy. As Christian mystic Meister Eckhart taught in the thirteenth century, God lives in every individual's soul. We are not separate from what is sacred; we are part of it and it is part of us.

In fact, Deity is our soul's partner! Here is how twelfth-century Sufi mystic Ibn Arabi expressed this truth:

> Man [humankind] alone reflects back to the Absolute all . . . of the Divine qualities; it is for this reason that man is the . . . receptacle and the mirror of the Divine qualities, the "other" to whom and through whom these qualities are revealed. The function, then, of an apparent "other" . . . is to make possible . . . self-knowledge.[3]

With each dynamic of the unconscious we bring to light we join forces with mystics from every religion who have said that humanity contains all the qualities of the Divine. They have expressed again and again that the ultimate, initially shocking, conclusion to draw from this is: "To know oneself is to know God."

Listen for example to the fourteenth-century Christian anchorite Mother Julian of Norwich:

"The purpose of the Incarnation . . . is not so much to scrub away an original sin as to heal the two sides to our nature."[4]

"Just as God is truly our Father, so also is God truly our Mother."[5]

"We are in God and God whom we do not see is in us. We are of God. That is what we are. I saw no difference between God and our Substance but as if it were all God."[6]

"We can never know God until we first know clearly our own soul."[7]

Julian's God was a loving Father and Mother, a mature King and Queen. And how was Julian to know God? By knowing *her own soul.* Why have mystics always believed this? Because they have found out for themselves that with every shadow quality they accept, God feels more like a friendly intimate and less like a dangerous judge. This is why the struggle to know who we are is a spiritual quest. This is why Jesus said that the Kingdom of God is at hand and within us.

Because it really is.

Because ultimately, *we* are the sovereigns of our own spirits and souls.

Empowerment to act on this truth is the seventh gift of integrated wisdom.

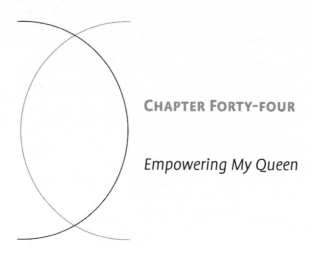

Chapter Forty-four

Empowering My Queen

AS A SENSITIVE and spiritually oriented young woman I looked to my religion for confirmation that I was okay. After decades of trying, I finally realized it didn't have the slightest idea how to help me come to terms with my authentic self. By the time of my Serpent Power dream, I'd been re-prioritizing my values for several years. Painfully aware of my dogged devotion to heroes and authorities from whom I'd expected so much but received so little, I could no longer go to church without getting a stomach ache. So I stopped going.

Today I realize that wasn't necessary. A stronger and wiser person could have carried on her inner work within the framework of a well-intentioned and supportive spiritual community. But at the time this wasn't an option for me. I wasn't giving up on God. I was just trying to wake up instead of numbing out. This was about claiming my own authority while I was still lucky enough to be alive. It was about submitting to no one else but God.

I redirected my focus from the outer world to the inner, and from the past and future to the present, hoping to accomplish two things. First, I needed a reprieve from the unrelenting burden of anxiety and guilt about never being good enough. Second, I craved a more intimate connection with what truly felt sacred to me—that which inspired, was personally meaningful, elicited awe and comfort, fueled my energy instead of draining it, and helped me become a more authentic and compassionate person. I was ready to become reacquainted with the Divine Mother from whom

I had been separated since early childhood. This time I wanted to know her consciously!

I found tools I needed in Jungian psychology. Bible study had shown me my spiritual goals, but memorization and willpower hadn't helped me reach them. What did help was various kinds of mental training that developed greater self-knowledge and helped me tame my dragons. Along with my writing and Jungian studies I regularly practiced dreamwork, meditation, and yoga. To this date, dreamwork and writing continue to be my primary spiritual practices. They never fail to heighten my awareness of my connection with the Sacred.

Exploring the unconscious is slow work, though—at least for me! I love it every bit as much as archaeologists must love dusting every grain of sand off a long-buried artifact, but it can take me a long time to figure out how the find relates to my everyday life. For example: Despite more than twenty years of inner work, only in the last few years have I understood that my most problematic dragons are related to a wounded sense of self-worth; and it was only in working on this book that I realized how my dream of the Lone Ranger foresaw this! (Yes, twenty years. That's some pretty serious unconsciousness, right?)

Giving names to these parts of my shadow helps me recognize them more readily. Accepting them without letting them shame me into submission and squelch the development of my authority makes my Queen more confident and courageous. I'd like to introduce three of them to you with the hope that my example will inspire and motivate you to conduct your own inner archaeology and release your own sovereignty.

May I have a drum roll please? Ladies and gentlemen, please give it up for Spiritual Bully, Orphan, and Heroine Addict. Ta daaaaa!

Spiritual Bully

Every positive quality has the potential to develop a negative shadow if it becomes obsessive. This is true of institutions and societies as well as individuals. The conscious aims of our cultural heroes and religions couldn't be more worthwhile. There's no question about the hope, help, and healing genuine spiritual heroes bring to countless lives. But we all know this isn't the whole story. We've also seen the shadow side of patriarchal religions—which can be authoritarian, imperialistic, elitist, misogynistic, homophobic, racist, dogmatic, judgmental, perfectionistic, self-righteous, superior, and devoid of genuine compassion. Just like us.

Of course, these are extreme examples. Patriarchy's Spiritual Bully is far more subtle in some of us. Most growing, socially conscious egos don't like him, so we try to hide him from public view. But sometimes he escapes: We might act kind and loving but secretly feel superior to people who aren't as "spiritual" as we are. We may think we're being very wise, tolerant, and understanding toward another's beliefs and ideals, but our attitudes and body language show that we equate spirituality with correct belief and rigid morality. We may not openly criticize or speak ill of others, but sometimes unconsciously dismiss or patronize people who don't quite live up to our "higher" standards.

I would like very much to believe the Spiritual Bully isn't a strong factor in how I relate in the world. But he keeps showing up in my dreams, so he obviously sneaks out in ways of which I'm totally unaware. Naturally, this knowledge is disturbing, which is why I'm working so hard to understand him. And in my inner life? The truth is he's a tyrant: a scrupulous perfectionist with an earnest desire to be helpful and a compulsive need to criticize me for not living up to his standards. With balance and moderation, self-criticism can build character; but when it's continuous and intense it can really bring you down and thwart your efforts to become more confident.

My sense is that many people wrestle with a Spiritual Bully. We need to get a handle on this guy because I believe he's the main culprit in our cultural repression of the Queen. To help you see yours, I'd like to share a brief explanation of how mine came to have such a powerful influence over me.

My father was a really good guy and my personal hero. For me, his cultural counterpart was the Lone Ranger. Daddy loved horses and introduced me to them; Silver was the epitome of horse magnificence. Daddy was a policeman devoted to supporting the laws of the land, keeping the rules, and saving others; this was the Lone Ranger's passion as well. Daddy was raised in a religious environment of scrupulous morality and strong idealism. If the Lone Ranger was religious we never knew it, but there's no doubt about the ferocity of his ideals: If the laws of the land couldn't tame the bad guys, then he'd simply do it all a-*Lone*! (Well, with a little help from Silver and Tonto.)

Finally, like the Lone Ranger, my father wore a mask. Not a physical one, but a psychological one based on society's conventions and morality. Behind it there existed not a hero, but a real, flawed mortal man. He never gave any evidence of it, but I now suspect that behind that mask he struggled mightily with his own Spiritual Bully—who finally won the battle when Daddy died of his third heart attack three months after divorcing Mama and immediately remarrying. Moral guilt can be a very dangerous adversary; especially for a man sworn to uphold the law.

At ten I couldn't see his mask, but something in me knew it was there. If Daddy was a hero, why wasn't he home to guide and protect *me*? Why away for such long periods of time? Was he roaming the countryside like the Lone Ranger and Tonto (if they had wives and children, we never knew that either) righting wrongs and saving victims? Something in my young heart felt the injustice of this but didn't want to see it. That would mean admitting my hero was flawed: Maybe he didn't care as much about me as I believed.

Is that why the Lone Ranger shot me? To show how I was beginning to feel about myself in relation to my Father, and to the masculine values that ruled my world? That my male heroes saw me as an insignificant and expendable little girl? Was he also demonstrating that idealizing him would be toxic to me? Both interpretations resonate deeply. In my dream the Lone Ranger embodied the Spiritual Bully: outwardly an admirable, well-intentioned hero but inwardly a stern and unrelenting judge. He stood for a ruthlessly strong conscience and the intense moral guilt that plagued my father . . . and that I was inheriting from him.

I didn't understand this then. I didn't understand it after Daddy died, either, when my heroic ideals and sense of vulnerability only intensified. My daddy had died and I could, too. As I saw it (mostly unconsciously, of course), my hopes for survival lay in pleasing outer authorities and becoming more scrupulous about adopting their values so they wouldn't shoot me. Thus was born my very own Spiritual Bully, whose job was to push me to ever greater heights while continually pointing out how far short I fell from his ideals.

I'd known a bit about him in me for a while, when working on a series of dreams helped me see him clearly. In these dreams he deliberately pestered me when I was trying to teach, criticized my work, intruded on my privacy, dumped his garbage on my property, assaulted a helpful Asian woman, stalked and threatened me in a darkened classroom, judged me for being wimpy, harassed me for sex, withdrew his approval when I inconvenienced him, possessively reprimanded me for being overly friendly to a stranger, and rudely interrogated me.

Despite all this unpleasant stuff, I sense that his power over me, considerably weakened after several years of dreamwork, is nearing an end. Why? Well, for one thing, in a particularly delightful dream in the same series he played the role of a traditional macho cowboy sheriff/hero who was killed by an outlaw! I love it! Daddy was a deputy sheriff, and the Texas Rangers—the Lone Ranger's outfit—have the same powers as sheriffs. I think the macho sheriff represented the negative aspects of my Epoch II hero worship and loyalty to patriarchy. I think the outlaw symbolized a part of me that had grown strong enough to overcome them, even though this meant breaking the laws (the killer was working *out*side the *law*) of my overly strict conscience!

Have I conquered this issue, fully owned my own sovereignty, tamed this bully for all time? Not by a long shot. He still tries to undermine my confidence and make me feel bad about everything imaginable, but I'm getting better at hearing his voice in the self-critical thoughts that run through my head like rodents on a never-ending loop. When I do, I imagine I'm talking to him and say something like: "Okay. I know you think you have to criticize me to perfect me. But you're too strict and I'm only human, and God knows I'm doing my best! So why don't you just take a rest and give me a break?" Usually, he does. For a while.

Orphan

Spiritual Bully has had power over me for so long because of an equally potent shadow character that is almost his exact opposite: the Orphan. She is my personal version of what spiritual bullies do to little princesses who grow up without Kingly fathers to keep them safe or Queenly mothers who are strong, positive models of feminine ego strength and confidence.

Was my Orphan also prefigured in my Lone Ranger dream? Of course. If being shot by my hero was my first encounter with Spiritual Bully, being his victim was my first experience of orphanhood. What else is an orphan but a vulnerable child who has lost the protection of her parents? Why was I all alone (not only in my dream, but also most of the time in waking life as well)? Where was my mother? What did the Lone Ranger represent if not the shadow of a culture that devalues and sometimes preys upon the feminine?

Like my mother I found it difficult to see the worth of things that are small, tender, delicate, unformed, passive, soft, vulnerable, receptive, sensitive, emotional, or feminine. I felt deeply uncomfortable when I sensed these tendencies in myself. I feared that if let in they would most certainly make me a victim. So I overcompensated by trying to develop their opposites.

I couldn't respect or feel compassion for my Orphan. So she hid in my unconscious, where I couldn't see her. There, covered in darkness, all the pathetic, unworthy, "childish" emotions a good little soldier represses began to coalesce and grow into a powerful orphan complex. Mine came to include fear of my unworthiness, sadness, hopelessness, depression, neediness, anxiety, vulnerability, self-pity, and insecurity. I was pretty good, though, at creating a social mask (persona) of confidence and poise. So I don't think many people suspected I harbored feelings like this, not even my mother. It actually took several years of inner work before I could even see them myself.

My Spiritual Bully had the sanction of mainstream society and the authority of traditional religion. Appearing to conform to his standards brought my Orphan hope, reassurance, relief from anxiety, and a sense of security. Way up in the conscious realms of my psyche (think head), I was unaware of my Orphan. But I was grateful for the release of pressure in my gut when she felt safe, and I happily agreed with the bully when he said I was not worthy. Like the Lone Ranger, he was my hero, and I thought his criticisms of me were valid and in my best interest. I was wrong.

For a long time my Orphan appeared in dreams as sad, needy, neglected little girls who were always alone and wanted my attention. Once she was a tattered ragamuffin who kept blocking my way; another time, a lonely, precocious little girl who recited poetry to impress me. The obvious neediness of these children made me uncomfortable.

As far as my waking ego was concerned, I was strong and independent. There was no way I was like them, so I generally ignored them. In the natural correspondence between outer and inner, my dream ego tried to ignore them as well. But they kept showing up in dream after dream, and I gradually got the message.

As I began trying to help them in my dreams, they began to evolve. In one dream my Orphan appeared as a dark little Asian girl whom I had agreed to adopt. Later on she was a happy little girl who proudly introduced me to her mother, a detail which suggested she wasn't an orphan anymore.

By the way, in an extraordinary synchronicity, the day after I had the dream of the little Asian girl I was offered the opportunity to unofficially "adopt" a girl from Nepal. As her sponsor I would make it possible for her to leave her remote village in the Himalayas and attend a boarding school in Kathmandu where she would receive health care and an excellent education. I was thrilled to have this opportunity to honor my Orphan in a very real way in waking life, and happily took the responsibility. Sonam and I communicate regularly. We have met and enjoy each other's company enormously, and at this writing she has successfully completed a post-high school course that qualifies her for an excellent job.

Now I have a similar relationship with my inner princess who rarely appears as an Orphan anymore. She did return ten days after my mother died as a sad and lonely girl who was desperate for my attention. But when I pulled her to me and held her in a warm embrace, she grew older and happier and then was suddenly gone. This dream reminded me to honor my sad feelings. I took that advice and haven't dreamed of my Orphan since.

Heroine Addict

The year I discovered Spiritual Bully I also met my Heroine Addict. She is another inevitable outcome of the powerful repressive forces dramatized in my Lone Ranger dream. At age ten I sensed I was vulnerable to male aggression and sexual invasion. I was also pretty sure I'd never get to be a hero myself. This was the early 1950s when girls still had little hope of becoming sheriffs, lawyers, doctors, or presidents. A year later the trauma of my father's death created wounds so deep that I'm still working to heal them.

So how was I to gain safety and prove my worth? Paying close attention to how people in authority reacted to me, doing my best to meet their expectations, being very careful not to offend, and excelling in school and the roles allowed to me seemed like a plan. Again, most of this "reasoning" went on very deep in my unconscious. My ego wasn't aware of it.

By the time I left adolescence behind I felt strong, full of myself, and occasionally even a little rebellious. As a young adult I devoted most of my energy to becoming a heroine: the perfect wife, the perfect teacher, the perfect mother, the perfect homemaker, the perfect community volunteer, the perfect daughter of God, and later on, the perfect television producer, graduate student, and college professor.

Now I know I truly was addicted to being heroic instead of just being myself. By the time I finally began a serious program of inner work, my heroine's attitudes and motivations were so integral to my personality, and her behaviors so habitual in every aspect of my life, that I was no more aware of her than of the beating of my wounded heart. But she was as real as my heart, and by 2005 I had accumulated enough data from my dreams to prepare the way for her dramatic debut.

After a few dreams featuring women whose immoderate behavior embarrassed my dream ego, I had an important one that prefigured the

Big Reveal! In this dream she appeared as someone I know in waking life. Like me, she's a hardworking and demanding perfectionist and occasionally can be a bit harsh and insensitive. (*Okay! Okay! I get it.*) But she also can be playful and laugh at herself. In the dream I was stressing over being unprepared for a play in which we both were to perform that afternoon. Meanwhile, she was sitting on a silly, life-sized metal horse, intensely struggling to make her noble steed gallop around a large room.

My dream ego's anxiety about the play underscored similar feelings I'd been having in waking life about an upcoming presentation. But what in the world did the woman represent? Now I think this dream was a clever parody of masculine heroic activity (my heroes always ride horses) in which she was playing a sort of female Don Quixote to get my attention. She was working like crazy to get that silly thing to gallop around the room. Riding a flesh-and-blood horse requires a partnership between rider and animal, both of whom contribute to the experience. But this woman was getting no help at all from the instinctual world. It was all about her steel will and determination. Ouch! Sound familiar?

The subtle allusion to heroic behavior in that dream was a hint, but I still didn't see the big picture. Then came the dream that cracked the code. In it I was chatting with someone at a party when a beautiful, flamboyant woman walked into the room and announced that she was a reformed *heroin* addict. Apparently expecting rejection, perhaps even inviting it, she seemed touched that I didn't visibly recoil at her revelation. She walked across the room to talk to me. Her need to talk about herself was embarrassing and her intensity made me uncomfortable, but I wanted to be understanding and didn't want to hurt her by turning away. Instead of doing what I really wanted to—which was go talk to a handsome artist whose sister had just said he wanted to spend time with me—I stayed to talk to her.

It took weeks of living with the strange woman before I got Dream Mother's joke about her. Why was she a heroin addict? I've never tried heroin and the only things I've been addicted to are cigarettes, writing, goodness, popcorn, and perfection!

Then I got it. Goodness. Perfection. *Heroin* was a very clever pun, a homophone for *heroine!* She was addicted to being heroic—not real, not honest, not emotionally authentic, and definitely not vulnerable—but *heroic!* What could more aptly portray the toxic consequences of an obsessive identification with masculine values? I wonder if that was Joan of Arc's drug of choice as well.

Many Epoch II egos, especially religious ones, believe the way to enlightenment or salvation lies in perfection. Many of us are terrorized by spiritual bullies who insist that only perfection makes us worthy. Perfection may be a realistic goal in a musical performance or Olympic competition, but not in human nature. When it comes to the psyche, imperfection isn't bad. It's the human condition.

Heroic psycho-spiritual perfection is a masculine ideal, perpetuated by a masculine theology, based on masculine reasoning and a masculine God-image. The feminine emphasis is on completion, which jibes with the theory of evolution. Humans, like everything else in Nature, are still evolving as a species—not only physically, but also psychologically and spiritually.

We are not born in sin, as some of our ancestors thought; we're just born incomplete.[8] We're not meant to aspire to somebody else's notion of perfection, but to grow into our own completion. We are to evolve as Nature wants us to evolve—that is, into greater integration and expanding consciousness. We are not to resist change because we have only one standard of perfection and everything else falls short. Yet, despite the evidence of Nature and our own experience, we cling to the ideal of perfection. Why?

Most of us know orthodox Christianity's take on it. The Sky God created a perfect world but the Earth woman Eve spoiled it by wanting to become morally conscious. As a result of her disobedience we are born in sin. This belief was so deeply entrenched in the minds of many early Church fathers that they imposed it on the teachings of Jesus who supposedly said, "Be ye therefore perfect, even as your Father which is in heaven is perfect."[9]

As Neil Douglas-Klotz says in *The Hidden Gospel,* the meaning of the Aramaic word that later on was translated into perfect is not "flawless and spotlessly pure," but actually "completed" or "whole!" The true meaning of that admonition is that we connect with Sacred Otherness by becoming complete human beings. Why? Because as long as we remain incomplete, the mysterious God/Nature energy of life remains incomplete. The Divine Knowing, Growing, Parenting force of the cosmos completes itself in *us*![10]

My deep feminine understands this, but sometimes my ego still struggles with it. This is why the Heroine Addict had such a hold on me for so long. But luckily Dream Mother tells me the truth about myself and my ego is learning to listen and trust.

Am I finished with my inner work? Not by a long shot. There are still way too many missing spaces in my puzzle. Most likely I'll never be completely free of my Spiritual Bully, Orphan, or Heroine Addict. But I can forgive myself for not being perfect. I've discovered the sterility of that Kingly goal when it's not partnered with my life-giving Queen. And I'm getting better at empowering her. The more I do that, the more I believe I really may be the lovable, worthy, and sovereign spiritual being she says I am.

No matter what the Lone Ranger thinks.

Notes

1. Lyonpo Jigmi Y. Thinley, "Values and Development: Gross National Happiness," keynote speech delivered at the Millennium Meeting for Asia and the Pacific, October 30–November 1, 1998, Seoul, Republic of Korea.

2. John Dominic Crossan and Richard G. Watts, *Who Is Jesus?* (Louisville, KY: Westminster John Knox Press, 1996), 102.

3. Reza Shah-Kazemi, "The Metaphysics of Interfaith Dialogue," in *Paths to the Heart: Sufism and the Christian East*, James S. Cutsinger, ed. (Bloomington, Indiana: World Wisdom, Inc., 2002), 153.

4. Brendan Doyle, *Meditations with Julian of Norwich* (Santa Fe, New Mexico: Bear & Company, 1983), 12.

5. Ibid., 89–90.

6. Ibid., 98.

7. Ibid.

8. I am indebted to retired Episcopal Bishop John Selby Spong for this insight which I first heard at his HIARPT (Highlands Institute of American Religious and Philosophical Thought) lectures in Highlands, NC, August, 2005. For more on this theme, see his book, *A New Christianity for a New World* (San Francisco: HarperSanFrancisco, 2001).

9. *Holy Bible*, King James version, Matthew: 5:48.

10. Neil Douglas-Klotz, *The Hidden Gospel: Decoding the Spiritual Message of the Aramaic Jesus.* (Wheaton, IL: Quest Books, 1999), 129–30.

The Eighth Gift
Meaning

Life becomes infinitely more meaningful when the focus of our existence changes from separating to connecting. The more opposites we unite, the more conscious we become. The wiser we grow, the more sacred significance we see . . . and the more deeply we experience our lives.

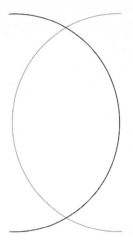

CHAPTER FORTY-FIVE

The Brain's Role in Epoch II Thinking

IN HIS BOOK *The Alphabet Versus the Goddess,* vascular surgeon Leonard Shlain presents a startling new theory about the two hemispheres of the human brain. He says that since the invention of writing and the alphabet, the West has progressively moved into a left-hemisphere mode of thinking, and that the dominance of this side of the brain has given rise to the dominator mode of social governance which causes so much of the world's suffering.

As most of us know by now, the left brain specializes in thinking that is analytic, discriminatory, linear, and abstract. It's concerned with doing and controls the vital act of willing. But it is poor at discerning holistic patterns and intolerant of right-brain thinking and values.

Shlain calls the right brain the portal to the world of the invisible. Its principal attributes concern being, images, holism, and music. The right brain can conjugate images, and is better than the left in making judgments as to balance, harmony, and the composition of holistic patterns. Metaphor is the right brain's unique contribution to the left brain's language capability. Shlain also notes that there is compelling evidence that certain aspects of dreaming occur primarily in the right brain.

Comparing the brain's hemispheric specializations with traditional ideas about gender, Shlain says that the left hemisphere aligns with what we think of as the masculine principle, and the right, with the feminine. He believes that the intolerance of the left brain for the right explains the misogynistic messages in religions that rely heavily on the written word. Dr. Shlain writes, "There is something inherently anti-female in the written word. Men obsessed with the written word tend to be sexist."[1] Citing numerous examples, he points out that throughout history rising literacy has been associated until very recently with misogyny. Inversely, whenever the influence of the written word has declined, there have been dramatic improvements in the fortunes of women.

He further says that conceiving of a deity who had no concrete image prepared the way for the kind of abstract thinking that inevitably led to a dualistic philosophy that cleaved the older right brain's integrated sense of wholeness—which resulted in humans creating a distinction between *me-in-here* and *world-out-there*.[2] This detached subject/object split enhanced the skills of who needed to separate themselves from the hunted, and strengthened their ability to stay motionless while focusing on a single task.

These developments came at the expense of attributes like holistic awareness and emotional depth. As Shlain says, "The dispassion inherent in dualism, a viewpoint indispensable for killing, is the opposite of a mother's binding love for her child."[3]

The patriarchs knew they were flawed. They knew something beautiful and noble was missing from their lives. They yearned for it with all their hearts, and they did the best they could to connect with it. But ruled by the drive for self-preservation and the left hemispheres of their brains, they were in an Epoch II mode: They saw themselves as separate, vulnerable creatures living in a hostile universe. This perspective inevitably leads to misdirection and tragedy.

As spiritual guide Eknath Easwaran has written,

> Separate creatures are cut off from everything that gives life meaning: a sense of unity, a purpose for living that is larger than ourselves, and the lasting, loving relationships we must have to be human and whole.
>
> Every human being hungers for these things, yet these are inner needs which can never be filled by the material goods that industrial civilization is made to offer.[4]

In today's world the Epoch II ego is still disconnected from the natural gifts of the right hemisphere of the brain. Unaware that its imaginative, mythical way of seeing is the language of our souls, our egos hunt prey that can't nourish them.

Logos and Mythos (or Sense and Nonsense!)

Plato was the first great thinker in Western history to define the modes of thinking that are the specialties of the two hemispheres of the brain. He called them *logos* and *mimesis*. Following the lead of psychologist Gisela Labouvie-Vief, I will call the latter *mythos*. The left hemisphere of the brain specializes in logos; the right, in mythos.

Mythos thinking is symbolic, metaphoric, instinctive, imaginative, visual, intuitive, and emotional. Receptive to chaos, mystery, newness, and change, mythos is a compass that points us to the eternal and the universal. Mythos is the mother of original thinking, self-discovery, spiritual growth, and personal meaning. It is the basis for all forms of creative expression and every form of inner work that leads to self-knowledge.

Although Plato loved mimesis/mythos and was himself very imaginative, inner-directed, and spiritually oriented, he considered reason a more advanced and mature form of knowing. He preferred logos to mythos for two reasons: because of mythos's appeal to the emotions—which can be dangerous and uncontrollable when they are not made conscious—and because he thought logos was fostered by written language, which he considered an advancement and refinement over oral language.

Plato passed this bias on to Aristotle, Aristotle passed it on to us. From the enormous influence of these men on Western philosophical thought, today virtually everyone but artists and mystics vastly underrates the contributions and potential of *one half* of our brains: in essence, the "feminine" half! I find it bizarre that we still haven't overcome this prejudice against qualities of our own brains!

Following Plato's example, the writer of the Christian Gospel of John proposed that logos is cosmic reason and the self-revealing thought and will of God. The cause-and-effect relationship between the left brain's masculine hunter/warrior mentality, logic, reason, the written word, dualistic thinking, the dominator mode of governance, and the repression of women and minorities might tempt some to blame the masculine God and his logos for the world's problems! But the dilemma doesn't originate with God and his logos. If Shlain is right, the root problem is the intolerance the left hemisphere of our brains has for right-brained otherness!

If logos is the language of God's masculine side, mythos is the language of God's feminine side. But mythos is of no practical use to a warrior who needs to be emotionless, task-oriented, focused, and factually precise. To a warrior, mythos is pointless, impractical nonsense.

Associated with all that's mysterious, unconscious, felt, organic, and personally compelling, mythos voices truths of the body, heart, spirit, psyche, and soul. Using mythos to explore enigmas of the outer and inner universes brings enormous psychological and spiritual advances, because it is inherently integrating and self-validating. Mythos helps us unveil the unconscious dimensions of ourselves and the feminine side of God.

But neither the unconscious self nor a feminine God-image is of any help to a hunter, either. For him, they are merely *other*: the enemy. Prey.

As the *word* is the basic unit of logos, so the image, or *symbol*, is the basic unit of mythos. The ego artificially creates words and uses them to try to *understand* life's mysteries; the Self naturally and spontaneously creates symbols and images that bring the ego into a *meaningful relationship* with the mysteries.

Author and former nun Karen Armstrong says, "The only way we can conceive of God, who remains imperceptible to the senses and to logical proof, is by means of symbols, which it is the chief function of the imaginative mind to interpret."[5] And Jungian analyst Connie Zweig writes, "In effect, the life of the imagination *is* the spiritual life."[6]

Meaningful symbols are keys to hidden chambers of the unconscious. When the ego uses these keys it both discovers and creates spiritual meaning.

But of what use is a symbol to a hunter? Personal meaning doesn't result in the kill. Imagining a web of life and being able to see how our prey fits into it doesn't put food on the table. What makes a hunter or warrior successful is knowing where the prey is and what its characteristics are, and having the focus and discipline to get the job done. Logic is what makes sense to a warrior, and an Epoch II ego that is dominated by the Warrior archetype often has a profound distrust of mythos.

Mythical narratives address questions about our relationship to the gods and the ultimate value of life. The symbols of our myths awaken our dormant spirit, their rituals ease our pain and suffering. These new symbols become precious to us. They inspire us, bring new hope and vitality, and make us feel that our lives have meaning.

Do you think our earliest ancestors were looking for inspiration or meaning? Or did they just want to live? Sort of like dinosaurs, sharks, or tigers. They hunted for prey and killed and ate it and probably didn't worry one bit about if it meant anything. But we're not like that anymore. We've been changing since our ancestors squirmed out of the salty womb-soup of the maternal matrix. Since Eve ate of the tree of the Knowledge of Good and Evil.

Adam and Eve and the snake and tree symbolize a profound spiritual truth. Their myth says that in our unconscious Epoch I paradise, being fully enveloped by the God of our tribes greatly improves our chance of survival. Yet, our egos (Adam) are capable of questioning the rules and growing into greater consciousness of good and evil . . . *if we are willing to be led by the feminine (Eve) sides of our psyches and brains which are receptive to the ever-evolving energies of life (snake).*

Humanity no longer finds complete fulfillment in a survival mentality. Now we bring moral sensibility to the table. We have questions about who we are and why we're here. We want our lives to have purpose. We're not hunting for prey to devour anymore. We're in search of our souls. To find them we need to engage both sides of our brains. Doing so brings us integrated wisdom's eighth gift of meaning.

Integrating Logos and Mythos

- You know the facts of your life, but if you were to write a myth or fairy tale based on your life what would it look like? Describe the theme. The characters. The time and place, or setting. Select three or four significant events to make up the plot. Include some symbols—animals, colors, helpful people, magical objects—to bring more meaning to the plot and events. Create the best possible ending.

- Now write your story.

- Share it with someone you trust and ask for their honest reaction.

- What did you learn about yourself?

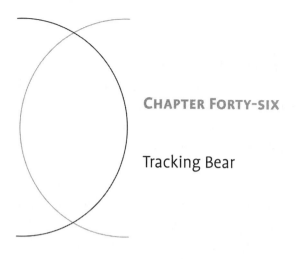

CHAPTER FORTY-SIX

Tracking Bear

NINE YEARS after my *kundalini* awakening, two dear friends introduced me to the work of Carl Jung and I was immediately hooked. From then on Jungian studies and practices like dreamwork and active imagination absorbed most of my free time. No other spiritual practices had brought so much joy, vitality, or spiritual meaning. As I became more responsive to my interiority I made associations between outer and inner, between the facts of my waking life and the symbolic life of my dreams, seeking insights and connections wherever I could find them. I was on the hunt for meaning.

One symbol, the bear, was particularly compelling. When I perceived the world solely through logos I saw no personal significance in bears, but my mythos side was beginning to understand the spiritual implications of profound feeling. Jungian analyst Janet Dallett writes, "The religious part of the psyche is at work whenever you pay attention to something that is numinous to you, whether or not other people feel it is important."[7]

For reasons I didn't understand, I was deeply drawn to bears. Bears have ancient associations with religion. At first I tended to associate them with my old masculine God-image, but gradually I was drawn to their maternal aspects. Now I think my fascination with the mother bear signaled my readiness for a more mature God-image. I read more about bears, surrounded myself with images of them, sought out flesh and blood examples in my waking life, and studied ones that visited my dreams. Over time, I came to understand that bears express archetypal themes about the human journey.[8]

One theme is *introspection*. The bear emerged at a time when I was attending weekly classes on Jungian psychology, studying my dreams, and recording my most meaningful insights. Just as bears spend long periods of time in inward-focused hibernation each year, so was I thoroughly immersed in my inner world. And it was the most exciting place I had ever visited!

Another theme is *endings and beginnings* and the times of *transition* between. In their simple willingness to shake off their unconscious sleeps, abandon the dark caves of their births and hibernations, and make their solitary ways into the forest, bears demonstrate that transitions from known to unknown are not to be feared as obstacles or punishments, but embraced as thresholds to enriched living. Metaphorically, I felt that I, too, had been abandoned by the mother bear to make my solitary way down the tree and into the forest. Painful as it was, it was also the most spiritually significant and transforming experience of my life. I learned to trust that every death makes way for a new birth, and times of transition are not punishments to be stoically endured but opportunities to mine for meaning.

As large animals that are so human-like and yet so strangely *other*, bears evoke reverence for the *instinctual life* of the body and soul. Bears remind us that we ourselves are animals.

As one who had spent most of her life in her head, I don't have words to describe how meaningful my growing awareness of my body and instinctual self has been. How could I have ignored this extraordinary container of my soul for so long? How could I not have understood what a miracle the life in my body is?

My interest in symbols led to the study of myths. Through the writings of Joseph Campbell and several Jungian analysts I learned that religions have always used myths and symbols to express the soul's truths. I discovered the Gnostic Gospels and learned they were written by early Christians trying to express fundamental religious ideas through new myths that were more compatible with the evolving psyche. These documents were eventually characterized as heretical by Orthodox Christian Literalists.

To the religious leaders who couldn't see through the veil of left-brained literalism to the kingdom within, Gnostics were dangerous others who had to be destroyed. There are still people today who think that using metaphors and symbolic language to describe the Absolute is somehow heretical—yet they do it every time they wear a cross, light a menorah, or wear white to Friday prayers and listen to readings from a Qur'an bound in green. This is no more heretical than dreaming or using symbols and metaphors to express the underlying meaning of a story or work of art!

As Timothy Freke and Peter Gandy note in their bold book, *Jesus and the Lost Goddess,*

> From our exploration of the secret teachings of the original Christians it is clear that Christianity was not always the safe, pre-packaged, off-the-shelf religion it has become. The Christian Way was once travelled by philosophical adventurers who proclaimed life to be an opportunity for self-discovery, for spiritual creativity, for living our own myths. Christianity may have ended up a power-crazed Literalist religion spreading guilt and fear, but it began as a movement of mystical enthusiasts with a beautiful vision of the meaning and mystery of life.[9]

My inner work was giving me a glimpse of this vision and I couldn't get enough of it. I was a serious seeker and after thirty years, approaching my spiritual needs with only my left brain was no longer enough for me. I needed to engage my right brain, too.

Words were not enough. I needed images that connected me to my feelings.

Logic was not enough. I needed imagination and myth to show me the meaningful relationships between my outer and inner realities, between myself and God.

Knowledge of other people's theories was not enough. I needed what motivated, inspired, and filled me with awe.

Beliefs were not enough. I needed a heartfelt connection to the Mystery that permeates and surrounds me.

The symbols of my religion were not enough. I needed the symbols from my dreams that depicted my soul's dramas and charged my waking life experiences with special significance.

I needed self-knowledge.

I needed personal meaning.

I needed to track Bear.

Integrating Fact and Symbol

- List the colors you surround yourself with. List the animals you are drawn to. List the objects you collect. List the activities you find most interesting and fulfilling. List some symbols from your dreams.

- Consult a dictionary of traditional symbols to research the symbolic meaning of as many of these things as you can.

- Look for connections between the meanings of your symbols and the facts of your life, both outer and inner.

- Record your insights so you won't forget them.

- Pay attention to how and when your symbols appear.

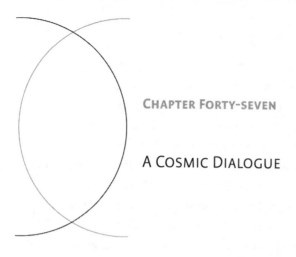

CHAPTER FORTY-SEVEN

A COSMIC DIALOGUE

It's holiday season in many parts of the globe. God and Goddess are sitting on their lawn thrones, observing the many rituals their children on Earth have created to celebrate their Mystery.

There are preparations: lists drawn up, duties assigned, purchases made, rehearsals attended. There are cleansings, confessions, sacrifices, fastings, prayers, meditations, and retreats. Spaces are beautified with lush plants and sanctified with symbolic objects. Bodies are decorated with specific clothes, jewelry, head-coverings, or artful adornments. Some prepare their souls by secluding themselves, others in activities with family and community.

There are celebrations: pageants that commemorate holy events; processions with sacred objects; concerts and recitals of music, song, and dance; parties with friends; meals with special foods prepared and shared in ritualistic ways; the giving of gifts.

There are sacraments: rites of separation, reconciliation, contrition, transition, union, reunion, birth, death, restoration, and renewal. There are ceremonies with openings, statements of intention, prayers, offerings, chants, songs, confessions, movements, teachings, vows, readings, blessings, pronouncements, and closings.

There are altars, flowers, candles, plants, banners, art, holy objects, sacred symbols, relics, special vessels and utensils, ritual activities using water, earth, air, and fire. There is food, music, color, texture, scent, darkness and light. And in the hearts of some participants, there are quickenings of sacred meaning.

God can see that Goddess has something on her mind. "You aren't enjoying this as much as I am, are you?" he asks. "What's the matter?"

"Well, the reverence and beauty and good intentions are very heart-warming. I adore our children when they're like this. They're trying *so* hard. But for some of them, none of this is making any difference."

She gestures to several spots on Earth. "Look at that place of worship over there. And those over there. And those. I see some hearts glowing with promising light, but do you see how many are almost completely smothered in darkness? I'm hurting for them, the ones for whom the traditional rituals are just duty, habit, entertaining diversions, or ways of maintaining social relationships. They aren't *experiencing* Us. The rituals may bring comforting memories and warm nostalgic feelings, but beyond that they have no *meaning*. And if there's no meaning, there's no transformative power."

God nods. "You're right. I was so captivated by the outer observances that I wasn't noticing their hearts. That's always been your specialty."

Goddess continues. "It's just so sad to see how they're so held by the past and so worried about the future that they're numb to the present. They don't even see their fear, their anxiety, their lack of joy and passion, their hopelessness. They come to these events wanting to feel some spark of inspiration or hope, and so many of them leave with disappointment and guilt.

"Look at them," she continues. "So many are just sitting there, repeating words that mean nothing to them. Smiling at people they don't even like. Worrying about whether they're wearing the right clothes or saying the right thing. They're actors. Puppets. Why aren't they paying attention to what really feels sacred to them?

"That one over there should be out hiking. The only meaningful connection she ever felt to Us was on a mountaintop. And him? He should be writing the original music that's in his head right now. It's the only thing that inspires and excites him, yet he's too busy doing things he hates to do the one thing he loves.

"And that couple. She's a brilliant teacher; he's a gifted therapist. They're mature spirit persons with so much to offer. They're dying to be of service, but there are no opportunities for them in their place of worship.

"Why don't they create some new rituals with symbols and myths that speak personally to them and invite some friends with similar interests to participate? Don't they get it that they don't have to betray you to honor me? Most of them have no problem with loving both of their physical parents. Don't they know they can love us both at the same time too? Don't they know they honor us both by honoring the life in their bodies, their creativity, the true gifts of their souls that we gave them at birth? Their passions? Their genuine spiritual needs? Don't they understand that they worship us every time they love and nurture new life in themselves and each other?"

Goddess begins to cry. "My poor, poor children. Some of them try so hard to please you by keeping up appearances. But how many of them will leave their bodies without ever appreciating the life in them? Without enjoying the beauty and diversity of that exquisite planet? Without knowing themselves? Without discovering their passions? Without creating anything original or fulfilling their purposes or fully living their unique lives? It's such a tragic waste!"

Sadly, tenderly, God holds Goddess as she weeps for her lost children, the Orphans who will never know the love of their Divine Mother.

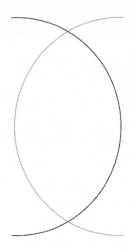

CHAPTER FORTY-EIGHT

The Divine Feminine as Meaning

THE SCHOLAR and Wisewoman archetypes have the same goal—release from delusion. But each has a different approach.

We can think of the Scholar as representing our left brain. He specializes in reason, distinguishing details, discriminating differences, and objectively processing factual information with logic, comprehension, analysis, synthesis, and evaluation. This mode of thought is what we normally consider intelligence and measure with I.Q. tests. It is indispensible to our growth as individuals and progress as a species, but by itself it does not produce wisdom.

The Wisewoman symbolizes our right brain, which uses mythos/analogical thinking. Some of her specialties are holistic awareness, imagination, intuition, metaphor, imagery, symbolism, emotion, personal valuing, and subjectivity. This way of processing information is largely ignored by mainstream education with the exception of certain courses in literature, art, and psychology. These courses intentionally use symbols and metaphors to express truths that go deeper than literal, known facts. Many people see no value in this way of thinking. But consider this observation attributed to Albert Einstein: "The intuitive mind is a sacred gift and the rational mind is a faithful servant. We have created a society that honors the servant and has forgotten the gift."[10]

From a psychological perspective, the gift has been forgotten because society is currently dominated by the Epoch II ego. We know from Einstein's writings that he valued his imagination and intuition (mythos) more than logic and knowledge (logos)—although, of course, he always consulted his reason in his work and tested his theories. Obviously he had integrated the gift of feminine wisdom.

The Wisewoman is our missing link to wisdom. She connects us with unconscious aspects of ourselves, otherness, and the realm of the Sacred. Her holistic awareness enables us to work with input from everything within and without—including our emotions, bodies, the Self, and nature— in imaginative ways to create new ideas and images. The resulting wisdom provides guidance, offers insights, validates choices, and brings meaning. She lives within each of us, female and male, skeptic and seeker, sinner and saint. She does not orate, preach, or teach. She whispers. If we don't hear her, it is not because she's not doing her job, but because the ears of our souls are closed.

Every religion has an exoteric and an esoteric tradition. Travelers on the exoteric path tend not to be aware of their Wisewoman; they defer to externally sanctioned intermediaries for God. Deeply embedded in hierarchical power structures, this is still the path for most organized religion in the West. It's more than enough for many, if not most spiritually oriented Westerners.

But there are always seekers for whom it's not enough. These follow the inner, individual way of the mystic. By trusting their Wisewoman—that is, their intuitive guidance—and heeding her messages, they are led to personal encounters with God; something like what Abraham, Moses, Buddha, Jesus, Mohammed, and countless other spirit persons have experienced.

In the East, which has explored the inner universe for several thousand years, the fact that some people are more suited for this path is taken for granted. But this is not so in the West. Our cultural bias against feminine ways of knowing is woven so tightly into the fabric of our religions that few seekers even know about the mystical path. Fewer still receive any guidance about it. If we should have a brush with something mysterious that fills our lives with meaning, we tend to interpret the experience in accordance with our religious tradition. Or we discount the messages of our own bodies and souls! And when do we take them seriously, our pastors, priests, and rabbis are usually the last people we go to for help. We stoically deny ourselves the antidote to the aridness of the Western soul.

This antidote is meaning. With meaning, there's nothing we can't bear;

without it, there's nothing to live for. There is nothing logical or objective about meaning. We can't see it, explain it, measure it, or prove it to anyone else's satisfaction. Nevertheless, it's real.

Meaning is the "Aha!" of understanding; the "Eureka!" of discovery; the thrill of wonder and awe when we discover that someone we love loves us back; the flood of bliss, joy, and energy that comes from pursuing a passion that ignites our creativity. Meaning is the salt that heightens the flavor of life, the light that brings enlightenment. Meaning affirms, invigorates, and provides purpose for our souls. The more we experience meaning, the more deeply we experience our lives and dwell in the spiritual realm. Meaning is the ultimate gift of new life from She who births all life.

What is the secret to meaning? Why do so many of us lack it? How can we acquire it? I find guidance in a deceptively simple phrase by the novelist E.M. Forster: "Only connect." With these two words he succinctly summarized both the motivation and the genius of all the feminine arche-types, particularly of the Wisewoman.

Let's explore what connecting has to do with spirituality. In Hinduism a centuries-old concept, the "Diamond Net of Indra," presents the universe as a vast net. At every point where one thread crosses another there is a diamond, and each facet of each diamond reflects every other diamond. If you look at one face of one diamond you see everything in the entire universe; if you shake one diamond, the entire net reverberates.

This symbol of a cosmic net speaks to an underlying, holistic structure of intricate connections between self and other, visible and invisible. It sug-gests that if there were no connections, each of us would truly be alone, like an island floating in a vast, meaningless universe with nothing to love, no one to teach or inspire us, and nothing else to learn from. It suggests that because there *are* connections among all things, we can continue to grow and evolve into the Divine Oneness that is our greatest spiritual hope.

The ancient East didn't have a monopoly on this idea. In 600 B.C.E. Hesiod wrote of the ancient creative trinity comprised of Gaia, Chaos, and Eros who created the world together. None of these great beings works alone; each is so intimately connected with the others that they are impos-sible to separate. Their *connectedness* is what makes new life possible.

In our own time, David Bohm, a twentieth-century physicist, likewise held that the universe is comprised of three orders. He called them the *explicate*, which is the world of matter that we recognize with our senses (this corresponds to Hesiod's Gaia); the *implicate* (Chaos), which is a sea of energy beneath the surface; and the *superimplicate* (Eros). The latter he described as the underlying source for the organization and creative activity of the implicate order, determining how its energy will manifest in space, time, and matter.[11]

Bohm believed that through the continuous action of unfolding and enfolding, all three orders of the universe interact with one another in such a way that the universe is, in effect, a hologram in which every single particle contains information about, and is connected with, every other particle. Here too, existence is an intimately connected, undivided totality.

What metaphors could describe this sophisticated new scientific theory more aptly than the East's Diamond Net of Indra or Greece's creation trinity—concepts arrived at centuries ago, not through the scientific method of logos, but through the luminous insight of mythos?

This is cool enough as it is, but there's more. Bohm believed that the physical and mental are two aspects of one overall reality, and that each reflects and implies the other.[12] Physicist Wolfgang Pauli arrived at the same conclusion: "To us ... the only acceptable point of view appears to be the one that recognizes both sides of reality—the quantitative and the qualitative, the physical and the psychical—as compatible with each other, and can embrace them simultaneously ... "[13]

Now for the best part (whew!): In pondering the nature of the connection between physical and psychical, and hence between the three orders of the universe, Bohm concluded that their relationship is carried out through *meaning*.[14] As Norman Friedman writes,

> I believe it is fair to say that meaning [as Bohm uses it] is a form of being, and being is that which has actuality (material or nonmaterial). In this sense, meaning is the essential feature of consciousness, and matter and everything else is permeated with meaning. From this one can conclude that an elementary particle [of matter] has meaning, but is not necessarily self-aware.[15]

But the human ego *is* self-aware, and has the capacity to discern meaningful connections between the inner life of the mind and the outer life of matter. Jung has called these connections *synchronicities*, or meaningful coincidences. If everything visible and invisible is linked, then what could be more natural than for objects and events outside ourselves to coincide exactly with our inner subjective reality?

This does not mean that our ego selves caused these events by willing them (as in, you pray hard enough for a parking space, and *poof* it magically appears!) but only that the three orders of the universe are interacting and connecting with us via the Self to actively support our spiritual growth. Synchronicities occur because of the benevolent nature of the universe. They are evidence that your consciousness has expanded enough to experience your link to everything in it.

This is simply how the universe works. Being shocked when a synchronicity occurs is like being amazed when your heart takes another beat. Our reason for being is the soul's blossoming into conscious union with all that is. The processes of life support it, just as they work to heal our body's wounds and sustain our health. Meaning is in everything and we are *supposed* to find evidence of it everywhere we look.

The "Aha!" of meaning which is the essence of a synchronistic event is an intellectual insight with an emotional impact. In Native American and other pre-industrial cultures, the inner knowing of the "Aha" was treated as an unquestioned truth. It is only one-sided scientific rationalism that fails to see the sacredness in nature or the spiritual value of meaningful quickenings of the soul. Because an "Aha" connects the intellect with emotion and meaning, it is, like all mediations and connections, a product of Wisewoman. It is a guide that counsels us, points us in new directions, and opens new gates that were previously closed to us.

To the logical mind such ideas feel dangerously ignorant and superstitious, but to the analogical mind they make perfect sense. There is no reason or need to choose between one way of thinking or the other, for we are meant to use both. With balance, maturity, and a healthy regard for objective reality, we do not need to be afraid to honor the personal meaning we discover in synchronistic events *as long as we do not impose our meanings on others or use them to justify manipulating or hurting others.*

Synchronicity is a spiritual aid for the individual, maturing seeker. Does it really matter if my synchronistic event is "true" according to your definition of truth? Not a whit! Not if it fills me with joy and vigor and empowers me to persevere in my journey toward the destiny I believe to be mine.

Life becomes infinitely more meaningful when the focus of our existence changes from separating to connecting. The more opposites we unite, the more conscious we become. The wiser we grow, the more sacred significance we see in ourselves, in others, in the processes of nature, in life.

Why is that?

I believe it's because meaning *is* the Divine Feminine; the Divine Feminine is *meaning*! She is our mediatrix between the sacred and the profane, the most evolved manifestation of the Self's feminine potential. She lies dormant until our egos begin to accept and empower our feminine archetypes. As she and the ego strengthen their sacred union, together they create consciousness, connecting self with other, inner with outer, invisible with visible, unconscious with conscious, fact with image, masculine with feminine, heaven with Earth. She is not just a personal or religious symbol, but a scientific reality, an actual form of *being* that permeates *everything*.

Why are the lives of so many contemporary people so meaningless? Because by clinging to our Epoch II separations we have lost our connection with the feminine, and if there is no connection to her, there can be no meaning to our lives.

How can we find spiritual meaning? By opening to our souls and pursuing paths that are meaningful to us, thus honoring God's feminine side.

By nurturing the sacred marriage.

Only connect.

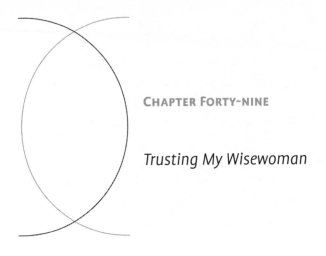

CHAPTER FORTY-NINE

Trusting My Wisewoman

SEVERAL years ago I experienced a set of synchronistic events that were instrumental in the formation of this book. The initial idea came during a meditation early in January 1993. At first I thought the title would be something like *The Sins of the Father God are Visited on the Daughters*. At the thought of working on such a subject I began to cry great heaving sobs. Something very important was going on here. One thing I knew for sure was that this subject was deeply painful. I also realized I was afraid to write about it, afraid of the criticism I would get from certain corners in organized religion. As I closed my meditation I set my intention to be open to guidance in whatever form it might take.

At the time I was reading Brooke Medicine Eagle's book, *Buffalo Woman Comes Singing*.[16] In it, she writes about rainbow medicine—her name for the blending together of all colors, all races, all religions, and "All My Relations" (a Native American term meaning the entire Body of creation) in a bridge of understanding. Partly because of that book I was becoming deeply interested in Native American culture. So, that morning when I saw in the paper that there was a powwow at the fairgrounds, I got very excited and decided to see what it was all about.

After stopping by my office I drove to the fairgrounds. I watched the dancers for a while then decided to check out the exhibits. As I walked toward the exhibit tent I saw a huge, perfect rainbow arcing over the lake behind the fairgrounds. I gasped in amazement. It was awesome—the biggest, brightest, most brilliant rainbow I have ever seen.

A rainbow is a common symbol of joining and mediation. As a bridge that connects heaven with earth to remind us of God's covenant with humanity, the rainbow symbolizes our contact with sacred energies. In *The Woman's Dictionary of Symbols and Sacred Objects,* Barbara Walker notes that Australian and African mythology both contain creation stories in which the Rainbow Serpent Mother or Rainbow Goddess made the world and gave birth to people.[17] In Eastern mythology, the rainbow's colors represent seven veils of Maya, the goddess who manifests the many-colored material world.[18]

For Carl Jung, the colors of the rainbow represent the entire spectrum of human experience, from the infra-red of instinct and emotion to the ultraviolet of spiritual transcendence. In Greek mythology rainbows embodied the goddess Iris, the messenger of heaven who was sent to gather up the souls of women. These are all aspects of the Great Mother I've been calling the Wisewoman. She is the divine presence that connects heaven and earth and pervades the whole of creation, utterly involved with humanity and delighting to be with us.

I had been reading about rainbow medicine that morning. God's sign to Noah was a rainbow. Could it be my sign too? Was I meant to help build a bridge between the old form of Christianity and a new one that knows and values the feminine as much as it has valued the masculine? Shivers went through my body as I thought about these things. Yet, even though the appearance of this rainbow coincided exactly with my inner spiritual condition and felt deeply meaningful, I was reluctant to take seriously the powerful "Aha" it evoked. After all, the rainbow was there for everyone else at the fairgrounds too.

It's just a coincidence, I thought. *Just a beautiful, natural phenomenon of nature that has absolutely nothing to do with me. Only a truly self-centered and incredibly superstitious ego would take such a thing personally!* proclaimed the logos-oriented, scientifically trained part of my mind. But meanwhile, my mythos mind was alert and watchful: *It feels like something important could be happening here,* it thought. *Wait and see.*

I walked on to the exhibits. After browsing through several booths, my attention was drawn to a lovely painting titled "Spirit Horse." It depicted a white horse running through a desert of blue and green sand. The horse is a very important symbol to me. It has appeared in many of my dreams. I've come to understand that the instinctual power the horse presents—which is very wild and strong but can be controlled by reason and cooperates willingly with the human ego—is the energy behind my writing and my passions. Furthermore, I had once owned a white horse, and blue is my favorite color.

For all these reasons, plus others I didn't understand, I was strongly attracted to this painting. As I honored this attraction by looking at the painting more closely, I was suddenly reminded of a recent dream that had felt especially meaningful.

In this dream, my childhood home had been totally renovated and redecorated. Instead of the shabby little frame house I grew up in, I saw a delightful bright bungalow with new rooms, new carpeting and wallpaper, and a gorgeously landscaped front yard teeming with lush foliage and colorful flowers. In the center of the front yard was a circular driveway that had not been there in waking life.

The woman who had redone the house called my attention to this circle (a classic symbol of wholeness and the Self) and asked me what I thought of it. I loved it. Then I saw that the front wall to my old bedroom had been opened up with the addition of two French doors. Inside, the walls were covered with beautiful wallpaper made up of repeating patterns of a field in blue and green, in the same arrangement as the painting, with something white in the center that I couldn't distinguish.

As I reflected on this dream while looking at the painting of the spirit horse, I wondered: *Could the something white in the wallpaper of my dream a few days earlier have been a spirit horse?* Was this a *déjà vu* in which I was seeing a physical manifestation of my dream image? Did this spirit horse have something to do with the spirit behind my writing as well as the spiritual direction of my life?

Don't be ridiculous! I told myself. *You're just making things up, trying to create meaning in things that have nothing to do with you.* Again, I was reluctant to take these compelling coincidences seriously; but deep within, despite my rational critic, hope was stirring.

Feeling emotionally moved but mentally skeptical, I pondered these things as I left the powwow and drove back to my office. When I was a few blocks away, my attention was drawn to a very pregnant woman in a buttery yellow shorts outfit walking through the light rain along the side of the road. She appeared to be Native American. With a jolt I realized I had seen this exact same woman walking in the exact same direction a few hours earlier when I had driven to the fairgrounds.

Why was she out in the rain like this, walking with no umbrella or raincoat, and why was she headed in the same direction she had been going before? Waves of chills washed up my shoulders and neck. My personal dream symbol for my new books has always been new birth. How much of a coincidence was it to see the same woman, pregnant with new life, walking in the same direction, not only when I was headed toward a powwow but also when I was returning from it, at a time when I was reading a book by a Native American woman, *on the very day I had been inspired to write a new book?*

Again, the coincidence coincided exactly with my inner spiritual state. My reluctance to attach significance to it didn't completely disappear, but I could no longer deny the mounting feelings of pleasure, enthusiasm, awe, alertness, and yes, confidence.

By now I had experienced *four* synchronistic events that coincided perfectly with what was going on in my head in the course of three hours. The sheer number of meaningful coincidences should have been enough to speak for themselves, even without considering the powerful inner resonance and shifting of energies I was experiencing. How much harder did I need to be hit over the head? I decided this was enough for me. I needed to move ahead with my idea.

Even so, for the next eighteen days I couldn't start writing. Then, one morning at breakfast I noticed something walking toward me from the left corner of the newspaper I was reading. It was a ladybug. Odd, I didn't remember ever seeing a ladybug in our house before. As I carefully let her out the back door, I wondered about her.

Brooke Medicine Eagle's book had awakened me to the possibility that everything in nature can have spiritual meaning for those who are alert and aware. I had just seen a *lady*bug; could she be a messenger from the feminine aspect of God? If so, what was she trying to tell me? Maybe she had come to announce some new direction in my life that was imminent. Did this have something to do with my proposed book?

Later that morning, right after my meditation, the first draft of the myth which concludes this book hit me all at once with the impact of a powerful revelation. Six hours later it was finished, having poured out of me as fast as my fingers could type. It appeared that the ladybug did indeed have a message for me!

Taken together, all these synchronistic events made a profound impact. They were too numerous, too *meaningful* to write off as mere coincidence. They moved me in an important way. They made me feel I was receiving guidance from something much greater than myself. I decided to trust this guidance and write about my chosen subject as honestly and respectfully as I could.

As it turned out, I still wasn't ready. In today's world, the sacred feminine is so deeply unconscious that we have great difficulty bringing her into consciousness, let alone capturing her in words. It took eighteen years of false starts, sidetracks, meditating, listening, learning, writing and revising several manuscripts for this final version to emerge. But the groundwork was done and the seeds had been sown.

Ever since I made the choice to take my inner life seriously, many synchronistic events have heightened my awareness of God the Mother. Now I know it's possible to have a reciprocal relationship with the sacred realm, to receive help and guidance from the feminine aspect of the Mystery that pervades and sustains physical life and informs us of the sacredness of matter with every gift she sends our way—including rainbows and insects.

Notes

1. Leonard Shlain, "A Penguin Readers Guide to *The Alphabet Versus the Goddess*," 6, in Leonard Shlain, *The Alphabet Versus the Goddess* (New York: Penguin/Compass, 1998); also at http://us.penguingroup.com/static/rguides/us/alphabet_versus_goddess.html (accessed March 30, 2012).

2. Leonard Shlain, *The Alphabet Versus the Goddess* (New York: Penguin/Compass, 1998), 22.

3. Ibid., 23.

4. Eknath Easwaran, "Three Harmonies," *Parabola*, 16, no. 4 (Nov. 1991), 51.

5. Karen Armstrong, *A History of God* (New York: Ballantine Books, 1993), 233.

6. Connie Zweig, *The Holy Longing: The Hidden Power of Spiritual Yearning* (New York: Jeremy Tarcher, 2003), 226.

7. Janet O. Dallett, *The Not-Yet-Transformed God: Depth Psychology and the Individual Religious Experience* (York Beach, Maine: Nicolas-Hays, Inc., 1998), 3.

8. This and the following material about bears is used with permission from Jean Benedict Raffa, "Following Bear," *Pilgrimage*, 27 (2001–2002), 75–79.

9. Timothy Freke and Peter Gandy, *Jesus and the Lost Goddess: The Secret Teachings of the Original Christians* (New York: Three Rivers Press, 2001), 185.

10. This quotation came to me via e-mail from a friend. It appears in several places on the Internet including http://www.alberteinsteinsite.com/quotes/einsteinquotes.html and www.sfheart.com (under the topic, "On Education").

11. Norman Friedman, *Bridging Science and Spirit* (St. Louis, MO: Living Lake Books, 1994), 64–69.

12. Ibid., 78.

13. Wolfgang Pauli, quoted in Robert G. Jahn and Brenda J. Dunne, *Margins of Reality: The Role of Consciousness in the Physical World* (Harcourt Brace Jovanovich, Orlando, 1987), 267.

14. Friedman, *Bridging Science and Spirit*, 79.

15. Ibid.

16. Brooke Medicine Eagle, *Buffalo Woman Comes Singing* (New York: Ballantine Books, 1991).

17. Barbara G. Walker, *The Woman's Dictionary of Symbols and Sacred Objects*. (New York: HarperSanFrancisco, 1988), 349.

18. Ibid., 840.

The Ninth Gift
Mandorla
Consciousness

The world-wide polarization in religious and political dialogue is frightening. But beneath the chaos, individuals and nations are making unprecedented progress in healing the sacred divide. Our species is evolving and we are beginning to unite the opposites. Welcome to Epoch III: the era of mandorla consciousness.

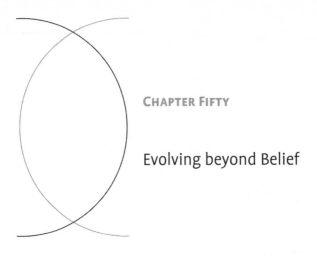

CHAPTER FIFTY

Evolving beyond Belief

OUR EGOS won't give up their unexamined beliefs without a struggle. To some Epoch II egos, organized religion is the only way to God and the idea of self-exploration as a spiritual path appears misguided. Some people think that the latter is irresponsible and narcissistic—a danger to the survival of great accomplishments in moral development humanity has made through the millennia from honoring certain duties to the God of our religions. A very real concern of critics of the inward path is that it's a lightweight, watered-down, self-indulgent form of spirituality in which everything becomes "all about me" instead of being all about the glory of God.

Theologian Marcus Borg reminds us that to insist on following the traditional beliefs is to follow the "broad" way of conventional wisdom. In his words,

> . . . the broad way is the way most people live most of the time. It is not that most people are "wicked," but that most live lives structured by the conventions of their culture, by taken-for-granted notions of what life is about and how to live, by what "everybody knows."[1]

Borg contrasts the broad way of convention with the narrow way of which Jesus spoke. The narrow way consists of a radical return to, and centering in, God. In this manner of living,

> the word "repent" . . . [means] to *return from exile* and *to think/see*

anew. It means to return from a condition of estrangement and exile to the presence of God. And it means to acquire a new way of seeing and thinking that goes beyond the conventions of culture.[2]

In the broad way as Borg explains it, our reference point is behaviors and beliefs of others that we adopt as our own. In the narrow way we aren't centered in *ideas* about God, we're centered in God. We don't just *believe* in the way, we *follow* the way. Religion is born not in *beliefs about* God, but in an awakening ego's *experience of* God. Beliefs come later, as the ego tries to make sense of its experience and conveys it to others in words that are substitutes for the real thing.

To travel the broad way is to live an unexamined life. To not understand the value of self-reflection. To not see that the individual, experiential journey toward expanding consciousness is exactly what empowers the genuine spirit persons we so admire. For such a person, "It isn't enough to believe in the love of God, as a doctrine; you must experience the love of God."[3]

Whatever else Jesus may have been, he was a model of enlightened consciousness who experienced the love of God in a culture that over-valued masculinity and disowned femininity. Having fully opened to his whole Self, he understood and loved the feminine side of himself, God, and life, and wanted to help others experience this mystery for themselves.

Let's examine some of his messages. The following are from the King James version of the Holy Bible unless otherwise noted. Some are paraphrased for the sake of brevity and clarity.

- My purpose is to help you live an abundant life (John 10:10). *(God wants all of us to live lush, complete, powerful, joyous, creative, fulfilled, and happy lives; not one-sided lives of guilt, fear, and powerlessness.)*

- God is love. If you live in love you live in God and God lives in you. (I John 4:16). Love one another (John 13:35). *(God's fundamental nature is love. You can experience God's realm [kingdom] for yourself by loving yourself and nurturing loving relationships with others.)*

- . . . the Kingdom of heaven is at hand (Matt. 3:2) . . . the kingdom of

God is within you (Luke 17:21) . . . The kingdom of God is within you and it is outside you. When you know yourselves then you will be known, and you will understand that you are children of the living Father. But if you do not know yourselves then you live in poverty, and you are the poverty (The Gospel of Thomas: Saying #3). *(God lives both outside of and within you. The inner journey to self-knowledge and consciousness is a spiritual path to God's realm in which you become God-centered, learn how to live a meaningful life, and become who you really are.)*

- Don't be like the hypocrites who do everything for appearances. Do the caring, loving, morally responsible thing without boasting about it (Matt. 6:2, 5:20, 16; Matt. 23:28). *(Authentic spirituality is genuinely caring more about being truly compassionate than gaining status and approval.)*

- But I say unto you, That ye resist not evil (Matt. 5:39) . . . See the log in your own eye instead of pointing to the mote in the eye of another (Matt. 7:3). *(Wrestle with your own demons. Discover and befriend your shadow instead of projecting it onto others and making them scapegoats.)*

- Love your enemies (Matt. 5:44) *(Behave with kindness and compassion toward those who criticize and attack you.)*

- Heal the sick (Luke 9:2; 10:9) . . . Befriend the disenfranchised. (Romans 12:16) . . . Share the wealth. (Matt. 5:42) . . . Embrace diversity (Matt. 5:47; 19:12) *(Work for social justice by recognizing, helping, and honoring the significance of those who are different and/or less fortunate than you.)*

- God created males and females to be united in equality as one entity. (Matt. 19: 4–6, 8–9).

Leonard Shlain finds it significant that neither Jesus nor any of his disciples committed any of his teachings to writing and that his method of teaching, with its aphorisms and parables, was more right-hemispheric than left. These things, plus respect for all life, "love, compassion, Free

Will, and nonviolence combined with a disregard for laws, money, and power expressed a feminine agenda such as no Western religious leader had ever before espoused."[4]

Jesus had at least one spiritual predecessor with a similar agenda: Father Abraham. Author and editor Christopher Bamford writes,

> It is perhaps surprising to find that such "feminine" receptive qualities as faith, responsibility, hospitality, silence, compassion, and love lie at the source of the Abrahamic path, usually thought of as so quintessentially patriarchal. . . . The Abrahamic path is . . . feminine at its core: that is its unspeakable secret.
>
> Abraham's femininity is evident, finally, not only in the qualities he manifests, but also and above all in that he walks the way of Wisdom, Sophia or Hochma, as taught in the Wisdom Books.[5]

The way of Wisdom was Jesus's path as well. But during his time the average ego was not yet ready to hear, let alone understand this radical message. Nor were the bulk of his followers able to relate it to their own feminine sides! Thus, over time the most powerful and repressive Epoch II males distorted it into a written-down, dogma-driven, belief-based religion that often bore little resemblance to its true essence.

Today, mistrust of the inner spiritual path originates in the unconscious influences of these distortions. Critics of this path would make us believe our current problems have nothing to do with a five-thousand-year-old tradition of male dominance and feminine repression, but with the weakness of a society that lacks the moral fiber to return to traditional values and follow the "tough-minded exemplars of the Bible and history."[6]

It's usually overlooked that our tough-minded exemplars are responsible for as much war, abuse, rape, theft, deceit, enslavement, and genocide as anything and anyone else. The Inquisitors believed in returning to traditional values and following the tough-minded exemplars of the Bible. They hated evil and couldn't see their own capacity for it. They thought they were carrying out God's will by torturing people they considered guilty of heresy— "incorrect" or unorthodox belief. But as their actions clearly showed, insisting on correct belief doesn't destroy evil; it perpetuates it.

How so? If we obsess over one side of our natures and project our feared and despised qualities onto others, we eventually turn into that which we most hate. Have you ever really considered the implications of this well-known psychological principle? If not, here's a contemporary example.

Some fundamentalist branches of Christianity are fascinated by the book of Revelation, the most mystical and metaphorical book of the New Testament. In their interpretations of its prophecies about the end times, the battle of Armageddon, and the anti-Christ, they single out various "bad guys" (other people, nations, and religions) whose identities change as political boundaries and affinities change. But one thing never changes: The winners, the "good guys" are always "us," the true believers.

But what if the anti-Christ is not some nation, group, or person outside our country or Church? What if it's not even outside of "us?" What if it's a metaphor for a destructive, anti-spiritual, anti-life attitude *within* us—a way of thinking that's the exact opposite of the one Jesus talked about and manifested in his life? A way that doesn't embrace otherness but rejects it? A way that separates, divides, and points fingers in the name of a masculine God-image about which there's only one correct set of beliefs?

Matter/anti-matter. Christ/anti-Christ. If anti-matter is the absence of matter, anti-Christ is the absence of Christ. If Christ is about sacred new life, anti-Christ is the absence of sacred new life. If Christ is about love, anti-Christ is the absence of love. If Christ is about social justice, anti-Christ is the absence of social justice. If Christ is about forgiveness, anti-Christ is the absence of forgiveness. If Christ was someone who lived fully and authentically, anti-Christ is the absence of full, authentic living. If Christ accepted all others, anti-Christ is the absence of acceptance of otherness.

What if the anti-Christ is the negative shadow of Christianity—a one-sided mind-set that denies the feminine softness and fertility of the soul and aborts the sacred new Christ-life that wants to be born in us?

You decide.

Has finding spiritual meaning in my own experiences and trusting the guidance of the Self turned me into someone for whom "God and his glory are not the center of attention"? Quite the contrary. The farther I travel, the greater my awareness and devotion grow for the authority of a

Sacred Other and the more centered I am in That. Only now I experience this authority not as a set of rules and beliefs but as an inner Beloved that compels me to learn how to love, explore the depths of my being, fully experience the miracle of my life, and live it authentically. I don't worry about what other people believe any more. I don't worry about what I believe either. I'm just grateful that the Mystery I seek to engage more fully has a soft, open, all-encompassing, gently accepting feminine side. And that I'm discovering the mandorla way of experiencing her for myself.

Integrating Belief and Experience

Most of us have had mystical experiences that were so meaningful and unusual—perhaps even "mind blowing"—that they felt sacred. Think about experiences like this you've had.

- Choose one and describe it as honestly and clearly as you can, without embellishment or religious bias, without holding back.

- Find a meaningful way to record it, whether in writing, on tape, or in art, so that you can return to it whenever you want to.

- Compare/contrast this experience to your spiritual/religious beliefs. Was it in accordance with your beliefs or did it challenge them? What knowing or gnosis did this experience bring? Describe the differences in your thinking it made.

- What did this experience mean to you? Why was it so meaningful? Would it mean as much to you if it happened to someone else who told you about it? Why or why not? What accounts for the different impact?

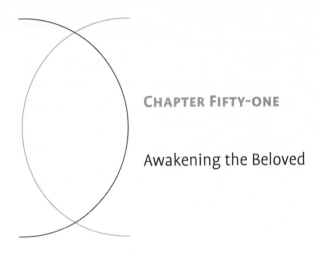

CHAPTER FIFTY-ONE

Awakening the Beloved

THE TERM *beloved* connotes many different things. In your physical life it can mean the person you love above all others and with whom you enjoy sexual intimacy.

Psychologically the Beloved is the feminine archetype that is partner to the Lover. Together, the Lover and Beloved represent the masculine (dynamic) and feminine (magnetic) aspects of the instinct for sex with its goals of love and pleasure. Among the Beloved's many attractive features are our soul's essential goodness, beauty, benevolence, hospitality, mystery, desirability, receptivity, emotional integrity, and inherent worth.

In Christianity the Beloved often refers to Jesus, since when he was baptized a voice came from heaven saying "This is my beloved Son, in whom I am well pleased."[7] Sometimes it means the Church, the body of Christ, who are God's beloved: feminine matter wedded to masculine spirit. But this term is not confined to Christianity. The Sufi poets of Islamic mysticism have a long tradition of writing love poetry about the Beloved to symbolize their union with God.

Beloved can also be an encompassing term for the feminine archetypes that make up the feminine side of the Self. Or, as the sum-total of our masculine and feminine sides and the personal and collective unconscious, it can mean the Self itself: the spiritual essence of each individual, our mystic center, the sacred Other, the Christ within, the immanent God which is beloved of us and God.

As we integrate these seeming paradoxes we approach a Sacred Mystery. The Beloved is *our* Beloved—the aspect of God that indwells every soul and compels us to evolve into oneness. And we ourselves are *God's* Beloved. As such, we have a profoundly sacred mission to complete ourselves. For in doing so, we complete our Divine Lover.

Many fairy tales feature a prince who knows something is missing and goes on a search for a princess. Usually she is either a captive (in which case he must rescue her) or asleep (in which case he awakens her with a kiss). A literal interpretation of stories like this suggests that our search for love is a rather short-lived event that takes place in our youth and culminates when we find the person of our happily ever after. In truth, the beloved people with whom we enter into intimate relationships can help guide us to our destination, but they are not themselves the destination.

Like parables and myths, fairy tales always have a deeper meaning. There is an outer search for physical union and human love, and an inner one for Divine Union and Spiritual Love. This means that our ego/Lover sometimes takes two journeys: the outer one in the early days of Epoch II and the inner one in its latter days, when we begin to realize something is missing. In the second journey, our ego is conscious of the divided self and intentional in its search for psycho-spiritual unity. This is when the Beloved represents the magnetic allure of the feminine unconscious where the Self resides and with which the ego needs to unite in order to become whole. She is the ultimate object of our Lover's search.

A classic example of the two journeys of the Lover is provided by Dante Alighieri, the greatest poet of the Middle Ages. Beatrice was a simple, lovely girl whom Dante met just twice in his life. His first glimpse of her on the Ponte Vecchio bridge in Florence when she was only a girl electrified his emotional life and changed him forever. In the lightning flash of that brief, momentous meeting, Dante's Lover was awakened and he acquired an image of his Beloved. Unfortunately, Beatrice died before Dante's twenty-seventh year, after which he married another woman, took up politics, and led a relatively ordinary life for many years.

But when Dante reached midlife his Lover reawakened and he found himself in a dark wilderness of pain, confusion, and alienation. This time he got the message. Instead of wasting all his Lover energy pining away for Beatrice, the human person whose physical presence was forever lost to him, he internalized her image. She became the muse that guided his spiritual initiation. Dante understood the spiritual basis of his yearning. What he truly desired was not the woman, but what she represented to him: the unknown feminine parts of himself, his personal and collective unconscious, his spiritual essence, his Beloved.

So he began the second journey. It transformed his soul from a condition of childlike passivity, fantasy, and yearning into ecstatic, passionate, extraordinarily creative maturity. This was a journey to his own Beloved which Beatrice, a human woman, inspired him to take. He recorded it for her sake with touching brilliance in his metaphorical masterpiece, *Divine Comedy.*

With rare insight, Dante somehow knew that Beatrice's importance to him did not lie in the woman herself, but in his capacity to experience and honor the reality of his own being—down to the roots of his deepest, darkest, most secret true self with all its shameful weaknesses and flaws and disowned emotions, including those he had always considered "feminine." The deepest meaning of his story, and of all the fairy tales and myths that feature seeking princes, is that when the Lover withdraws his projections from outer realities and succeeds in awakening the Beloved, the result is a joyful and empowering reunion, a coming home.

Our attachment to surface interpretations and solutions is certainly one reason our Lover can't find our Beloved. But perhaps the greatest obstacle to discovering and awakening her is the wilderness of self-hatred. In his book *Life of the Beloved,* Catholic theologian Henri Nouwen writes that it is extremely difficult to hear the voice of the Beloved

> . . . in a world filled with voices that shout: "You are no good, you are ugly; you are worthless; you are despicable, you are nobody— unless you can demonstrate the opposite."
>
> These negative voices are so loud and so persistent that it is easy to believe them. That's the great trap. It is the trap of self-rejection. Over the years I have come to realize that the greatest trap in our life is not success, popularity or power, but self-rejection.[8]

The challenge is to listen to the unfulfilled desire of our Lover and follow it to our Beloved. We need to trust and believe that no matter what others tell us, no matter what we look like on the outside, no matter what our inner critics tell us about ourselves, there lies buried deep in our core something awesomely sacred, exquisitely delicate, supremely magnificent, and breathtakingly beautiful. She is there. She is. She is our sacred inheritance and our right and our gift just for being alive.

The Beloved is how we imagine and feel with the deepest recesses of our soul, the most alluring, fascinating, and compelling being we could ever hope to meet. She represents our divine nature, the immanent God, that which connects us to eternity. Through honoring her within us, we begin to feel that we are known and loved by something beyond ourselves, something sacred and very beautiful.

Ultimately, our Beloved is the only thing that can truly and completely satisfy human desire. The Greeks personified her in the goddess Aphrodite. In *The Goddess Within,* Jennifer and Roger Woolger describe Aphrodite's association with the human heart:

> A Jewish saying runs, "God wants the heart." Nothing could be more true of Aphrodite; we should also say of her, "The Goddess wants the heart." For the heart symbolizes all that is authentic and true of our deepest, least-defended selves. And when two hearts are open to each other, then the magic of eros can flow between them. This is Aphrodite's greatest gift, the commingling of two hearts in harmony with the great sensual commingling of our physical beings. When both channels are open, the goddess is truly present to us.[9]

This suggests that the key to love in any partnership is not just sexual intimacy but also emotional honesty. In this respect, the Beloved represents emotional integrity and total acceptance of who we are and who we are not. But we must remember that Aphrodite is an archetype, and we are mere mortals. For us it is neither wise nor prudent to express our raw emotions as freely as the immortal goddess does. Emotions are neither good nor bad in and of themselves, but when humans act out powerful emotions untempered by moral sensibility (a mature King and Queen), they can be extremely dangerous. As an archetype, Aphrodite represents not just the beauty and truth of honest emotions, but also the danger and destructiveness of emotion in its most primitive, uncivilized states. The

Beloved has her negative aspects like every other archetype.

As the recipient of God's love, our healthy Beloved sees her Lover in the everyday aspects of life. She experiences all of them as sacred, mysterious gifts of Divine Being. The Beloved knows that God dwells not only in us, but also in other people, nature, the world. She trusts The All to be behind and beneath every event, no matter how painful some events are to the ego. All of nature is sacred to her. She experiences intimate moments of rapture in the velvety nuzzle of a gentle horse, a nest filled with wee speckled eggs, or the mysterious hush of a shadowy oak grove.

Above all, the Beloved knows that God indwells the body. Her way of connecting with God is to experience God's love in the Now by being receptive through the physical senses, aware of God's presence in the physical phenomena of creation. She appreciates the smell of freshly cut grass, the curve of a lover's neck, or the curl of a fine wine around the tongue. Ultimately, for the Beloved, enlightenment is embodiment.

Since the Lover and Beloved are fueled by the need to give and receive love and pleasure, nurturing this pair to maturity on the physical plane is often our entry into the spiritual domain. This love connection is why sages and mystics often say that sexual and spiritual energy are the same thing. It is also why every step we make toward spiritual maturity brings us so much love and pleasure.

For most of us our Beloved remains hidden behind a veil of illusion. We see what we've been conditioned to see or what our egos can tolerate. We focus on the physical dimensions of sexual love and ignore the holy work of creating a loving heart. We emphasize physical beauty and can't see the genuine beauty of our souls. Our egos push us to extreme lengths to appear physically attractive and desirable to others, while we neglect the inner gifts that provide infinitely more love and pleasure. We've evolved to where we *could* be aware of the Beloved, but few of us dare make the inner choices she requires.

The more we obsess over outer images of the Beloved archetype and ignore the real thing, the more power we give to her negative shadow. Examples include being so preoccupied by our appearance that we take unduly drastic steps to improve it, having distorted body images, being indiscriminately receptive to sexual advances, being overly seductive, creating emotional dramas to get the attention we crave, people pleasing, pretending, and performing.

A Lover who obsessively searches for love and pleasure in the outer world while ignoring the psychological and spiritual dimensions of relationships is equally misguided. In seeking physical remedies for psycho-spiritual ailments, we might jump enthusiastically from one pleasure to another without making lasting commitments or changing in any meaningful way. We might try to stay young, innocent, and irresponsible forever. Our treatment of our partners might be unfeeling and self-serving. We might exhibit predatory behavior, sexual aggression, and all sorts of addictions, including sexual addiction.

Why are we attracted to certain kinds of people to the exclusion of others? At birth our archetypes are just empty patterns, like the outlined shapes in a child's coloring book. Throughout our youth our ego fleshes them out with colors and behaviors based on our experiences with people around us. One person's Lover becomes cocky and flashy; another's is gentle and giving. One Beloved is sexy and seductive; another is sweet and shy.

Our image of the perfect partner never completely fits the person onto whom we project it. While there are some similarities, our partner often turns out to be quite different from our expectations. Until we become conscious of the immaturity of our Lover and the reality of our projections, we'll blame our partner for our relationship problems. Moreover, as long as we fail to develop a direct relationship with our inner Beloved, our authentic selves will be covered in layers of ignorance, habitual reactions, denial, and blame.

Fortunately, the people we love are mirrors that reflect valuable information back to us. Conflicts with our partners reveal the problematic aspects of our personal and collective (archetypal) shadows. Their love validates our true beauty and worth.

Our soul mates are not people who will make us happy forever by always being exactly what we want them to be. Our true soul mate is one who is so committed to our relationship that s/he chooses to tolerate the inevitable tension of the search for intimacy without withdrawing love. Remaining in a relationship with someone who cares this much challenges both partners to grow into their fullest potential. Then it becomes a win/

win situation because in accepting our shadows and establishing honest relationships with each other, both partners develop healthier Lovers and become more connected with their own Beloveds.

Consciousness of your Beloved brings healing new life. Old insecurities begin to melt away. You stop interrupting and denying and start listening and understanding. You feel more compassion and appreciation for your partner who is no longer an object or image, but a unique individual who is also seeking his or her own Beloved. Your personality, behavior, and relationships become easier and softer around the edges. Your life acquires meaning and you feel grateful for the simple pleasures of being.

This does *not* mean your work is over or that you will live consciously ever after. The inner universe is as vast as the outer, and there will always be more aspects of your shadow and Beloved to discover. This is the human condition, and it's okay. You can forgive yourself for being incomplete. But you will have the tools for fully and freely participating in your life. If you keep at it, there will be times when just being alive, just being *conscious* of your Beloved gives you all the happiness and pleasure you need.

Integrating Your Shadow Beloved

People with a strong Shadow Beloved have a deep mistrust of their inner selves. They emphasize external beauty and perfection while being unable to trust and express their soul's true feelings and truths in ways that reflect the positive qualities of a mature, secure Beloved.

- Identify some true feelings or emotions you have that you would like to be able to express honestly and openly.
- Select one or two that have the most potential for healing your relationships.
- If the feelings are negative, imagine an honest way of expressing them that will cause the least amount of pain.
- Journal your ideas for accomplishing this.
- Act on your desire to communicate your feelings more effectively and authentically.

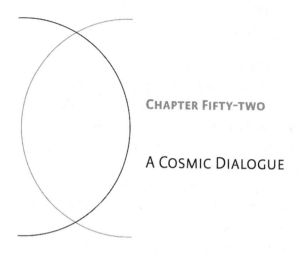

Chapter Fifty-two

A Cosmic Dialogue

God is in his receiving room, listening to prayers. He files the green ones that are dutiful renditions of old formulas under "Well-Meaning but Still Unconscious." He files the red ones saturated with self-righteousness, mean-spiritedness, and pride under "Needs Humility." The blue ones prompted by faith and spiritual hunger he puts in "Needs Attention." The prayers motivated by fear of his retribution are brown and go under "Pitifully Misguided." And he files the yellow ones overflowing with praise and gratitude under "To Read When I'm Feeling Sad."

Then one prayer surrounded by a soft glow of indigo/violet light attracts his attention. It's coming from a woman whose soul is suffering profoundly and whose heart is utterly sincere. "Teach me how to love. Please, teach me how to love. I give you my complete and unqualified permission to do whatever you have to. Giving you this power terrifies me, but I mean it. I mean it. Just teach me how to love," she says over and over again.

When Goddess comes home from work she finds God in his receiving room and is immediately drawn to the same prayer. "Oh yes. I know that one," she says. "I've been working with her for years now."

"I knew you must have been," says God.

"I've been meaning to talk to you about her," says Goddess. "I think she's ready. She's beginning to sense my presence and that will make her strong enough to endure the fire."

They go on to discuss the details of their plan. When the time is right, Goddess returns to Earth and merges with the spark of light she has been nurturing in this soul for many years. Coiling around the base of the woman's spine, Goddess turns up the heat of her evolutionary energy and begins to move through her body, awakening every cell and breaking down every barrier as she goes.

Thus is the anti-Christ expelled from one more soul. Thus is the new life of the Christ within conceived. The woman enters a Dark Night that lasts for nine years. Nine, the number of Goddess. Nine, the number of gestation and completion. During this time she discovers that the way to the light lies through the valley of the shadow of death. That the depth of your suffering is a measure of your capacity for growth. That your willingness to purge your shadow is a measure of your spiritual integrity. That self-knowledge is a requirement for God-knowledge. That self-acceptance is a requisite for love.

Thus is the Christ within delivered from the prison of one more frightened ego.

God and Goddess watch with great anticipation to see what will happen to this woman who is opening the door to their light. When she emerges from the darkness, annealed by the fire, once again the world seems bright and hopeful. She is growing, growing, and the knowledge fills her with joy. Maybe, just maybe, her prayer is being answered at last.

God and Goddess embrace. They look forward to enjoying communion with each other in this beloved soul that is opening to life.

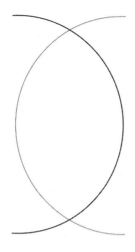

CHAPTER FIFTY-THREE

The Divine Feminine as the Christ Within

TODAY'S world is in thrall to two toxic weapons of the anti-Christ: obsessive masculinity and repressed femininity. This has created an extremely volatile situation. Obsessive masculinity begets dominator systems that repress and destroy others. The obsessive King can be so controlling that freedom, fairness, and justice are lost. The obsessive Warrior eliminates everyone and everything he fears then sets up idealistic new regimes that become as toxic as the old ones. The obsessive Scholar enforces rigid belief and squelches feminine spontaneity, intuition, and personal meaning. The obsessive Lover loses himself in his passions and uses and abuses women.

On the other side, repressed femininity is self-destructive. Life without the Queen's compassion, conscience, and mature social ethic corrodes virtue. Without Mother's creativity, nurturing, and openness to growth and change, our bodies, souls, and spirits shrivel and die. Without Wisewoman's knowing and honoring of our soul's realities we live the meaningless lives of puppets. And if we can't enjoy our Beloved's lovableness, worth, and beauty we succumb to hopelessness, victimization, depression, mental and physical illnesses, and every kind of self-destructive behavior including suicide.

Growing appreciation for the feminine principle is bringing new spiritual life to individuals and revitalizing many branches of organized religion. This is only natural, for to quote Heinrich Zimmer,

> The idea of redemption is everywhere associated with the . . .
> mysteries of the Great Mother—is it not to be expected that the
> soul, in its highest aspiration, should turn to the great ancient

goddess and, childlike, look to her motherliness for what it feels incapable of obtaining by its own strength?[10]

We are recognizing the reality of the Divine Feminine—whether we think of her as the Holy Spirit, Sophia, the Beloved, Wisdom, Meaning, or the sacred contents of the feminine unconscious, the Christ within. We will no longer be denied the promise of spiritual transformation that is our birthright. Religious groups that can't accept this will, to use a term I heard from Episcopal Bishop John Shelby Spong, wither away under the weight of their own irrelevancy.

We see this trend in widespread recent interest in Mary Magdalene, whom some believe to have been Jesus's beloved and maybe even wife. More important to me than this kind of speculation is the hard evidence of the Gospel of Mary, a second-century apocryphal text. Whether we understand it as fact or metaphor, it takes this woman very seriously indeed—depicting her as one of the disciples Jesus singled out for special teachings. Theologian Karen King says this work shows an early Christianity that was radically different from what it has become. In particular, it interprets the teachings of Jesus as about the inner path to spiritual knowledge, a path that directs us to the power of the true self and frees the soul from the fear of death.[11]

In his summary of this gospel, James M. Robinson calls attention to Jesus's teaching that sin derives not so much from moral ignorance as from the soul's inability to properly balance the material and the spiritual.[12] Esther De Boer says that after telling this to his disciples, Jesus advises them

> not to be distracted by looking here and there, but rather to look within themselves, where the child of humanity (or son of man, as the phrase traditionally has been translated) is to be found. This should be the gospel the disciples preach, not a legalistic set of rules and regulations.[13]

At one point in the gospel, Jesus tells Mary that a vision she had of him came not through the soul or spirit, but through the mind, or consciousness, which is *between* the soul and spirit.[14] He also says that where the mind is, there is the treasure. This is a truly profound statement. What it means is that *consciousness* connects the human soul with Divine Mystery. *Consciousness* is our treasure, our bridge to Christ. God is not to be found in a particular belief, religion, God-image, or way of worshiping, but by shedding light on our inner darkness. *Consciousness.*

From a psychological perspective, the Torah, Bible, Qur'an and myths and scriptures of every tradition say the same things about humanity:

- We have the capacity to grow in love and consciousness.

- We are made in such a way that our egos hunger for intimate union and partnership with the Beloved, or Christ within.

- Throughout history we've projected our intuition of our Beloved onto such figures as the Divine Androgyne, the Great Mother, Earth Mother, Brahma, Vishnu, Shiva, Shakti, Buddha, Isis, Osiris, Sky God, Abraham, Moses, Zeus, Persephone, Athena, Apollo, Jesus, Sophia, Holy Spirit, Mary the Mother of Jesus, Mary Magdalene, and Mohammed to help us understand and give birth to the new spiritual life for which we yearn.

- The repressive ego that refuses to acknowledge its shadow and become more conscious of its true nature is the source of the pride, ignorance, confusion, imbalance, conflict, violence, and evil that generates divisiveness in us and the world.

The religious patriarchs could not have had better intentions! Judaism sought to keep the ego and shadow under control through *law*. Christianity tried to do it with *faith*. Islam is founded on *law* and *belief*. Jungian analyst Edward Edinger believes that

a new mode is on the horizon, namely depth psychology. *The new psychological dispensation finds man's relation to God in the individual's relation to the unconscious.* This is the new context, the new vessel with which humanity can be the carrier of divine meaning. . . . God is now to be carried experientially by the individual.[15]

To Epoch II sensibilities the implications of this are mind-blowing and revolutionary. We've been afraid that if we look within we'll discover the unworthiness of our true selves. We thought self-examination would make us even more egocentric than we already are! We thought questioning our old beliefs and opening to new ideas would send us straight to Hell! What we never could understand is that making the unconscious conscious is a spiritual path in which the masculine ego works in partnership with the Deep Feminine, and that together they lead us into the sacred realm where we become Godcentric.

We are beginning to understand that the world problem is an individual problem: Our own disowned material separates us from the Christ within. The spread of democracy, elevation of women into positions of power, increased respect for diversity, and related trends point to the ego's healing of its dysfunctional relationship with feminine otherness—both human and divine, within and without. As a result of our growing consciousness, more people than ever before have the hope of healing the sacred divide and participating in the sacred marriage. In them lies the hope of our species and the world.

What does it look like to be Godcentric? To have an inner knowing of your sacred core? To be united with it? Earlier I mentioned that having loving relationships with otherness is one measure of mature spirituality and that there are two others. All three are expressed in a new definition of God proposed by retired Episcopal Bishop Spong, one of the most courageous spiritual pioneers on the planet today.

Spong describes the theistic God-image of Epoch II spirituality as "a being, supernatural in power, dwelling outside this world and invading the world periodically to accomplish the divine will."[16] He believes, as I do, that this God-image is no longer relevant for Westerners who are looking for new ways to imagine and experience God that are congruent with evolving consciousness.

I have deliberately built upon this anthropomorphic God-image for the mythical cosmic dialogues in this book. I did so in the hope of expanding readers' awareness of the fuller potential of that which we think of as God. But I also wanted to demonstrate that *no* God-image or religious symbol can be taken literally. *Every* symbol is a metaphor for a far more profound spiritual mystery. This is the same mystery to which the Couple, the Self, the Beloved, the Christ within, and the sacred marriage also point. This mystery is what Bishop Spong attempts to describe.

He also notes that the Torah with its theistic, left-brained God-image also contains a non-theistic, non-literal way of imagining God. I've identified this subtext as feminine, right-brained mythos, and highlighted it when discussing some of Jesus's messages. Here is the new image of God that Bishop Spong offers us:

God is the Source of Life who is worshiped when we live fully.

God is the Source of Love who is worshiped when we love wastefully.

God is the Ground of Being who is worshiped when
we have the courage to be.[17]

Loving wastefully! Don't you love that term? I wept the first time I heard it. This is what I meant by saying that having loving relationships with otherness is one of three measures of mature spirituality. The other two are living fully and being who we are. All three require consciousness, and for that we need the full participation of our feminine sides. This is how we restore balance to our souls. This is how we create peace.

How might Christians view their heritage in the light of this new understanding? For Bishop Spong,

Jesus is a God-presence, a doorway, an open channel. The fullness of his life reveals the Source of Life, the wastefulness of his love reveals the Source of Love, and the being of his life reveals the Ground of All Being. That is why Jesus continues to stand at the heart of my religious life. That is also why I continue to call him "my Lord" and to call myself a Christian. But I am a Christian who can no longer live inside the exclusive claims of my traditional theistic past.[18]

Ditto.

The beauty, brilliance, and saving grace of this new vision of God is that it's not limited to Christianity or any one religion. The mandorla way heals the divides within ourselves and between each other by connecting with otherness. Every connection brings greater consciousness of our fuller potential to live fully, love wastefully, and be who we really are. This path is available to all. It transcends religious doctrines and symbols. It is a point upon which every religion and every spiritual seeker can agree. You don't have to be a rabbi, priest, bishop, pastor, imam, guru, yogi or any kind of religious leader to create consciousness. You don't have to join a new religion or desert the one that nourished your spirit, set it on fire, and fostered new life.

Rabbi Azriel ben Menahem, Isaac Luria, Meister Eckhart, Mother Julian of Norwich, Teresa of Avila, Ibn Arabi, Rumi, and countless other spirit persons did not leave their religions after connecting with their Beloved and discovering the deeper meaning of their scriptures. Rather, they welcomed her gifts of wisdom and enjoyed the sacred marriage within the context of their religions. They blessed their communities with newfound wisdom and worked to create healthier connections and greater unity.

The feminine holiness that indwells us can't be confined within one religious tradition. It sings the same song to all who listen:

> Your spiritual destiny is to create consciousness and
> you are the God crucible within which consciousness evolves.
> You unite with the Absolute by uniting the opposites in yourself.
> You contribute to the healing of the world by healing yourself.
> The struggle to know who you are is the spiritual quest.
> God is your Father and God is your Mother
> and you are their
> Beloved.
> Awaken! Connect!
> God indwells your soul!
> Live life. Practice love. Be who you are.

Do you really want to know God? Then know yourself! *You* are the Holy Grail. *You* are the Beloved. *You* are the God crucible of spiritual transformation, a container of sacred new life which is the Christ within. And you can give birth to this new life by healing the sacred divide. Open to God's feminine side. Let her fill you with her wisdom. Create an ongoing, never ending dialogue with her. Integrate every healthy potential she represents to celebrate a sacred marriage within your soul.

• • •

I opened this book with an invitation for you to join me on the radical middle path to spiritual maturity. Now I leave with the hope that I've shed enough light on it for you to make your own next steps forward. The world-wide polarization in religious and political dialogue is frightening. But beneath the chaos, individuals and nations are making unprecedented progress in healing the sacred divide. Our species is evolving and we are beginning to unite the opposites.

Welcome to Epoch III: the era of mandorla consciousness.

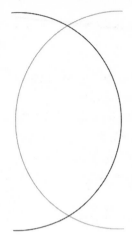

CHAPTER FIFTY-FOUR

Healing the Sacred Divide: A Modern Myth of New Beginning

LONG AGO and far away, in a time and place where you and I have never been, only a great and powerful Source of energy existed. It constantly renewed Itself through unfolding and enfolding, unfolding and enfolding, in a ceaseless vortex of unified, integrated movement. The two kinds of movement were completely one with each other.

Neither recognized itself or knew that the other existed. It was impossible to tell where one left off and the other began. The part that unfolded simply reached out, and there she was, his partner, reaching in to embrace him and bring him back to the center. Together and complete, they danced a blissful dance of endless love.

The movement that unfolded and reached out was called Manifestation, or Man. The movement that enfolded and reached in was called Womb of Wisdom, or Wom. Wom and Man had equal power, as the two beats of a heart.

Wom's was the all-embracing power of flowing, abundant discourse, revelation, and wisdom. Although she did not yet know it, she was the power of all the gods who would populate the earth. She was all-nourishing and all-devouring, the all-moving universal energy of Great Mother that is generated in every creature and in the impulse of every creature. As the mother of all enlightened beings she was destined to dwell in eternal, timeless, loving embrace with her partner, the universal God. Together they would create the sensory world of the outward eye, as well as the inner vision of the crystal-clear detachment of illumination and freedom. Together, they would move through history, evolving and changing until the last age of the world when all would be transfigured in spiritual transcendence.

But she did not know any of this yet. Nor did her partner, Man.

Man was the power to manifest and penetrate, to think and to act. Man had the ability to unfold, reach out, build, separate, divide, discriminate, aim, labor, move matter and channel it into useful forms. His was the energy that recognizes potential: the power of focused thought, the hunger that emboldens individual effort, the differentiation that shapes individuality, the idealism that generates perfection, the self-disciplined and goal-oriented activity that, with the help of Wom's energy, would make heroic accomplishments. His wisdom was the wisdom of the head, and although he did not yet know it, he was the Father of Life.

Wom was the poem; Man the poet. She was the cathedral; he the builder. She was the music of the cosmos; he the musician who plays it. She was the pieces of the puzzle: he the one who solves it. Together they were dynamite (she the powder he the flame). But Man's power to act was useless without her creativity and Wom's energies were useless without his ability to manifest.

One day, after eons and eons of unconscious immersion in their blissful dance, the most amazing coincidence occurred. (Was it coincidence?) At the exact same instant, just as Wom was reaching in to Man and Man was reaching out to Wom, each of them had a glimmer of consciousness.

"I exist," thought Man, "and I wish to know myself."

"There is another here," Wom sensed, "and I want to connect with it."

This is how thought and feeling were born. So complete was their interrelation that in thinking their separate thoughts and feeling their separate feelings, each communicated to the other. Such was the nature of their combined power that as their messages met, an incredible thing happened: something new was created, a tiny spark of light. This was so completely unexpected to both of them that they could not help but notice it, and in the noticing they became curious to see if they could make it happen again.

Again they thought their separate thoughts and felt their separate feelings and communicated. Again a spark of light was created, and immediately it joined with the first spark to create a tiny flicker. Over and over they tried it, each time gaining a little more awareness of what they were doing and how it was happening. Each spark they created joined with the earlier ones until what began as a flicker turned into a flame. The flame grew and grew until it was so vast and shed so much light that, with the utmost sense of wonder and awe, they beheld each other for the first time.

"This is me, this is my beloved," each one thought and felt in beholding the other. "How magnificent we are." Thus they discovered their ability to think and feel.

Owing to the nature of his unfolding, and inspired by Wom's creative potential, Man could not contain his exuberance. He was ready to reach out and do something. "Just imagine what we can *do* with these thoughts," he said to himself and his beloved. "Why, we could make something, couldn't we? Let's do it!"

"Yes," Wom answered. "Let's create a universe. It will be orderly and beautiful and filled with life. I have tons of ideas." And because she, with her preference for enfolding, especially enjoyed the exhilarating sensation of feeling, she added, "How good it feels to be with you; how excellent it will be to work together."

Man agreed completely, for Wom was part of him, as he was part of her. It was good.

They had been bound together in darkness without knowing. Now, in the full light of the day they created, and with joyful awareness, they made a conscious commitment to one another. They called their commitment the Sacred Marriage, and vowed that they would love, honor, and serve one another.

The result was new life. Together they created the entire magnificent cosmos in their own image: day and night, sun and moon, sky and earth, fire and water, spirit and soul, male and female, head and heart, thought and feeling. All that is and was and ever shall be was a reflection of God and became permeated with their sacred spark of light and life.

For a long time Wom and Man were blissfully happy. Their time of dark unknowing was over. They had found their opposites, and together they had joyfully created a universe filled with many healthy, happy offspring. What more could they want? What more, indeed? This is where "happily ever after" should surely go.

But an obstacle of life-and-death proportions arose.

Life and death were, in fact, the exact obstacle that confronted Wom and Man. It all started innocently enough. One day, after an especially long and particularly troublesome day, Man sat down as was his wont to review his accomplishments. Perhaps because the demands on him had been enormous and he was unusually tired—or maybe he was just changing with the natural flow of things—a new awareness entered his thoughts. This world they had created had seemed perfect to him. But today it occurred to him that there might be something a little imperfect about the cycles they had created—largely at Wom's insistence, if he remembered correctly. He understood the birth and rebirth part, but death? Was that absolutely necessary?

Wom had kept saying there had to be balance between the opposites, just as there was balance between the two of them, for the universe to run smoothly. If they were going to create life then they would also have to create death. But that would be okay, Wom said, because then death would be followed by rebirth. It was all a matter of wholeness and completion. The tension between the opposites would make the universe function, just as it had always made them function. Things just wouldn't work otherwise, she had said.

And anyway, that was the beauty of it: to become conscious enough to be able to integrate the opposites so their children too could reach their fullest creative potential. Wasn't that exactly what had happened to Wom and Man? Didn't it make sense to build a world on the same principles that had led to their own awakening and creativity?

At the time, Man had let it pass. Being embraced and contained by her warmth just as he was unfolding in all his magnificence had always been a little like dying and returning to the center to start over again, and it had certainly worked for them. But now he was getting a lot of complaints from humans who thought unfolding was everything and didn't understand the necessity for its opposite, enfolding. They were begging him to do something about it. A few were even challenging his authority and very existence.

On this particular day, Man was starting to see their point. After all, unfolding was his essence, and it was a little flattering to have them identify with him. And he had to admit that there were times when he secretly entertained the fantasy of unfolding into infinity without being constrained by her. Why did she always hold him back? Who knew how far he could go if she wasn't stopping him?

At the very moment Man was entertaining these thoughts, Wom was having some distressing thoughts of her own. Why hadn't Man come home yet? Why was he always working so late? It seemed like they rarely did things together anymore and she missed him. Was something wrong? What could it be?

When he finally came home that night, she nervously tried to find out what was wrong; but he was uncomfortable with his new feelings and at first wouldn't talk about them. Her questions became more avid and her embraces more fervent than ever. The harder she held on, the more he wanted to get away until he thought she would devour him with her hunger for him. When he could stand it no more he blurted out his concerns—a little indelicately due to all the holding back. Now it was Wom's turn to be affronted and annoyed.

They began to argue. The more they argued, the angrier they both got. Now, instead of unfolding gently and reaching out to her with happy expectance, Man lifted his arms reluctantly and grudgingly. Soon, instead of enfolding him with loving arms, Wom's embraces became more grasping and clinging. Man began to feel as if he were suffocating. Sometimes he could hardly breathe. He became distant and critical. Wom began to feel abused and rejected. Sometimes she could barely contain her rage. The cycle repeated again and again. Before long, they were barely speaking.

Then one day Man came home a few hours earlier than usual, and Wom was nowhere to be found. Startled, and a little worried, Man began to search for her. After scouring every room of the heavenly castle it occurred to him to check out Earth. That was where Wom spent most of her time while he was delivering orders to the angels and being praised by the seraphim and cherubim and other heavenly beings they had created.

That was something else that bothered him: It was almost as if she preferred Earth and the humans they had created to the castle they shared! What was that all about? There was no telling what she did down there. She might even be meddling about in human affairs in ways he wouldn't approve. He'd prefer that she stay home where he could keep an eye on her. As he approached Earth with these disturbing thoughts, in the distance he saw a strange silvery glow hovering over the trees in a particularly sinister-looking forest. So he headed in that direction.

After a while, the dark, dense grove of trees opened up into a place he had never noticed before. The clearing was filled with a misty fog that eddied and swirled in strange, malignant configurations, and it throbbed with the strangest music he had ever heard. There in the center of the clearing was Wom, naked as a snake, surrounded by a soft, luminous glow and dancing a wild and sinuous dance that made the hair on the back of his neck stand up and sent cold shivers up and down his spine. Frozen to the spot, Man stared with huge eyes, aware that every cell in his body prickled and tingled with erotic life.

As Wom danced, her head thrown back and her body writhing in ecstatic abandon, Man not only saw, but felt, the mystery of life and the horror of death in a way he had never seen them before. He saw spinning wheels of fire hurtling up the center of her spine and sparks cascading from the top of her head. He saw rattling skulls hanging from a necklace around her neck and dead bodies beneath her bloody feet.

Then Wom turned to him. What she saw was equally imposing. Man stood there in all his strength and majesty, his massive body taut with tension and gleaming with sweat from his exertion. Golden rays beamed from his sun crown and pierced the heavens, lighting up the universe beyond. With his magnificent sword in one hand and his jeweled scepter in the other, the light streaming from him was so brilliant and the power and vitality exuding from him so breathtaking that even she, the Queen of Heaven, could barely look at him.

For a moment, their eyes locked in an erotic embrace. Then, with a look of savage power mixed with a profound tenderness and longing, she held out her hand to him, inviting him to join in her dance. She had danced for him before, but this time it was different. This time he not only saw death, he felt it all around him. Worst of all, he felt it in his heart and gut. Icy fear twisted like a knife in his stomach.

Maybe it was the stunning realization that Wom had a way of experiencing life that was different from his. Maybe it was discovering that she had a space of her own that had nothing to do with him and in which he had no authority. Maybe it was the sudden awareness that her power was equal to his own, and that he was vulnerable to it, could even perish from it. Or maybe it was the shock of seeing a terrible truth in his most secret self: Despite all his ideals about perfection, despite his revulsion toward death, he wanted to join in her dance!

Whatever it was, and despite his violent need for her, Man could not move. Something in him was simply not ready to accept her as she was. He was suffocating. He could not breathe. He recoiled in terror. And suddenly he was filled with loathing. Dropping his eyes to the ground so as not to be tempted by her terrible allure, he turned away. And with a fierce determination that grew with every step he took from her, he headed back to the castle.

Man had had enough. How dare she challenge his power so brazenly! How dare she try to intimidate him like that! He sat down at his desk and drew up a formal proclamation. "Be it henceforth known . . ." he began. Then he stopped and thought a minute, erased his words, and started over. "I do hereby proclaim . . ." Yes, this was much better. "I do hereby proclaim that I, Man, shall, from this day forward be known as the one, the only God. Wom shall no longer bear that name, nor shall she partake of any of the fruits of *my* labor. She is no longer the mother of *my* children. They are mine alone, and she is henceforth banished from *my* *King*dom."

Man read the proclamation and smiled to himself, for it was good. Now, without her interference, he could make the world perfect, the way it should be. He was very full of himself, and the hot air from his inflated state fueled his anger. He thought for a minute, then added, "If Wom ever tries to return to my kingdom, let her be persecuted relentlessly, for she has plotted to share my wealth while actually contributing very little, and she pretends to have power which is mine alone. For I am the only God and anyone who says different is a heretic who deserves to be burned at the stake!"

He added these last words with a flourish, and signed his name at the bottom of the document. Then, in a state of self-righteous fury at the thought of all the indignities Wom had heaped upon him, he marched out the door and nailed the document to it.

"Wom," he roared with a voice like thunder, "as of this moment, we are divorced!" And he slammed the door and locked it behind him.

Wom was devastated. But her suffering was ignored by Man, for he had thoroughly convinced himself that she was evil and must be stripped of all power and authority. After a season of reaching in to him again and again, only to be rebuffed by his closed mind, she gave up. At last she understood that his need to separate himself from her was an inevitable consequence of his essence, which was to assert and develop itself. And with her inherent preference for creating new life, she intuited that this phase of growth and change was necessary and desirable: Without her inhibiting presence he would go into a phase of accelerated development.

Now that this process was activated, he would have to go on alone, as far and as high as he could. He would reap what he had sown until there was nothing left to sow, until he experienced the full extent of the forces he had unleashed. For a moment or two she actually considered destroying him for his treachery. In the end she was utterly incapable of committing such an act—not for lack of anger or motivation, but because she knew that would be a betrayal of her own nature and of their creation's hope of evolving to completion. She had no doubt that his betrayal of her would cause a time of imbalance and destruction in the world they had created. But she also knew that it would ultimately be for the best.

So she decided to withdraw to the Unconscious Underworld. There unobserved by anyone, she could continue her work of supporting, mediating, and maintaining balance throughout the universe. Through ocean and desert, through mountain range and jungle wilderness she searched, on and on until at last she found the narrow entrance to the Unconscious Underworld that was invisible to human eyes. With a high head and determined step, she entered the stone tunnel that spiraled down to a central core and culminated in a magnificent crystal cave. There, alone and in the dark, she lay down and rested for a season, exhausted by her ordeal.

But she wasn't really alone, for the crystal cave swarmed with all manner of life. When she slept, tiny spiders descended from the ceiling on slender threads and wrapped her body in a lacy cocoon to keep it warm. Ladybugs nestled in the drapes of her robes. Mother bears bore their babies next to her breast in the arc of her gently curved body. Wolf cubs turned around three times in the space behind her bent knees and snuggled down for a nap while their mothers kept guard. Even the crystals themselves throbbed with invisible life, life that could not help but continue in the presence of the Mother of us all.

As she slept in the Unconscious Underworld, winter descended on the land above. Snow fell and icy winds blew and much of the land was covered with a thick, cold crust. Many plants and animals, including human animals, died while she slept.

When she was fully rested she awoke, and with a heart full of love for her beloved children of the Earth she began to dance. Dancing in the dark, she danced the ice into thawing and the snow into melting. Dancing in the dark she danced the rivers into flowing and the seeds into sprouting and the leaves into budding. Dancing in the dark, she danced the bees into buzzing and the eggs into hatching and the babies into birthing.

Dancing in the dark, she danced the languishing flames of humanity's soul back to life. A few souls were ready for the conflagration and blossomed like the flowers that were blooming all over Earth. These become empowered spirit persons who recognized and celebrated Goddess's return and strove to help others do the same. Others felt the change and wanted more of the sacred warmth, but not badly enough to change their ways. Most escaped in denial and obsessions, terrified of the Unconscious Underworld, unaware of its significance. They had lived so long in coldness that they no longer felt or understood real warmth.

On and on Wom danced throughout the seasons. When she grew tired she would rest, and winter would come again. But despite her great pain which never abated, she always awoke and began dancing again. She lived this way for thousands of years.

Meanwhile, aboveground things weren't going as well as Man had expected. He still went off to work in heaven every day as he had before. But with an absentee father for a parent, and seemingly deprived of the daily ministrations of their wise and loving mother, the human children they had created became more and more unruly. They began to fight among themselves over trifling issues, like who crossed over whose boundary, who had the bigger piece of pie, and who got to make the rules of the games.

Gradually they forgot that they were brothers and sisters and became increasingly suspicious of one another. What was once a happy family began to disintegrate into a divisive den of vipers. Soon the children of the one-sided Father God were dispersing to the four corners of Earth, speaking different languages, drawing clear boundaries around themselves, and even going so far as to kill those who dared get too close. With the loss of their mother, they lost their sense of connection, their ability to cooperate, their belief in equality, their respect and compassion for each other, and their capacity for loving relationship.

The longer Wom was banished to the Unconscious Underground, the harder it became for her children to remember her heartfelt compassion and all the other qualities she had modeled for them. They lost the ability to wait patiently, to contain and simmer their ideas until they could implement them with wisdom. They forgot how to consider the welfare of their progeny and the planet before they acted and so did things that spread invisible toxic tentacles far into the future. They forgot how to care for others, and so lost their ability to protect themselves and each other from harm. They forgot how to listen to their deep, instinctive nature, and so lost touch with their souls.

As they gave more and more of their loyalty to a powerful father who ruled from the top of the heap, they began to compete against each other to see who could climb higher and closer to that power. They began to devise rules about how to get to the top and live there forever. They lost their respect for difference and individuality. They began to insist on rigid conformity to rules that simply got older and rustier and less useful.

Worst of all, as they forgot about their mother, they gradually lost all sense of meaning in their lives. There were still plenty of ideas to act upon, but action had lost its soulful purpose. Now, not even their father, Man (who still called himself God, believing in his utter *Goodness*) meant much to them anymore. Without his feminine partner, he lost not only his connection with his children, but also his own power to act in creative and beneficent ways for the well-being of all his relations.

With their mother banished from their senses, and with their father's power diminished as well, most of the children lost the ability for awe and reverence that comes from Wom's deep understanding of growth and change and the natural cycles of life. They forgot that new birth always follows death, and began to think of death as an end. They began to develop a terrible fear of death.

To make up for their loss of soul, and to help them forget their fear, they tried to recapture their lost bliss through alcohol, drugs, food, power, money, sex, material possessions, and work. They developed greedy appetites for temporary pleasures. As a substitute for life-renewing creativity, they used their soulless thinking to invent steely-cold machines, which they used to kill each other off more and more efficiently, ravage the Earth, and carelessly pollute the air and water.

This was the result of God's divorce. After thousands of years of this, Man could no longer deny what a terrible disaster it was. He began to realize that he was responsible for a one-sided world of suspicion, hatred, and greed in which their children were turned against one another and whole species were being killed off. God's divorce had destroyed the original wholeness and Earth, where Man's actions could be visible, was on the verge of extinction.

Now as everyone knows, all sacred holidays are preceded by an Eve. In Man's embarrassment over his failure, and in his great reluctance to humble himself and admit his mistake, he waited until the Eve of Destruction to act. Then, when he and his children could no longer ignore the inevitable, at last he swallowed his pride and strode out to find her.

At first his striding was random. But soon he found himself drawn to the forest where he had witnessed Wom's wonderful, terrible dance. It was darker there, and definitely more mysterious. But one of Man's most admirable qualities was his courage when in the grip of a holy cause, and he pressed on. He faced the fear of the unknown and of death which had haunted him for so long, ready at last to accept the truth about himself. He knew now that he needed Wom, for without her, he was incomplete. He would never rest until he righted his wrongs and completed himself by reuniting with her. He wanted his Beloved with all his heart, mind, and missing soul.

When the Divine Lover did not find his Beloved in the forest, on he went through dense undergrowth and up mountains heaped with boulders and through the waters of the seven seas. On and on he searched, and it seemed like decades before he finally found the invisible opening to the

Unconscious Underworld. When he felt the cool breeze emanating from within, with its delicate aroma of rose petals and lemon, patchouli and myrrh, he knew his journey was over.

Meanwhile, deep in the crystal cave, Wom was awakening from a restless sleep. Lately she had been feeling in every corner of her sensitive soul the danger seeping down through layers upon polluted layers of her beloved Earth. When she awoke, to her surprise the feeling that traveled through her body was not one of dull warning, but warm and delicious and tingly, like tiny shivers of electricity. She yawned and stretched and smiled to herself in sweet anticipation, for she knew exactly what was headed her way. With love for her partner filling her beautiful body, she began to prepare herself for his arrival.

As Man progressed down the tunnel and neared the cave, he too stopped to prepare himself. He ran his fingers through his hair, straightened his shoulders, took a deep breath to fill up his chest and give himself courage, and sucked in his stomach. Then he strode manfully through the threshold to the cave. As his eyes adjusted to the darkness, he began to perceive a form lying against the back wall. His heart was beating so loudly that he was certain Wom and all creation must hear it. Yet she did not stir, but lay so still that it seemed as if she were dead.

"Oh no," he thought fearfully. "Have I killed her, my Beloved, my partner, my soul, the one thing I love and need more than my own life?" With tears coursing down his face, he rushed to her and knelt by her side.

"Wom," he whispered softly. "Please wake up. I need you. Your children need you. I'm sorry I divorced you. I was too idealistic, too impressed with my thoughts and actions, too ignorant of the value of your wisdom. I didn't understand your compassion or your ability to accept the realities of the universe we created. I didn't understand the need for a relationship between the opposites, so I tried to make everything like me. I was afraid, Wom. Afraid of being swallowed up by you and falling back into the darkness. Afraid of the void, afraid of death. My fear turned me against you who are my life. Please forgive me."

In the darkness he didn't see the tiny smile at the corner of her mouth. She was smiling because in her prolonged season of dancing and resting she had seen many visions and dreamed many dreams and learned much from them. So she said in a fierce voice that echoed from the vaulted ceiling of the cave and seemed to emanate from the four corners of heaven itself, "Who are you to think you deserve my forgiveness?"

Man bowed his head and spoke the truth, "I am only Man. I am action without meaning, head without heart, spirit without soul. I am nothing without you, Wom."

Wom remained still. In a powerful voice that filled the cave with the vibrant energy of one who is confident of her own authority, she asked her second question: "And why should I trust you now?"

Man bowed lower in his misery. "Because I have learned from my mistakes. At last I understand the beauty and validity of your different kind of power and I no longer wish to control it or usurp it for myself. I truly desire that we should live together as equal partners for all eternity. This is the truth. I swear it on my life and on my love for you."

Wom's voice softened as she gently asked her third and last question, "And what, Man, is the meaning of this love for which you profess such reverence?"

Man lay on the earth beside Wom's warm and sweet-smelling body. He searched deep in his heart for his answer to this question. He knew it was a test that would decide his fate and the fate of the world. Then slowly and reverently, Man gave voice to the nine attributes of love it had taken him several millennia and untold suffering to learn.

Love is a conscious choice
to create partnerships between all opposites,
to participate joyfully in the sorrows of the world,
to support the growth of your Beloved without betraying yourself,
to tolerate tension between the opposites with honesty and courage,
to do everything in your power to avoid hurting self or others,
to respect the significance and sovereignty of otherness,
to share yourself with otherness,
to receive the gifts of otherness,
And to create as much consciousness as you can contain.

After saying these last words, Man lay quietly on the floor. He knew he had answered Wom's question with all the wisdom he was capable of at this point in the circle of eternity, and he awaited his judgment with humility. It seemed eons before he heard Wom's body rustle and stir, before he smelled the sweet perfume of her warmth and vitality, before he felt her gently rise, before he saw forgiving light shine from her eyes and tears of love stream down her cheeks.

Wom and Man embraced there in the darkness of the cave. Hours later they strode out into the fresh pink dawn of a new day.

Together they looked with joy at the greening world before them. A sparkling planet teemed with life that hadn't been destroyed after all. It was in the process of mending, just as their union was being healed, just as the souls of humans were being healed.

Together they walked off arm-in-arm toward a bold new life as two conscious individuals committed to creating a new spiritual paradigm: the sacred marriage.

The beginning . . .

Notes

1. Marcus J. Borg, *Jesus: Uncovering the Life, Teachings, and Relevance of a Religious Revolutionary* (New York: HarperOne, 2006), 194.

2. Ibid., 220.

3. Thomas R. Kelly. *Reality of the Spiritual World*, Pendle Hill Pamphlet 21. (Wallingford, PA: Pendle Hill Publications, 1942), 10.

4. Leonard Shlain, *The Alphabet Versus the Goddess* (New York: Penguin/Compass, 1998), 219.

5. Christopher Bamford,"The God of Abraham," *Parabola*, 33, no 2 (summer 2008), 46.

6. Shlain, *Alphabet Versus the Goddess*, 219.

7. *Holy Bible*, King James version, Matthew 3:17.

8. Henri J.M. Nouwen, *Life of the Beloved: Spiritual Living in a Secular World* (New York: Crossroad, 1996), 26–27.

9. Jennifer Barker Woolger and Roger J. Woolger, *The Goddess Within*. (New York: Fawcett Columbine, 1987), 174.

10. Heinrich Zimmer, "The Indian World Mother," in *The Mystic Vision: Papers from the Eranos Yearbooks*, Joseph Campbell, ed. (Princeton, N.J.: Princeton University Press, 1968), 83.

11. Karen L. King, *The Gospel of Mary of Magdala: Jesus and the First Woman Apostle* (Santa Rosa, CA: Polebridge, 2003), 3.

12. Karen L. King, "The Gospel of Mary," in *The Nag Hammadi Library*, 3rd ed., James M. Robinson, ed., (New York: HarperOne, 1990), 523.

13. Esther A. De Boer and Marvin Meyer, trans. *The Gospels of Mary* (NewYork: HarperSanFrancisco, 2004), 17.

14. Elaine Pagels, *Beyond Belief: The Secret Gospel of Thomas* (New York: Random House, 2003), 104.

15. Edward F. Edinger, *The Creation of Consciousness: Jung's Myth for Modern Man* (Toronto: Inner City Books, 1984), 90.

16. John Selby Spong, *A New Christianity for a New World* (San Francisco: HarperSanFrancisco, 2001), 21–22.

17. Ibid., 145.

18. Ibid.

About the Author

JEAN BENEDICT RAFFA is a former teacher, television producer, and college professor with a doctorate in Education from the University of Florida. In her late thirties she underwent a spiritual "dark night" that shifted her focus from the outer world of achievement and conformity to the authentic inner life of the psyche. The work of Carl Jung inspired intense study and led to the re-discovery of her passions for writing and self-knowledge. Since then she has been writing and teaching about psychological and spiritual matters from a perspective informed by Jungian psychology and personal experience. Her previous books on these subjects are *The Bridge to Wholeness* and *Dream Theatres of the Soul,* and her blog, *Matrignosis,* can be found at www.jeanraffa.wordpress.com. A mother of two and grandmother of five, she and her economist husband live in Maitland, Florida and Highlands, North Carolina.